Lecture Notes in Computer Science　　12628

Imari Sato · Bohyung Han (Eds.)

Computer Vision – ACCV 2020 Workshops

15th Asian Conference on Computer Vision
Kyoto, Japan, November 30 – December 4, 2020
Revised Selected Papers

 Springer

Editors
Imari Sato
National Institute of Informatics
Tokyo, Japan

Bohyung Han (iD)
Seoul National University
Seoul, Korea (Republic of)

ISSN 0302-9743   ISSN 1611-3349 (electronic)
Lecture Notes in Computer Science
ISBN 978-3-030-69755-6   ISBN 978-3-030-69756-3 (eBook)
https://doi.org/10.1007/978-3-030-69756-3

LNCS Sublibrary: SL6 – Image Processing, Computer Vision, Pattern Recognition, and Graphics

This Springer imprint is published by the registered company Springer Nature Switzerland AG
The registered company address is: Gewerbestrasse 11, 6330 Cham, Switzerland

Preface

We are very pleased to present the workshop proceedings of the Asian Conference on Computer Vision (ACCV), which took place during November 30 to December 4 in 2020. ACCV 2020 hosted four workshops on a variety of topics and formats and was successful, with many attendees. However, the number of accepted workshops was less than in the previous conferences because ACCV 2020 was a fully virtual meeting hosted during the COVID-19 pandemic. It is unfortunate that the researchers did not have the opportunity to have physical meetings and technical discussions in the workshops. Despite the small quantity, we accepted workshops of excellent quality. The list of workshops held in conjunction with ACCV 2020 is as follows:

- Webly-Supervised Fine-Grained Recognition Challenge (WebFG)
- Human Identification at a Distance (HID)
- Machine Learning and Computing for Visual Semantic Analysis (MLCSA)
- Multi-Visual-Modality Human Activity Understanding (MMHAU)

The workshops were primarily related to high-level computer vision, and covered interesting topics in terms of its applications. All workshops had invited speaker sessions, where leading researchers gave insightful talks. Two workshops hosted challenges and presented their results in their sessions.

We thank all the workshop organizers for their efforts to make these successful events, especially in the challenging environment of virtual hosting. We hope they continue to hold the workshops in future ACCVs. We also thank the publication chairs for putting together the papers presented in the workshops to make the workshop proceedings.

January 2021

Imari Sato
Bohyung Han

Organization

Webly-Supervised Fine-Grained Recognition Challenge (WebFG)

Xiu-Shen Wei	Nanjing University of Science and Technology, China
Yazhou Yao	Nanjing University of Science and Technology, China
Oisin Mac Aodha	The University of Edinburgh, UK
Wenguan Wang	ETH Zurich, Switzerland
Jian Yang	Nanjing University of Science and Technology, China
Jianxin Wu	Nanjing University, China
Chunhua Shen	The University of Adelaide, Australia
Grant Van Horn	Cornell Lab of Ornithology, USA
Shin'ichi Sato	National Institute of Informatics, Japan
Osamu Yoshie	Waseda University, Japan

Human Identification at a Distance (HID)

Shiqi Yu	Southern University of Science and Technology, China
Liang Wang	Institute of Automation, Chinese Academy of Sciences, China
Yongzhen Huang	Institute of Automation, Chinese Academy of Sciences, China; Watrix Technology Co. Ltd., China
Yasushi Makihara	Osaka University, Japan
Nicolás Guil	University of Málaga, Spain
Manuel J. Marín-Jiménez	University of Córdoba, Spain
Edel B. García Reyes	Shenzhen Institute of Artificial Intelligence and Robotics for Society, China
Feng Zheng	Southern University of Science and Technology, China
Md. Atiqur Rahman Ahad	University of Dhaka, Bangladesh; Osaka University, Japan

Machine Learning and Computing for Visual Semantic Analysis (MLCSA)

YongQing Sun	NTT, Japan
Xian-Hua Han	Yamaguchi University, Japan
Jien Kato	Ritsumeikan University, Japan

Multi-Visual-Modality Human Activity Understanding (MMHAU)

Zhigang Tu	Wuhan University, China
Junsong Yuan	University at Buffalo, State University of New York, USA
Zicheng Liu	Microsoft AI&R Ambience Intelligence, USA

Contents

Machine Learning and Computing for Visual Semantic Analysis (MLCSA)

Spatial and Channel Attention Modulated Network for Medical Image Segmentation

Wenhao Fang$^{(\boxtimes)}$ and Xian-hua Han

Graduate School of Science and Technology for Innovation,
Yamaguchi University, Yamaguchi, Japan
{b501vb,hanxhua}@yamaguchi-u.ac.jp

Abstract. Medical image segmentation is a fundamental and challenge task in many computer-aided diagnosis and surgery systems, and attracts numerous research attention in computer vision and medical image processing fields. Recently, deep learning based medical image segmentation has been widely investigated and provided state-of-the-art performance for different modalities of medical data. Therein, U-Net consisting of the contracting path for context capturing and the symmetric expanding path for precise localization, has become a meta network architecture for medical image segmentation, and manifests acceptable results even with moderate scale of training data. This study proposes a novel attention modulated network based on the baseline U-Net, and explores embedded spatial and channel attention modules for adaptively highlighting interdependent channel maps and focusing on more discriminant regions via investigating relevant feature association. The proposed spatial and channel attention modules can be used in a plug and play manner and embedded after any learned feature map for adaptively emphasizing discriminant features and neglecting irrelevant information. Furthermore, we propose two aggregation approaches for integrating the learned spatial and channel attentions to the raw feature maps. Extensive experiments on two benchmark medical image datasets validate that our proposed network architecture manifests superior performance compared to the baseline U-Net and its several variants.

1 Introduction

In modern and clinic medicine, medical images have played an important role for conducting accurate disease diagnosis and effective treatment. A large number of medical images using different imaging technologies, such as X-ray, computed tomography (CT), ultrasound, and magnetic resonance imaging (MRI) and so on, have made great contributions to research evolution for developing computer-aided diagnosis (CAD) systems [1] using image processing and machine learning [2–5]. On the contrary, the developed CAD system is prospected to conduct rapid analysis and understanding of large amount of medical data to reduce the doctor's interpretation time, and further extends the wide use of medical images in clinic medicine. The CAD systems can not only conduct fast screening for

© Springer Nature Switzerland AG 2021
I. Sato and B. Han (Eds.): ACCV 2020 Workshops, LNCS 12628, pp. 3–17, 2021.
https://doi.org/10.1007/978-3-030-69756-3_1

supporting doctors but also provide quantitative medical image evaluation to assist more accurate treatment. There proposed a lot of CAD systems in recent decades of years. Therein automatic medical image segmentation that extracts specific organs, lesion or regions of interest (ROI) [6–8] in medical images is a crucial step for the downstream tasks of medical image analysis systems. Traditional medical image segmentation methods mainly rely on hand engineered feature for classifying pixels independently. Due to large variation of uncontrollable and complex geometric structures in medical images, traditional methods usually lead to unsatisfied segmentation results. Inspired by the great success of deep convolutional neural network for image classification in recent years, deep learning [9] based methods has been widely investigated and provided impressive performance for different vision tasks including semantic image segmentation. In the last few years, numerous CNN [10] models have been proposed and validated that deeper networks generally result in better performance for different recognition and segmentation tasks. However, it is mandatory to prepare large scale of annotated samples for training very deep models, which is difficult in medical application scenario. Further the training procedure for a very deep model is usually unstable due to the vanishing or explosive gradient problems and needs rich experience for hyper-parameter turning.

In semantic medical image segmentation scenario, simple network architectures are most preferred due to small scale of annotated training samples. In 2015, a simple and easily implemented CNN architecture: U-Net [11] was proposed specifically for medical image segmentation, and has become a very popular meta architecture for different modalities of medical data segmentation. To boost segmentation performance, different variants of U-Net via integrating more advance modules such as recurrent unit, residual block or attention mechanism, have been widely investigated. Among them, the attention mechanism manifests promising performance for segmentation task on different CNN architectures including U-Net. Many existing attention approach usually investigate spatial attention via focusing on salient regions, which aid at better estimation of the under-studying target greatly while may neglect the possible different contribution in the learned feature maps. Thus it still deserves the further studying of exploring different attentions not only on spatial domain but also on channel direction.

This study proposes a novel attention modulated network based on the baseline U-Net, and explores embedded spatial and channel attention modules for adaptively highlighting interdependent channel maps and focusing on more discriminant regions via investigating relevant feature association. The two explored attention modules: spatial attention module (SAM) and channel attention module (CAM) can be employed to any feature map for emphasizing discriminant region and selecting important channel maps in a plug and play manner, and further can be combined as spatial and channel attention module (SCAM) for simultaneously conducting spatial and channel attention. In addition, we propose two aggregation approaches for integrating the learned spatial and channel attentions into the raw feature map. Extensive experiments on two benchmark medical image datasets validate that our proposed network architecture manifests superior performance compared to the baseline U-Net and its several variants.

2   Related Work

In the past few years, semantic medical image segmentation has been actively researched in computer vision and medical image processing community, and substantial improvement have been witnessed. This work mainly concentrates on the medical image segmentation using deep learning methods. Here, we briefly survey the related work.

2.1   Medical Image Segmentation

Semantic segmentation of medical images is a crucial step in many downstream medical image analysis and understanding tasks, and has been extensively studied for decades of years. Traditional medical image segmentation approaches generally employ hand engineered features for classifying pixels independently into semantic regions, and lead to unexpected results for the images with large variation in intensities. In the last few years, with the rapid evolution of deep learning technique, many medical image segmentation models based on convolutional neural network (CNN) have been proposed. Via replacing the fully connected layers of standard classification CNNs with convolutional layers, fully CNN (FCN) [12] has been proposed to conduct dense pixel prediction at one forward step, and successfully applied for generic object segmentation. Further, FCN employs skip connection among network for reusing the intermediate feature maps to improve the prediction capabilities. Later many variants inspired from the FCN such as SegNet [13], DeepLab [14] have been investigated for boosting segmentation performance and made great progress for generic image segmentation in computer vision applications.

On the other hand, U-Net architecture was firstly proposed specifically for semantic medical image segmentation, and has become very popular due to its simple implementation and efficiency for network training. In this architecture, there have contractive and expansive paths, where contractive path is implemented using the combination of convolutional and pooling layers for learning different scales of contexts while expansive path employs the combination of convolutional and upsampling layers for mining semantic information. Then, similarly as in FCN [12], skip connections are used to concatenate the context and semantic information from two paths for accuracy prediction. To further improve segmentation results, different variants of U-Net models have been proposed. Kayalibay et al. [10] proposed to integrate multiple segmentation maps and forward feature maps from different paths, and then predict the final segmentation results from the integrated maps. Drozdzal et al. [15] explored and evaluated the importance of skip connections for biomedical image segmentation while Reza Azad et al. [16] proposed to employ convLSTM unit to integrate the feature maps from two paths instead of simple skip connection. Chen et al. [17] proposed a deep contour-aware network (DCAN) to extract multi-level contextual features with a hierarchical architecture while McKinley et al. [18] designed a deep dig-like convolutional architecture, named as Nabla-Net for biomedical image segmentation. Further, several works [19,20] embedded recurrent and residual structures into the baseline U-Net model, and showed impressive performance.

The other research direction is to extend the conventional U-Net to 3D counterpart for 3D medical image segmentation tasks. V-Net: a powerful end-to-end 3D medical image segmentation model [21], has firstly been proposed via combining FCN [12] and residual connections while a deeply supervised 3D model [22] was explored attempting to employ multi-block features for final segmentation prediction. To refine the segmentation results from CNN model, Kamnitsas et al. [23] integrated fully connected CRF into a multi-scale 3D CNN for brain tumor segmentation. Residual structure in the 3D CNN model was also extensively studied for medical image segmentation such as High-Res3DNet [24] and Voxresnet [25].

2.2   Deep Attention Network

Attention mechanisms are capable of emphasizing important and relevant element of the input or the under-studying target via learning strategy, and thus have become a very popular component in deep neural network. The integration of these attention modules have made great progress in many vision tasks such as image question-answering [26], image captioning [27] and classification [28]. Attention mechanisms have also been integrated into semantic image segmentation networks, and proven performance beneficial for this pixel-wise recognition tasks [29–34]. For instance, Zhao et al. [30] proposed a point-wise spatial attention network (PSANet), which allows a flexible and dynamic aggregation of different contextual information by connecting each position in the feature map with all the others through adaptive attention maps. Fu et al. [31] investigated a dual attention network for scene segmentation. Despite the growing interest on exploring attention mechanisms for image segmentation of natural scenes, there are still limited work for adopting to medical images segmentation. The existed study for integrating attention mechanisms into medical image segmentation networks [35–39], generally employ simple attention models, and the improvement are limited.

3   Spatial and Channel Modulate Network

This study aims to explore a novel spatial and channel modulate network. We combine attention mechanism with U-Net to propose a attention modulate network for semantic segmentation of medical images. The schematic concept of the proposed SCAM-Net is given in Fig. 1. The mainstream of the proposed SCAM-Net follows the encoder-decoder architecture, and various feature maps, which

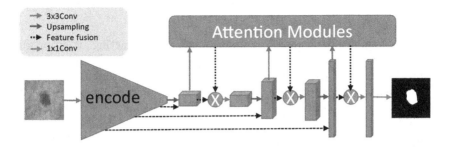

Fig. 1. The schematic concept of the proposed SCAM-Net

may contribute differences to final prediction, can be learned for representing different contexts. To adaptively learn more effective contexts for better predicting target in the model training procedure, we propose to leverage attention mechanism, which can emphasize important and relevant elements among the learned maps. We explore two attention modules: spatial attention module (SAM) and channel attention module (CAM), which can be employed to any feature maps of the main encoder-decoder architecture (U-Net), and then combine them as spatial and channel attention module (SCAM) for simultaneously conducting spatial and channel attention. Next, we would introduce the mainstream of the encoder-decoder architecture, and then describe the spatial, channel attention modules and their combinations.

3.1 The Mainstream of the Encoder-Decoder Architecture

The used main backbone network follows U-Net architecture consisting of two paths: encoder and decoder. Both encoder and decoder paths are divided into four blocks, and each block is mainly implemented in 3 convolutional layers with kernel sizes 3*3 following RELU activation function after each convolutional layer. The channel numbers of feature maps are increased to double and feature maps sizes are decreased to half via employing MaxPooling layer with a 2*2 kernel in horizontal and vertical directions, respectively, between blocks of the encoder while decreasing to half of channel number and increasing to double of map sizes are inversely implemented with up-sampling layers between blocks of the decoder. It is known that the encoder generally extracts multi-scale features retaining detail structures of the input while the decoder learns multiple features with more semantic information for predicting the target. However not all semantic features learned by the decoder path aid to prediction of the specific under-studying target and may have different contributions to the final result. Thus we employ attention mechanism to emphasize discriminant region and select important channel maps for boosting performance.

Let us denote the learned feature map of a block of the decoder as $\mathbf{X} \in \Re^{W \times H \times C}$, we implement a series of transformations for extraction attention map of $\mathbf{X}$, and then add the explored attention map to the raw feature for emphasizing important context, which is formulated as the following:

$$\bar{\mathbf{X}} = \mathbf{X} + f_{AM}(\mathbf{X}) \tag{1}$$

where $f_{AM}(\cdot)$ denotes the transformation operators for extracting attention map. With the attention module in Eq. (1), it is expected that more discriminant features for prediction of the target can be adaptively and automatically emphasized in model training procedure. Further the attention module can be feasibly employed to any learned feature of the decoder in a plug and play manner. Next, we would describe the detail implementation of our proposed spatial and channel attention modules.

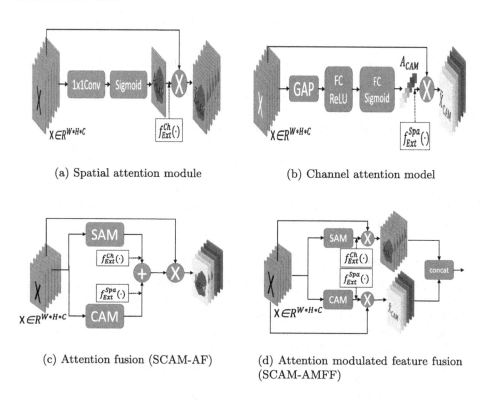

(a) Spatial attention module   (b) Channel attention model

(c) Attention fusion (SCAM-AF)   (d) Attention modulated feature fusion (SCAM-AMFF)

Fig. 2. Different attention modules

3.2 Spatial Attention Module (SAM)

The simple up-sampling process of the decoding path in the mainstream architecture may lead to un-expected spatial information and detail structure lost. To solve this problem, U-Net employs skip connections to combine (concatenate) the feature map with detail spatial information in the encoding path and the feature map of the decoding path. However, this simple concatenation brings many redundant low-level features. Therefore, we leverage a spatial attention module (SAM) in the decoding path to effectively suppress the activation regions with little discriminant information and thereby reduce the number of redundant features. The structure of the proposed SAM is shown in Fig. 2(a).

Given a feature map extracted by a block of the decoder as $\mathbf{X} \in \Re^{W \times H \times C}$, we implement the spatial attention mechanism via firstly employing a convolutional layer with 1*1 kernel and output channel 1, being formulated as:

$$\mathbf{X}_{SAM} = f_{Conv1*1}(\mathbf{X}) \tag{2}$$

where $\mathbf{X}_{SAM} \in \Re^{W \times H}$ has the same spatial size with $\mathbf{X}$. Then a non-linear transformation is conducted to generate the spatial attention map with magnitude range [0, 1] using an activation function, where a coefficient close to 1 indicates more relevant features. The activation operation is expressed as:

$$A_{SAM} = \sigma(\mathbf{X}_{SAM}) \tag{3}$$

where $\sigma(\cdot)$ is sigmoid activation function. Finally, the extracted spatial attention map is employed to the raw feature map $\mathbf{X}$ for emphasizing discriminant regions:

$$\bar{\mathbf{X}}_{SAM} = \mathbf{X} \otimes f_{SAM}(\mathbf{X}) = \mathbf{X} \otimes f_{Ext}^{Ch}(A_{SAM}) \tag{4}$$

where $f_{Ext}^{Ch}(\cdot)$ extends the spatial attention map in channel direction to the same size of $\mathbf{X}$ for being combined with the raw feature map. After that, it is passed normally into the mainstream.

3.3   Channel Attention Module (CAM)

Recently, the channel attention module has attracted a lot of interest and has shown great potential for improving the performance of deep CNN. The core idea is to automatically learn the indexed weights for each channel of feature map, so that the feature maps with more important information for final result prediction have larger weights while the feature maps with invalid or less discriminant information have small weights.

We implement the channel attention via exploring the correlations between different channels of features. The learned feature maps $\mathbf{X}$ in the decoder's block are aggregated to generate channel contribution index by employing global average pooling, formulated as:

$$m_k = \frac{1}{W \times H} \sum_{w=1}^{W} \sum_{h=1}^{H} x_k(w, h) \tag{5}$$

where $x_k(w, h)$ denotes the feature value on the spatial position (w, h) and the channel k of the feature map in $\mathbf{X}$, and m_k represents the global information of the $k - th$ channel of feature map. Then the channel-wise dependencies are investigated via using two fully connected (FC) layers. The first FC layer encodes the channel global vector $\mathbf{m} = [m_1, m_2, \cdots, m_K]^T$ to a dimension-reduced vector with reduction ratio while the second FC layer recovers it back again to the raw channel K as an the channel attention vector $\mathbf{X}_{CAM}$, which is expressed as the following:

$$\mathbf{X}_{CAM} = \mathbf{W}_2(\mathbf{W}_1\mathbf{m}) \tag{6}$$

where $\mathbf{W}_1 \in \Re^{\frac{K}{r} \times K}$ and $\mathbf{W}_2 \in \Re^{K \times \frac{K}{r}}$ represent the parameters of the two FC layers, respectively, and the r represents the ratio of scaling parameters. In our experiment, there is a compromise between accuracy and parameter amount($r = 16$).

Then, similar as in the SAM, a non-linear transformation is conducted to generate the attention map with magnitude range $[0, 1]$ using a sigmoid activation function $\sigma(\cdot)$, which is expressed as:

$$A_{CAM} = \sigma(\mathbf{X}_{CAM}) \tag{7}$$

Finally, the channel attention modulated feature map is formulated as:

$$\bar{\mathbf{X}}_{CAM} = \mathbf{X} \otimes f_{CAM}(\mathbf{X}) = \mathbf{X} \otimes f_{Ext}^{Spa}(A_{CAM}) \tag{8}$$

where $f_{Ext}^{Spa}(\cdot)$ extends the channel attention map in spatial direction to the same size of $\mathbf{X}$. Similar as in SAM, it will be passed normally into the mainstream.

3.4   Spatial and Channel Attention Module (SCAM)

In view of the above two attention modules, it naturally leads to the consideration of combining these two attention modules to generate a spatial and channel attention module for simultaneously emphasizing discriminant regions and selecting useful channel features. We explore two aggregation strategies, and the conceptual diagrams of the two methods are shown in Fig. 2(c) and Fig. 2(d), respectively.

The flowchart of the first aggregation method, called as attention fusion based SCAM (SCAM-AF), is shown in Fig. 2(c), which intuitively integrates the extended spatial and channel attention maps using element-wise addition, as expressed in the following:

$$\mathbf{A}_{SCAM} = f_{Ext}^{Ch}(A_{Spatial}) + f_{Ext}^{Spa}(A_{Spectral}) \tag{9}$$

Then, the attention map is added to the raw feature map for generating attention modulated feature map:

$$\bar{\mathbf{X}}_{SCAM} = \mathbf{X} \otimes \mathbf{A}_{SCAM} \tag{10}$$

The second combination method, called as attention modulated feature fusion (SCAM-AMFF), fuses the separately modulated feature maps by the SAM and CAM using a concat layer shown in Fig. 2(d). The approach also combines the feature maps of the two attention modules. It is also possible to give more weight to the space and the more effective areas in the channel at the same time, as expressed in the following:

$$\bar{\mathbf{X}}_{SCAM} = Concat(\bar{\mathbf{X}}_{SAM}, \bar{\mathbf{X}}_{SAM}) \tag{11}$$

In general, the two aggregation methods can conduct both special and channel attention to adaptively learning discriminant information, and thus benefit for more efficient training of our medical image segmentation model. In addition, the attention modulated modules can be integrated with any feature map extracted in decoder's blocks, and is expected to learn more effective features for predicting the under-studying target.

4   Experimental Setup and Results

4.1   Database

Lung Segmentation Dataset: The used lung segmentation dataset was presented in 2017 at the Kaggle Data Science Bowl in the Lung Nodule Analysis (LUNA) competition. This dataset consists of 2D and 3D CT images with respective label images for lung segmentation. In this paper, we used a total of 1021 slice images with size 512×512 extracted from the 3D images as the dataset. We use 70% of the dataset as the train subset and the remaining 30% as the test subset. Since the lung region in the CT image have almost the same Hausdorff value with non-interested object: air region but contains interference factors such as alveoli and blood vessels in small regions, it would be difficult to perfectly distinguish the lung from the region with the same Hausdorff value. It is known that the lung is surrounded by other body tissues anatomically and the regions outside body tissues are air. Thus it is prospected to achieve better performance via taking the lung and air regions as the same class, and other tissue region as the other class for segmentation learning. After obtaining the results of the lung and air region segmentation, it is very easy to get the lung region due the complete separation by other body tissues between the two regions. The used ground-truth mask for network training in our experiment are shown in Fig. 3.

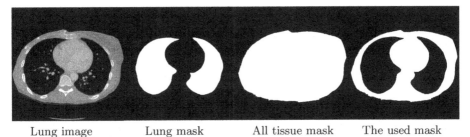

Lung image   Lung mask   All tissue mask   The used mask

Fig. 3. The used ground-truth mask in our experiments for lung segmentation.

Table 1. Performance comparison of the proposed attention modulated networks and the state-of-the-art methods on LUNA dataset.

Models	F1-Score	Sensitivity	Specificity	Accuracy	AUC
U-Net	0.9658	0.9696	0.9872	0.9872	0.9784
RU-Net	0.9638	0.9734	0.9866	0.9836	0.9800
R2U-Net	0.9832	**0.9944**	0.9832	0.9918	0.9889
SAM	0.9736	0.9890	0.9955	0.9922	0.9918
CAM	0.9634	0.9936	0.9860	0.9873	0.9898
SCAM-AF	**0.9841**	0.9823	**0.9971**	**0.9946**	0.9897
SCAM-AMFF	0.9800	0.9902	0.9938	0.9932	**0.9920**

Skin Segmentation Dataset: The ISIC dataset is a large-scale dermoscopy image dataset, which was released by the International Dermatology Collaboration Organization (ISIC). This dataset is taken from a challenge on lesion segmentation, dermoscopic feature detection, and disease classification. It includes 2594 images, in which we used 1815 images for training, 259 for validation and 520 for testing. The training subset consists of the original images and corresponding ground truth annotations. The original size of each sample is 700 × 900, and was resized to 256 × 256 in our experiments.

Table 2. Performance comparison of the proposed attention modulated networks and the state-of-the-art methods on ISIC dataset.

Models	F1-Score	Sensitivity	Specificity	Accuracy	Precision
U-Net	0.647	0.708	0.964	0.890	0.779
Attention U-Net	0.665	0.717	0.967	0.897	0.787
RU-Net	0.679	0.792	0.928	0.880	0.741
R2U-Net	0.691	0.726	0.971	0.904	0.822
SAM	0.773	0.699	0.970	0.913	0.866
CAM	0.851	0.779	**0.986**	0.942	0.938
SCAM-AF	**0.870**	**0.817**	0.983	**0.948**	0.931
SCAM-AMFF	0.869	0.809	**0.986**	**0.948**	**0.940**

4.2 Evaluation Results

We evaluate the experimental results using several quantitative metrics including accuracy (AC), F1-Score, sensitivity (SE), specificity (SP), precision (PC) and area under the curve (AUC). The true positive (TP), true negative (TN), false positive (FP), and false negative (FN) values are needed for calculating the evaluation metrics, which is expressed as:

$$AC = \frac{TP + TN}{TP + TN + FP + FN} \tag{12}$$

$$PC = \frac{TP}{TP + FP} \tag{13}$$

$$SE = \frac{TP}{TP + FN} \tag{14}$$

$$SP = \frac{TN}{TN + FP} \tag{15}$$

$$F1 - score = \frac{2SE * PC}{SE + PC} \tag{16}$$

To evaluate the effectiveness of the proposed SCAM-Net, we provide the compared results with several state-of-the-art methods including the baseline U-Net [11], Recurrent Residual U-Net [19], Attention U-Net [40], R2U-Net [20], and our proposed network with SAM or CAM for both skin lesion segmentation (ISIC) and lung segmentation dataset.

Table 2 and Table 1 provides the compared quantitative evaluations on two datasets, which demonstrates improved results compared with the baseline U-Net and its variants. At the same time, the proposed network with only one attention module can also achieve better performance than the baseline U-Net method, and better or comparable results with the extended version of U-Net. Meanwhile, it can be seen from Table 1 and 2 that CAM performs better than SAM in the ISIC dataset regard with the quantitative evaluation while SAM performs better than CAM in the LUNA lung segmentation dataset. Thus different attention models may be applicable to different datasets and deserved to be further investigated. Next, we conducted experiments on both datasets using the combined attention modules (SCAM-AF and SCAM-AMFF), and the compared results are also provided in Table 1 and 2, which manifests that the quantitative evaluation with the proposed SCAMs is better than not only the baseline U-Net but also the proposed networks with only one attention module (SAM or CAM). Finally, the visualization results of segmentation for two example images on both the LUNA and ISIC datasets, are shown in the Fig. 4, which manifests the segmentation results using the proposed networks with different attention modules are very similar to the ground-truth annotation.

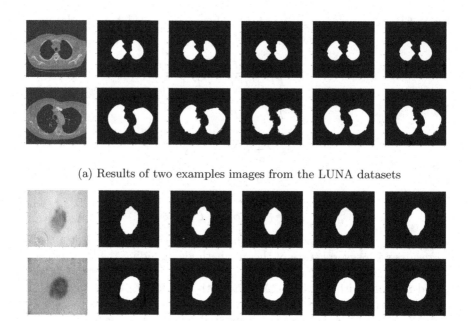

(a) Results of two examples images from the LUNA datasets

(b) Results of two examples images from the ISIC datasets

Fig. 4. The segmentation results of two example images from the LUNA and ISIC datasets, respectively, using the backbone network with different attention modules. (a) Results of two examples images from the LUNA datasets. (b) Results of two examples images from the ISIC datasets.

5   Conclusion

This study proposed a novel spatial and channel attention modulated network for effective segmentation of medical images module. To emphasize discriminate regions and adaptive select more important channel of feature maps, we explored both spatial and channel attention modules for integrating into the main encoder-decoder architecture in a plug and play manner. Further, we proposed two aggregation strategies to combine the two attention modules into a unified unit in the mainstream network for boosting segmentation performance. Comprehensive experiments on two benchmark medical data sets showed that our proposed method not only obtains better performance than the baseline U-Net and its variants, but also manifested encouraging performance compared with a single space or single channel attention module.

Acknowledgement. This research was supported in part by the Grant-in Aid for Scientific Research from the Japanese Ministry for Education, Science, Culture and Sports (MEXT) under the Grant No. 20K11867.

References

1. Roth, H.R., et al.: Spatial aggregation of holistically-nested convolutional neural networks for automated pancreas localization and segmentation. Med. Image Anal. **45**, 94–107 (2018)
2. Cerrolaza, J.J., Summers, R.M., Linguraru, M.G.: Soft multi-organ shape models via generalized PCA: a general framework. In: Ourselin, S., Joskowicz, L., Sabuncu, M.R., Unal, G., Wells, W. (eds.) MICCAI 2016. LNCS, vol. 9902, pp. 219–228. Springer, Cham (2016). https://doi.org/10.1007/978-3-319-46726-9_26
3. Gibson, E., et al.: Towards image-guided pancreas and biliary endoscopy: automatic multi-organ segmentation on abdominal CT with dense dilated networks. In: Descoteaux, M., Maier-Hein, L., Franz, A., Jannin, P., Collins, D.L., Duchesne, S. (eds.) MICCAI 2017. LNCS, vol. 10433, pp. 728–736. Springer, Cham (2017). https://doi.org/10.1007/978-3-319-66182-7_83
4. Saito, A., Nawano, S., Shimizu, A.: Joint optimization of segmentation and shape prior from level-set-based statistical shape model, and its application to the automated segmentation of abdominal organs. Med. Image Anal. **28**, 46–65 (2016)
5. Bai, W., et al.: Human-level CMR image analysis with deep fully convolutional networks. ArXiv abs/1710.09289 (2017)
6. Shih, F., Zhong, X.: High-capacity multiple regions of interest watermarking for medical images. Inf. Sci. **367–368**, 648–659 (2016)
7. Sanchez, V.: Joint source/channel coding for prioritized wireless transmission of multiple 3-D regions of interest in 3-D medical imaging data. IEEE Trans. Biomed. Eng. **60**, 397–405 (2013)
8. Raja, J.A., Raja, G., Khan, A.: Selective compression of medical images using multiple regions of interest (2013)
9. Krizhevsky, A., Sutskever, I., Hinton, G.E.: ImageNet classification with deep convolutional neural networks. In: NIPS (2012)
10. Kayalibay, B., Jensen, G., van der Smagt, P.: CNN-based segmentation of medical imaging data. CoRR abs/1701.03056 (2017)
11. Ronneberger, O., Fischer, P., Brox, T.: U-Net: convolutional networks for biomedical image segmentation. In: Navab, N., Hornegger, J., Wells, W.M., Frangi, A.F. (eds.) MICCAI 2015. LNCS, vol. 9351, pp. 234–241. Springer, Cham (2015). https://doi.org/10.1007/978-3-319-24574-4_28
12. Khened, M., Varghese, A., Krishnamurthi, G.: Fully convolutional multi-scale residual DenseNets for cardiac segmentation and automated cardiac diagnosis using ensemble of classifiers. CoRR abs/1801.05173 (2018)
13. Badrinarayanan, V., Kendall, A., Cipolla, R.: SegNet: a deep convolutional encoder-decoder architecture for image segmentation. IEEE Trans. Pattern Anal. Mach. Intell. **39**, 2481–2495 (2017)
14. Chen, L.C., Papandreou, G., Kokkinos, I., Murphy, K., Yuille, A.: DeepLab: semantic image segmentation with deep convolutional nets, Atrous convolution, and fully connected CRFs. IEEE Trans. Pattern Anal. Mach. Intell. **40**, 834–848 (2018)
15. Drozdzal, M., Vorontsov, E., Chartrand, G., Kadoury, S., Pal, C.: The importance of skip connections in biomedical image segmentation. In: Carneiro, G., et al. (eds.) LABELS/DLMIA -2016. LNCS, vol. 10008, pp. 179–187. Springer, Cham (2016). https://doi.org/10.1007/978-3-319-46976-8_19
16. Azad, R., Asadi-Aghbolaghi, M., Fathy, M., Escalera, S.: Bi-directional ConvLSTM U-Net with Densley connected convolutions. In: 2019 IEEE/CVF International Conference on Computer Vision Workshop (ICCVW), pp. 406–415 (2019)

17. Chen, H., Qi, X., Yu, L., Heng, P.: DCAN: deep contour-aware networks for accurate gland segmentation. In: 2016 IEEE Conference on Computer Vision and Pattern Recognition (CVPR), pp. 2487–2496 (2016)
18. McKinley, R., et al.: Nabla-Net: a deep dag-like convolutional architecture for biomedical image segmentation. In: Crimi, A., Menze, B., Maier, O., Reyes, M., Winzeck, S., Handels, H. (eds.) BrainLes 2016. LNCS, vol. 10154, pp. 119–128. Springer, Cham (2016). https://doi.org/10.1007/978-3-319-55524-9_12
19. Alom, M.Z., Yakopcic, C., Hasan, M., Taha, T., Asari, V.: Recurrent residual U-Net for medical image segmentation. J. Med. Imaging **6**, 014006–014006 (2019)
20. Alom, M., Hasan, M., Yakopcic, C., Taha, T., Asari, V.: Recurrent residual convolutional neural network based on U-Net (R2U-Net) for medical image segmentation. ArXiv abs/1802.06955 (2018)
21. Milletari, F., Navab, N., Ahmadi, S.A.: V-net: fully convolutional neural networks for volumetric medical image segmentation. In: 2016 Fourth International Conference on 3D Vision (3DV), pp. 565–571 (2016)
22. Dou, Q., et al.: 3D deeply supervised network for automated segmentation of volumetric medical images. Med. Image Anal. **41**, 40–54 (2017)
23. Kamnitsas, K., et al.: Efficient multi-scale 3D CNN with fully connected CRF for accurate brain lesion segmentation. Med. Image Anal. **36**, 61–78 (2017)
24. Li, W., Wang, G., Fidon, L., Ourselin, S., Cardoso, M., Vercauteren, T.K.M.: On the compactness, efficiency, and representation of 3d convolutional networks: Brain parcellation as a pretext task. ArXiv abs/1707.01992 (2017)
25. Chen, H., Dou, Q., Yu, L., Heng, P.: VoxResNet: deep voxelwise residual networks for volumetric brain segmentation. ArXiv abs/1608.05895 (2016)
26. Yang, Z., He, X., Gao, J., Deng, L., Smola, A.J.: Stacked attention networks for image question answering. CoRR abs/1511.02274 (2015)
27. Pedersoli, M., Lucas, T., Schmid, C., Verbeek, J.: Areas of attention for image captioning. CoRR abs/1612.01033 (2016)
28. Wang, F., et al.: Residual attention network for image classification. CoRR abs/1704.06904 (2017)
29. Chen, L., Yang, Y., Wang, J., Xu, W., Yuille, A.L.: Attention to scale: scale-aware semantic image segmentation. CoRR abs/1511.03339 (2015)
30. Zhao, H., et al.: PSANet: point-wise spatial attention network for scene parsing. In: Ferrari, V., Hebert, M., Sminchisescu, C., Weiss, Y. (eds.) ECCV 2018. LNCS, vol. 11213, pp. 270–286. Springer, Cham (2018). https://doi.org/10.1007/978-3-030-01240-3_17
31. Fu, J., Liu, J., Tian, H., Fang, Z., Lu, H.: Dual attention network for scene segmentation. CoRR abs/1809.02983 (2018)
32. Li, H., Xiong, P., An, J., Wang, L.: Pyramid attention network for semantic segmentation. CoRR abs/1805.10180 (2018)
33. Yu, C., Wang, J., Peng, C., Gao, C., Yu, G., Sang, N.: BiSeNet: bilateral segmentation network for real-time semantic segmentation. CoRR abs/1808.00897 (2018)
34. Zhang, P., Liu, W., Wang, H., Lei, Y., Lu, H.: Deep gated attention networks for large-scale street-level scene segmentation. Pattern Recogn. **88**, 702–714 (2019)
35. Wang, Y., et al.: Deep attentional features for prostate segmentation in ultrasound. In: Frangi, A.F., Schnabel, J.A., Davatzikos, C., Alberola-López, C., Fichtinger, G. (eds.) MICCAI 2018. LNCS, vol. 11073, pp. 523–530. Springer, Cham (2018). https://doi.org/10.1007/978-3-030-00937-3_60
36. Li, C., et al.: Attention based hierarchical aggregation network for 3D left atrial segmentation. In: Pop, M., et al. (eds.) STACOM 2018. LNCS, vol. 11395, pp. 255–264. Springer, Cham (2019). https://doi.org/10.1007/978-3-030-12029-0_28

37. Schlemper, J., et al.: Attention gated networks: learning to leverage salient regions in medical images. Med. Image Anal. **53**, 197–207 (2019)
38. Nie, D., Gao, Y., Wang, L., Shen, D.: ASDNet: attention based semi-supervised deep networks for medical image segmentation. In: Frangi, A.F., Schnabel, J.A., Davatzikos, C., Alberola-López, C., Fichtinger, G. (eds.) MICCAI 2018. LNCS, vol. 11073, pp. 370–378. Springer, Cham (2018). https://doi.org/10.1007/978-3-030-00937-3_43
39. Roy, A.G., Navab, N., Wachinger, C.: Concurrent spatial and channel squeeze & excitation in fully convolutional networks. CoRR abs/1803.02579 (2018)
40. Oktay, O., et al.: Attention U-Net: learning where to look for the pancreas. ArXiv abs/1804.03999 (2018)

Parallel-Connected Residual Channel Attention Network for Remote Sensing Image Super-Resolution

Yinhao Li[1] , Yutaro Iwamoto[1] , Lanfen Lin[2(✉)] ,
and Yen-Wei Chen[1,2,3(✉)]

[1] College of Information Science and Engineering,
Ritsumeikan University, Kyoto, Japan
gr0278ps@ed.ritsumei.ac.jp, yiwamoto@fc.ritsumei.ac.jp,
chen@is.ritsumei.ac.jp
[2] College of Computer Science and Technology,
Zhejiang University, Hangzhou, China
llf@zju.edu.cn
[3] Research Center for Healthcare Data Science,
Zhejiang Lab, Hangzhou, China

Abstract. In recent years, convolutional neural networks (CNNs) have obtained promising results in single-image super-resolution (SR) for remote sensing images. However, most existing methods are inadequate for remote sensing image SR due to the high computational cost required. Therefore, enhancing the representation ability with fewer parameters and a shorter prediction time is a challenging and critical task for remote sensing image SR. In this paper, we propose a novel CNN called a parallel-connected residual channel attention network (PCRCAN). Specifically, inspired by group convolution, we propose a parallel module with feature aggregation modules in PCRCAN. The parallel module significantly reduces the model parameters and fully integrates feature maps by widening the network architecture. In addition, to reduce the difficulty of training a complex deep network and improve model performance, we use a residual channel attention block as the basic feature mapping unit instead of a single convolutional layer. Experiments on a public remote sensing dataset UC Merced land-use dataset revealed that PCRCAN achieved higher accuracy, efficiency, and visual improvement than most state-of-the-art methods.

1 Introduction

High-resolution (HR) remote sensing images with rich detailed geographic information and textures play a vital role in remote sensing image analysis, such as traffic flow monitoring, disaster analysis, and vegetation coverage. However, due to hardware limitations and factors such as the orbit altitude, revisit cycle,

© Springer Nature Switzerland AG 2021
I. Sato and B. Han (Eds.): ACCV 2020 Workshops, LNCS 12628, pp. 18–30, 2021.
https://doi.org/10.1007/978-3-030-69756-3_2

instantaneous field of view, and optical sensor, the spatial resolution of satellite images is usually unsatisfactory in ordinary civilian applications [1,2].

Super-resolution (SR), which aims to recover HR images with rich high-frequency details from the corresponding low-resolution (LR) counterparts using software, is capable of solving the problem of insufficient resolution of remote sensing images. So far, various methods, including interpolation-based [3,4], reconstruction-based [5], and learning-based [6–17] methods have been proposed to address image super-resolution (SR).

In recent years, single image super-resolution (SISR) based on convolutional neural network (CNN) has become the mainstream method due to its high performance and fast prediction speed [8–17]. In 2014, Dong et al. [8] proposed a neural network model consisting of three convolutional layers referred to as SR convolutional neural networks (SRCNNs). Then, Kim et al. proposed a very deep neural network for image SR (VDSR) [9], in which only the residual map between the LR image and HR image requires to be learned for restoring lost high-frequency details. Since most regions' residuals are close to zero, the model complexity and learning difficulty are reduced significantly. Motivated by local residual learning proposed by He et al. [18], several methods based on ResNet were proposed for the SR image [19–21]. The residual connection models with a deeper CNN structure yield higher accuracy. Zhang et al. [16] combined the advantages in the structure of residual connection and dense skip connection to propose a residual dense network (RDN). Zhang et al. [17] used the channel attention mechanism to optimize the residual block and proposed a residual channel attention network (RCAN) to further improve the performance of SR CNN models. Also, CNN-based models have been widely used in remote sensing image super-resolution tasks in recent years. For instance, to learn the multi-level representation of remote sensing images, Lei et al. proposed an algorithm called local-global combined network [22]. Haut et al. [23] proposed an unsupervised SISR method and presented a model using the generative adversarial network to learn the image distribution. Xu et al. [24] proposed a new method called deep storage connection network to reduce the time consumption of reconstructing the resolution of remote sensing images.

From the perspective of the development trend of CNNs, many SR methods have deepened the CNN for improved performance [15–17]. With increased depth, the features in the deep neural network layers become hierarchical with different receptive fields. Therefore, hierarchical features from the network can provide additional clues for image resolution reconstruction tasks. However, by blindly pursuing depth, the model will treat feature maps containing different receptive fields equally, thereby limiting the expressive ability of the model. In addition, complex deep models tend to have a high computational cost and training difficulty, which hinder their practical application.

To address these problems, a preliminary version of this work was presented [25,26], where we introduced the basic structure of parallel connected network. In this study, to demonstrate the effectiveness parallel connected network for remote sensing image SR, we propose a parallel-connected residual channel attention network (PCRCAN) that is more effective for feature representation and high-frequency detail restoration. Inspired by group convolution [27], we combined a new structure based on parallel connections to broaden the network (i.e., make deeper layers wider). To improve the information fusion between the main line and branch lines and enhance the expressive ability of the model, we propose information aggregation modules to perform secondary processing on the feature maps of the upper branch lines. In addition, the residual channel attention structure introduced in [17] effectively reduces the training difficulty of complex CNN models suffering from the vanishing gradient problem. Therefore, to replace the standard full convolution, we use the residual channel attention block (RCAB) as the basic feature mapping unit.

Our contributions consist mainly of the proposed unified end-to-end architecture and are summarized as follows:

- We propose a novel deep CNN for remote sensing image SR. The proposed model has a deep and wide structure, and fully integrates hierarchical feature maps, especially feature maps with large respective fields. Our results demonstrate that the proposed model outperforms state-of-the-art methods in terms of accuracy and efficiency.
- We propose a novel building block called the parallel module that contains a parallel-connected architecture and feature aggregation module. This strategy can reduce the network parameters and calculations without compromising the accuracy of the results. In addition, to reduce the difficulty of training a complex deep model, we use the RCAB as the basic feature mapping unit. Both the parallel module and the RCAB architecture improve the representation ability of the network.

2 Method

In this section, we describe the architecture of the proposed PCRCAN, including the parallel module and mathematical expressions. The feature aggregation module and RCAB in the parallel module are described in detail followed by the loss function used in this study.

2.1 Network Architecture

As shown in Fig. 1, the proposed PCRCAN consists of a parallel module, a global residual branch, and an upscale module. Let us denote the input and output of the PCRCAN as I_{LR} and I_{HR}, respectively. Here, we use one convolutional layer to extract shallow features as the same in [28]. The first convolutional layer extracting features I_0 from the low-resolution (LR) input can be obtained by

$$I_0 = H_{EX}(I_{LR}), \tag{1}$$

where $H_{EX}(\cdot)$ denotes the convolution operation. I_0 is then used for global residual learning. Many studies have demonstrated that the global residual learning

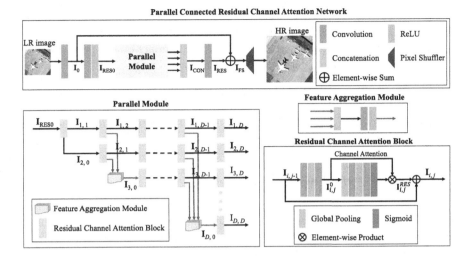

Fig. 1. Network architecture of proposed parallel-connected residual channel attention network (PCRCAN).

can effectively avoid gradient disappearance, reduce the training difficulty, and increase the training speed. Therefore, we focus on restoring the residual part of LR feature maps.

To further extract features and increase the number of channels for subsequent feature fusion, we add a convolutional layer inside the global residual branch, which can be represented as

$$I_{RES0} = \sigma(H_{EXD}(I_0)), \tag{2}$$

where $H_{EXD}(\cdot)$ and $\sigma(\cdot)$ refer to the convolution operation and rectified linear unit (ReLU) [29], respectively.

Then, we perform deeper feature extraction and fusion on I_{RES0} through our proposed parallel module. The operation can be obtained by

$$I_{PM} = H_{PM}(I_{RES0}), \tag{3}$$

where $H_{PM}(\cdot)$ denotes a composite operation using the parallel module, and I_{PM} represents the output of the parallel module. Further details about the parallel module are provided in Sect. 2.2.

For the two inputs of the global residual branch to be of the same size, we concatenate and filter the output feature maps of the parallel module. Thus, the residual information of the global residual branch I_{RES} can be formulated as

$$I_{RES} = H_{FIL}(H_{CON}(I_{PM})), \tag{4}$$

where $H_{CON}(\cdot)$ and $H_{FIL}(\cdot)$ denote the concatenation layer and the convolutional layer, respectively.

Finally, inspired by [13,16], we use a pixel shuffle layer introduced in [13] to directly output the corresponding HR image, which reduces the convolution operations and improves the speed with virtually no impact on the performance". Thus, the output HR image I_{HR} can be obtained by

$$I_{HR} = \mathcal{PS}(I_0 \oplus I_{RES}), \tag{5}$$

where $\mathcal{PS}$ denotes the pixel shuffle operation, and $\oplus$ denotes the element-wise sum operation.

2.2   Parallel Connection Module

In this subsection, we introduce the parallel connection module using the group convolution [27] and our proposed feature aggregation module. Figure 1 demonstrates that each branch can be viewed as separate from the upper branch using group convolution. Besides, to better integrate the feature maps of other branches, we use all the feature maps of the previous layer of other branches as input of a new branch, called the feature aggregation module. We demonstrate that the proposed model based on parallel connections can use features in deep layers more effectively. Furthermore, to reduce the difficulty of training complex models and improve the accuracy of the network, we use the RCAB as the basic feature mapping unit instead of a single standard convolution, as described in Sect. 2.3.

Supposing that we have D layers in the main line (first branch) of the parallel module, the output $I_{i,j}$ $(j \geq 1)$ of the j-th layer in the i-th line can be obtained by

$$I_{i,j} = H_{i,j-1}^{RCAB}(I_{i,j-1}), \tag{6}$$

where $H_{i,j}^{RCAB}(\cdot)$ denotes the operations of the j-th layer in the i-th branch using the RCAB.

To fully extract and fuse features, we propose a feature aggregation module that combines feature maps with the same receptive fields in other layers at the beginning of each branch. Thus, the input of the first layer of each branch $I_{i,0}$ can be represented as

$$I_{i,0} = \begin{cases} I_{RES0} & i = 1 \\ \sigma(H_{i,0}([I_{1,i-1}, I_{2,i-2}, \ldots, I_{i-1,1}])) & i = 2, 3, \ldots, D \end{cases} \tag{7}$$

where $[I_{1,i-1}, I_{2,i-2}, \ldots, I_{i-1,1}]$ refers to the concatenation of the feature maps produced by the $(i-1)$-th convolutional layer in the first branch (mainline), the $(i-2)$-th convolutional layer in the second branch, ..., the first convolutional layer in the $(i-1)$-th branch. In our SR model, the number of channels in each layer is K. $H_{i,0}(\cdot)$ denotes a convolution operation, which reduces the channel from $(i-1)K$ to K and performs preliminary fusion of the feature maps obtained from the other branches. σ denotes the ReLU activation function. Thus, we can obtain a series of feature maps $[I_{1,D}, I_{2,D-1}, \ldots, I_{D,1}]$ using the parallel module.

2.3 Residual Channel Attention Block

To further improve the network performance while reducing the difficulty of training a complex model, inspired by [17], we introduce the RCAB, which consists of a residual connected architecture and a channel attention module. The channel attention architecture can effectively improve the performance of the network; however, it increases the computational cost and complexity of the network, thereby increasing the difficulty of training a CNN. Therefore, using residual learning to prevent gradient disappearance can reduce the model training difficulty and increase the training speed.

According to the method described in [17], for the j-th RCAB in the i-th branch, we have

$$I_{i,j} = I_{i,j-1} + I_{i,j}^{RES} = I_{i,j-1} + H_{i,j}^{CA}(I_{i,j}^0), \tag{8}$$

where $H_{i,j}^{CA}(\cdot)$ refers to the channel attention module and $I_{i,j}^0$ is the output of preliminary mapping in the RCAB module. $I_{i,j}^{RES}$ is the residual of $I_{i,j}$ and $I_{i,j-1}$. $I_{i,j}^0$ can be obtained by

$$I_{i,j}^0 = H_{i,j}^{RCAB(2)}(\sigma(H_{i,j}^{RCAB(1)}(I_{i,j-1}))), \tag{9}$$

where $H_{i,j}^{RCAB(1)}(\cdot)$ and $H_{i,j}^{RCAB(2)}(\cdot)$ represent the first and second convolution operation in the j-th RCAB of the i-th branch, respectively, and $\sigma(\cdot)$ is the ReLU activation function.

The output $I_{i,j}^{RES}$ of the channel attention operation, which is a key step for generating different attention for each channel-wise feature, can be expressed by

$$I_{i,j}^{RES} = I_{i,j}^0 \otimes \delta(H_{i,j}^{CA(2)}(\sigma(H_{i,j}^{CA(1)}(H_{i,j}^{GP}(I_{i,j}^0))))), \tag{10}$$

where $H_{i,j}^{GP}(\cdot)$ represents the global pooling operation and $H_{i,j}^{CA(1)}(\cdot)$ and $H_{i,j}^{CA(2)}(\cdot)$ represent the first and second convolution operation in the channel attention module, respectively. $\delta(\cdot)$ refers to the sigmoid activation function. $\otimes$ refers to the element-wise product operation.

Based on the parallel module and RCAB, we can construct a very deep and wide PCRCAN for highly accurate image SR and achieve notable performance improvement over previous state-of-the-art methods.

2.4 Loss Function

In this study, our models are optimized by the L1 norm function. The absolute difference (L1 norm) between the output SR of the network and GND HR images can be expressed by

$$Loss_{L1} = \frac{1}{HW} \sum_{y=1}^{W} \sum_{x=1}^{H} |I_{x,y}^{SR} - I_{x,y}^{HR}|, \tag{11}$$

where I^{SR} is the SR output from the deep learning model, and I^{HR} is a GND HR image of size $H \times W$. Although the L2 norm is widely used in the image restoration due to its relationship with the peak signal-to-noise ratio (PSNR), the L1 norm offers better convergence and performance [16,28,30,31].

3   Experiments

3.1   Data Preparation and Parameter Settings

We followed the selection of [32] and used AID [33] as our training dataset. This dataset contained 30 land-use scene images, such as airports, deserts, and stadiums. We randomly selected 80 images of 600×600 pixels in each category to train the model, and used the remaining 20 images of 600×600 pixels in each category are used as the validation set. We used the initial images as GND HR images and degraded them to LR images at scale factors $\times 2$ and $\times 4$ in X and Y directions by bicubic interpolation. To evaluate the performance of our proposed method, we used the UC Merced land-use dataset [34], which included 21 land-use classes, including buildings, forests, and freeways. We converted raw red-green-blue (RGB) data to YCbCr space and used the Y channel to train and test all models. The SR results were evaluated with the PSNR and structural similarity (SSIM) [35] on the Y channel of the transformed YCbCr space.

We set the number of channels in the first layer of the proposed PCRCAN as 2 to the N-th power. N is equivalent to the scale factor. The number of channels of the second layer of PCRCAN and convolutional layers in the parallel module was set to 32.

We randomly extracted 16 LR patches with a size of 64×64 pixels as inputs in each training batch of our proposed PCRCAN. The other state-of-the-art models followed the settings in their corresponding papers. We used Adam as the optimizer and set the learning rate to 10^{-4}. We set the number of epochs to infinity, and stopped training when the loss function had 25 subsequent epochs without reduction. We implemented all the models in Keras with an NVIDIA Quadro RTX 8000 GPU. The operating system and central processing unit were Ubuntu 16.04 LTS and Intel Core i9-9820X, respectively.

3.2   Quantitative Results

Table 1 presents the quantitative results (i.e., mean PSNR, SSIM, number of parameters, and prediction time) of our proposed models, bicubic interpolation, and four state-of-the-art methods: SRCNN [8], VDSR [9], RDN [16] and RCAN [17]. We evaluated the performance of our proposed remote sensing image SR network PCRCAN on the UC Merced dataset with two different upsampling factors, $\times 2$ and $\times 4$.

The PSNR of our method was almost identical to that of RCAN. However, the number of parameters in our network was much smaller than that of RCAN. For instance, compared with RCAN, in the task of magnifying remote sensing

Table 1. PSNR (dB), SSIM values, prediction time, and number of parameters of different methods on UC Merced dataset for scale factors ×2 and ×4.

Method	Scale	PSNR	SSIM	#param. (M)	Time (s)
Bicubic	×2	30.60	0.8944	–	–
SRCNN [8]	×2	31.26	0.8985	0.008	1.346
VDSR [9]	×2	33.68	0.9215	0.666	1.568
RDN [16]	×2	34.03	0.9249	6.982	3.162
RCAN [17]	×2	34.09	0.9249	7.666	4.988
PCRCAN w/o RCAB (D = 10) [ours]	×2	33.80	0.9230	0.844	2.176
PCRCAN (D = 10) [ours]	×2	34.00	0.9243	1.452	3.810
PCRCAN (D = 12) [ours]	×2	34.06	0.9246	2.080	4.570
PCRCAN (D = 15) [ours]	×2	34.08	0.9252	3.232	6.361
Bicubic	×4	25.32	0.8051	–	–
SRCNN [8]	×4	25.77	0.8107	0.008	1.440
VDSR [9]	×4	26.93	0.8341	0.666	1.428
RDN [16]	×4	27.22	0.8393	6.982	2.873
RCAN [17]	×4	27.31	0.8407	7.666	4.611
PCRCAN w/o RCAB (D = 10) [ours]	×4	27.15	0.8381	0.882	1.807
PCRCAN (D = 10) [ours]	×4	27.33	0.8405	1.490	3.387
PCRCAN (D = 12) [ours]	×4	27.33	0.8407	2.125	4.244
PCRCAN (D = 15) [ours]	×4	27.33	0.8409	3.287	6.111

images twice, our proposed PCRCAN (D = 15) had higher SSIM while requiring less than half of the parameters. In the task of magnifying remote sensing images four times, our proposed models outperformed the state-of-the-art methods in terms of accuracy. Note that the element-wise sum and element-wise product operations in RCAB did not increase the network parameters, but the extensive use of RCAB increased the prediction time significantly. To solve this problem, our proposed PCRCAN (D = 10) used fewer parameters to outperform RCAN in terms of accuracy and efficiency. Although both the proposed PCRCAN and RCAN used RCAB as the basic feature extraction and fusion unit, the proposed parallel module enabled our models to obtain the same level of performance as the state-of-the-art methods in terms of accuracy, while less than half of parameters were required. As a result, the experimental results thus demonstrate that the proposed method based on the parallel module with feature aggregation and RCAB was better able to extract and fuse feature maps to reconstruct HR remote sensing images.

3.3 Visual Results

To fully evaluate the effectiveness of our method, we present several visual comparisons on scales ×2 and ×4 in Figs. 2 and 3, respectively. The results indicate that the proposed PCRCAN performed well in a real scenario. As illustrated in Fig. 3, for the large scale factor ×4, the bicubic upsampling strategy resulted in

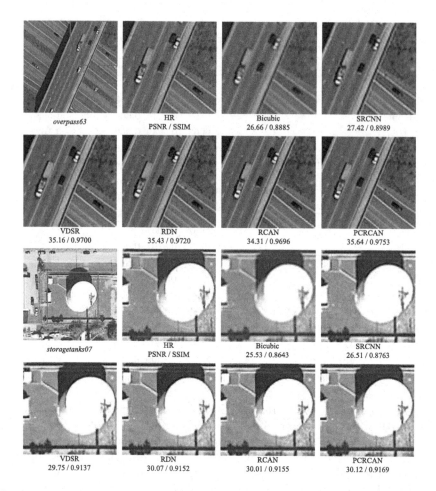

Fig. 2. Visual comparison of some representative SR methods and our model on ×2 factor.

loss of texture and thus produced blurry SR results. SRCNN and VDSR taking such bicubic interpolated images as network inputs will produce erroneous texture, resulting in low SR image quality. Although RDN and RCAN used the original LR image as input, they were unable to restore the correct texture structure, while our PCRCAN can recover more texture in the original corresponding HR image.

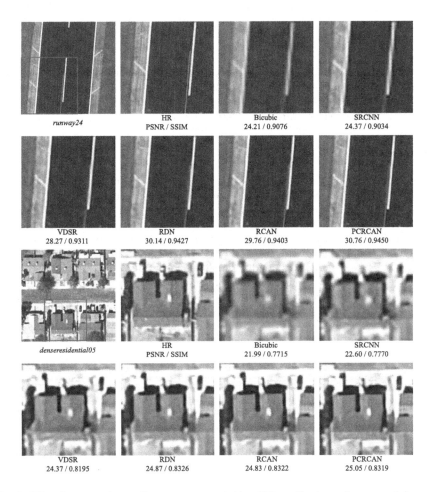

Fig. 3. Visual comparison of some representative SR methods and our model on ×4 factor.

4   Conclusions

In this paper, we propose a novel CNN called PCRCAN to improve the representation of deep CNNs and achieve improved performance in remote sensing image SR task. Specifically, we propose a parallel module as the core building module of our SR model for feature extraction and fusion. We use the RCAB as the basic feature mapping unit instead of a single convolution layer. This architecture can improve the network representation capability and stabilize the training. Furthermore, because the proposed parallel module is built based on group convolution and a feature aggregation structure, we can avoid the loss of accuracy due to poor channel circulation while constructing a lightweight model. The experimental results demonstrate that our proposed method obtained accurate results with fewer parameters and outperformed most state-of-the-art methods in terms of accuracy and efficiency.

Acknowledgement. This work is supported in part by Japan Society for Promotion of Science (JSPS) under Grant No. 19J13820, the Grant-in-Aid for Young Scientists (18K18078), Grant-in-Aid for Scientific Research (B) (18H03267) and Grant-in-Aid for Challenging Research (Exploratory) (20K21821).

References

1. Li, F., Xin, L., Guo, Y., Gao, D., Kong, X., Jia, X.: Super-resolution for GaoFen-4 remote sensing images. IEEE Geosci. Remote Sens. Lett. **15**, 28–32 (2017)
2. Xu, W., Xu, G., Wang, Y., Sun, X., Lin, D., Wu, Y.: High quality remote sensing image super-resolution using deep memory connected network. In: IGARSS 2018–2018 IEEE International Geoscience and Remote Sensing Symposium, pp. 8889–8892. IEEE (2018)
3. Zhang, L., Wu, X.: An edge-guided image interpolation algorithm via directional filtering and data fusion. IEEE Trans. Image Process. **15**, 2226–2238 (2006)
4. Hung, K.W., Siu, W.C.: Robust soft-decision interpolation using weighted least squares. IEEE Trans. Image Process. **21**, 1061–1069 (2011)
5. Zhang, K., Gao, X., Tao, D., Li, X.: Single image super-resolution with non-local means and steering kernel regression. IEEE Trans. Image Process. **21**, 4544–4556 (2012)
6. Peleg, T., Elad, M.: A statistical prediction model based on sparse representations for single image super-resolution. IEEE Trans. Image Process. **23**, 2569–2582 (2014)
7. Wang, L., Guo, Y., Liu, L., Lin, Z., Deng, X., An, W.: Deep video super-resolution using HR optical flow estimation. IEEE Trans. Image Process. **29**, 4323–4336 (2020)
8. Dong, C., Loy, C.C., He, K., Tang, X.: Image super-resolution using deep convolutional networks. IEEE Trans. Pattern Anal. Mach. Intell. **38**, 295–307 (2015)
9. Kim, J., Kwon Lee, J., Mu Lee, K.: Accurate image super-resolution using very deep convolutional networks. In: Proceedings of the IEEE Conference on Computer Vision and Pattern Recognition, pp. 1646–1654 (2016)
10. Kim, J., Kwon Lee, J., Mu Lee, K.: Deeply-recursive convolutional network for image super-resolution. In: Proceedings of the IEEE Conference on Computer Vision and Pattern Recognition, pp. 1637–1645 (2016)
11. Tai, Y., Yang, J., Liu, X.: Image super-resolution via deep recursive residual network. In: Proceedings of the IEEE Conference on Computer Vision and Pattern Recognition, pp. 3147–3155 (2017)
12. Tai, Y., Yang, J., Liu, X., Xu, C.: MemNet: a persistent memory network for image restoration. In: Proceedings of the IEEE International Conference on Computer Vision, pp. 4539–4547 (2017)
13. Shi, W., et al.: Real-time single image and video super-resolution using an efficient sub-pixel convolutional neural network. In: Proceedings of the IEEE Conference on Computer Vision and Pattern Recognition, pp. 1874–1883 (2016)
14. Dong, C., Loy, C.C., Tang, X.: Accelerating the super-resolution convolutional neural network. In: Leibe, B., Matas, J., Sebe, N., Welling, M. (eds.) ECCV 2016. LNCS, vol. 9906, pp. 391–407. Springer, Cham (2016). https://doi.org/10.1007/978-3-319-46475-6_25

15. Tong, T., Li, G., Liu, X., Gao, Q.: Image super-resolution using dense skip connections. In: Proceedings of the IEEE International Conference on Computer Vision, pp. 4799–4807 (2017)
16. Zhang, Y., Tian, Y., Kong, Y., Zhong, B., Fu, Y.: Residual dense network for image restoration. IEEE Trans. Pattern Anal. Mach. Intell. (2020)
17. Zhang, Y., Li, K., Li, K., Wang, L., Zhong, B., Fu, Y.: Image super-resolution using very deep residual channel attention networks. In: Ferrari, V., Hebert, M., Sminchisescu, C., Weiss, Y. (eds.) ECCV 2018. LNCS, vol. 11211, pp. 294–310. Springer, Cham (2018). https://doi.org/10.1007/978-3-030-01234-2_18
18. He, K., Zhang, X., Ren, S., Sun, J.: Deep residual learning for image recognition. In: Proceedings of the IEEE Conference on Computer Vision and Pattern Recognition, pp. 770–778 (2016)
19. Mao, X., Shen, C., Yang, Y.B.: Image restoration using very deep convolutional encoder-decoder networks with symmetric skip connections. In: Advances in Neural Information Processing Systems, pp. 2802–2810 (2016)
20. Han, W., Chang, S., Liu, D., Yu, M., Witbrock, M., Huang, T.S.: Image super-resolution via dual-state recurrent networks. In: Proceedings of the IEEE Conference on Computer Vision and Pattern Recognition, pp. 1654–1663 (2018)
21. Li, J., Fang, F., Mei, K., Zhang, G.: Multi-scale residual network for image super-resolution. In: Ferrari, V., Hebert, M., Sminchisescu, C., Weiss, Y. (eds.) ECCV 2018. LNCS, vol. 11212, pp. 527–542. Springer, Cham (2018). https://doi.org/10.1007/978-3-030-01237-3_32
22. Lei, S., Shi, Z., Zou, Z.: Super-resolution for remote sensing images via local-global combined network. IEEE Geosci. Remote Sens. Lett. 14, 1243–1247 (2017)
23. Haut, J.M., Fernandez-Beltran, R., Paoletti, M.E., Plaza, J., Plaza, A., Pla, F.: A new deep generative network for unsupervised remote sensing single-image super-resolution. IEEE Geosci. Remote Sens. Lett. 56, 6792–6810 (2018)
24. Xu, W., Xu, G., Wang, Y., Sun, X., Lin, D., Wu, Y.: Deep memory connected neural network for optical remote sensing image restoration. Remote Sens. 10, 1893 (2018)
25. Li, Y., Iwamoto, Y., Lin, L., Xu, R., Chen, Y.W.: VolumeNet: a lightweight parallel network for super-resolution of medical volumetric data. arXiv preprint arXiv:2010.08357 (2020)
26. Li, Y., Iwamoto, Y., Lin, L., Xu, R., Chen, Y.W.: VolumeNet: a lightweight parallel network for super-resolution of medical volumetric data. IEEE Trans. Image Process. (2020, submitted)
27. Krizhevsky, A., Sutskever, I., Hinton, G.E.: ImageNet classification with deep convolutional neural networks. In: Advances in Neural Information Processing Systems, pp. 1097–1105 (2012)
28. Lim, B., Son, S., Kim, H., Nah, S., Mu Lee, K.: Enhanced deep residual networks for single image super-resolution. In: Proceedings of the IEEE Conference on Computer Vision and Pattern Recognition Workshops, pp. 136–144 (2017)
29. Nair, V., Hinton, G.E.: Rectified linear units improve restricted Boltzmann machines. In: ICML (2010)
30. Ahn, N., Kang, B., Sohn, K.-A.: Fast, accurate, and lightweight super-resolution with cascading residual network. In: Ferrari, V., Hebert, M., Sminchisescu, C., Weiss, Y. (eds.) ECCV 2018. LNCS, vol. 11214, pp. 256–272. Springer, Cham (2018). https://doi.org/10.1007/978-3-030-01249-6_16
31. Zhao, H., Gallo, O., Frosio, I., Kautz, J.: Loss functions for image restoration with neural networks. IEEE Trans. Comput. Imaging 3, 47–57 (2016)

32. Zhang, D., Shao, J., Li, X., Shen, H.T.: Remote sensing image super-resolution via mixed high-order attention network. IEEE Trans. Geosci. Remote Sens. (2020)
33. Xia, G.S., et al.: AID: a benchmark data set for performance evaluation of aerial scene classification. IEEE Trans. Geosci. Remote Sens. **55**, 3965–3981 (2017)
34. Yang, Y., Newsam, S.: Bag-of-visual-words and spatial extensions for land-use classification. In: Proceedings of the 18th SIGSPATIAL International Conference on Advances in Geographic Information Systems, pp. 270–279 (2010)
35. Wang, Z., Bovik, A.C., Sheikh, H.R., Simoncelli, E.P.: Image quality assessment: from error visibility to structural similarity. IEEE Trans. Image Process. **13**, 600–612 (2004)

Unsupervised Multispectral and Hyperspectral Image Fusion with Deep Spatial and Spectral Priors

Zhe Liu[1]([✉]), Yinqiang Zheng[2], and Xian-Hua Han[1]iD

[1] Graduate School of Science and Technology for Innovation, Yamaguchi University, Yamaguchi, Japan
{b602vz,hanxhua}@yamaguchi-u.ac.jp
[2] National Institute of Informatics, Tokyo, Japan
yqzheng@nii.ac.jp

Abstract. Hyperspectral (HS) imaging is a promising imaging modality, which can simultaneously acquire various bands of images of the same scene and capture detailed spectral distribution helping for numerous applications. However, existing HS imaging sensor can only obtain images with low spatial resolution. Thus fusing a low resolution hyperspectral (LR-HS) image with a high resolution (HR) RGB (or multispectral) image into a HR-HS image has received much attention. Conventional fusion methods usually employ various hand-crafted priors to regularize the mathematical model formulating the relation between the observations and the HR-HS image, and conduct optimization for pursuing the optimal solution. However, the politic prior would be various for different scenes and is difficult to hammer out for a specific scene. Recently, deep learning-based methods have been widely explored for HS image resolution enhancement, and impressive performance has been validated. As it is known that deep learning-based methods essentially require large-scale training samples, which are hard to obtain due to the limitation of the existing HS cameras, for constructing the model with good generalization. Motivated by the deep image prior that network architecture itself sufficiently captures a great deal of low-level image statistics with arbitrary learning strategy, we investigate the deep learned image prior consisting both spatial structure and spectral attribute instead of hand-crafted priors for unsupervised multispectral (RGB) and HS image fusion, and propose a novel deep spatial and spectral prior learning framework for exploring the underlying structure of the latent HR-HS image with the observed HR-RGB and LR-HS images only. The proposed deep prior learning method has no requirement to prepare massive triplets of the HR-RGB, LR-HS and HR-HS images for network training. We validate the proposed method on two benchmark HS image datasets, and experimental results show that our method is comparable or outperforms the state-of-the-art HS image super-resolution approaches.

© Springer Nature Switzerland AG 2021
I. Sato and B. Han (Eds.): ACCV 2020 Workshops, LNCS 12628, pp. 31–45, 2021.
https://doi.org/10.1007/978-3-030-69756-3_3

1   Introduction

In recent decades of years, imaging technique has been witnessed significant progress for providing high-definition images in different applications from agriculture, astronomy to surveillance and medicine, to name a few. Although the acquired images with the existing imaging systems can provide the high-definition information in a specific domain such as spatial-, temporal- or spectral-domain according to the application requirement, it is difficult to simultaneously offer all-possible required detail distribution in all domains such as the high-resolution hyperspectral (HR-HS) images to meet the demand of the resolution enhancement in both spatial- and spectral- domains. It is well known that hyperspectral (HS) imaging employs both traditional two-dimensional imaging technology and spectroscopic technology for obtaining a three-dimensional cubic data for a scene, and enriches greatly the spectral information for being successfully applied in remote sensing [1,2], medical image analysis [3], and many computer vision tasks, such as object recognition and classification [4–6], tracking [7], segmentation [8]. However, the detail distribution in spectral domain (high spectral resolution) implies less radiant energy being able to be collected for each band of narrow spectrum. For guaranteeing acceptable signal-to-noise ratio, photo collection has to be performed in a much larger spatial region via sacrificing the spatial resolution. On the other hand, ordinary RGB cameras usually produce RGB images with high-resolution in spatial domain. Thus fusing the low-resolution HS image (LR-HS) with a corresponding high-resolution RGB (HR-RGB) image to generate a HR-HS image (called as multispectral and hyperspectral image fusion) has attracted remarkable attention.

Multispectral and hyperspectral image fusion is a challenging task due to its ill-posed nature in reality. Most existing methods mainly employ various hand-crafted priors to regularize the mathematical model formulating the relation between the observations and the HR-HS image, and conduct optimization for pursuing the optimal solution. Therein, one research line explores different spectral representation methods according to physical property of the observed spectrum such as matrix factorization and spectral unmixing motivated by the fact that the HS observations can be formulated as a weighted linear combination of the reflectance function basis and their corresponding fraction coefficients [8]. On the other hand, many work investigated sparse-promoted representation [9] as the prior knowledge for modeling the spatial structure and local spectral characteristic based on a dictionary trained on the observed HR-RGB and LR-HS images, and proved feasibility for HR-HS image reconstruction. Beside sparse constraint on spectral representation, low-rank technique has also been exploited to encode the intrinsic spectral correlation prior on the underlying HR-HS image for reducing spectral distortion [10]. There are also several work to explore the global spatial structure and local spectral similarity priors for further boosting the performance of the HS image reconstruction [11,12]. Although the promising performance with the hand-crafted priors such as mathematical sparsity, physical property of spectral unmixing, low-rank and similarity has been achieved, different scenes with highly diverse configurations both along space and across spectrum should have various effective priors for modeling and to figure out a proper prior for a specific scene is still difficult.

Recently, deep learning (DL) based methods have popularly been applied for the HS image reconstruction, and evolved into three research directions: 1) conventional spatial resolution enhancement with the observed LR-HS image, 2) traditional spectral resolution enhancement with the observed HR-RGB image, 3) fusion method with both LR-HS and HR-RGB images. Compared with the traditional prior-promoted methods, DL based methods do not need to rely on any assumption on the prior knowledge and can automatically capture the intrinsic characteristics of the latent HS images via data-driven learning. However, the DL based methods are generally used in a fully supervised way, and it is mandatory to previously collect large amount of training triplets consisting of the observed LR-HS and HR-RGB images, and their corresponding HR-HS images for learning optimal network parameters [13–15]. It is known that in the HS image reconstruction scenario, it is extremely hard to obtain large-scale training samples especially the HR-HS images as the label samples. In spite of the prospected advantage, the fully supervised DL scheme suffers from less generalization in real applications due to small number of the available training triplets. On one hand, Ulyanov et al. [16] advocated that the architecture of a generator network itself can capture quite a lot of low-level image priors with arbitrary learning strategy, and proposed deep image prior (DIP) learning with the deep network. The DIP method has successfully been applied to different natural image restoration tasks and manifested excellent results without any additional training samples.

Motivated by the fact that the deep network architecture itself carries large amount of low-level prior knowledge as explored in the DIP work [16], we propose a novel deep spatial and spectral prior (DSSP) learning farmework for HS image reconstruction. With a random noisy input, we attempt to learn a set of optimal parameters via searching the network parameter space to recover the latent HR-HS image, which is capable of approximating the observed HR-RGB and LR-HS images under a degradation procedure. In the network training step, we leverage both observed LR-HS and HR-RGB images of the under-studying scene to formulate the loss functions for capturing the underlying priors of the latent HR-HS image. Via employing the deep learned spatial and spectral priors, our proposed DSSP method can effectively recover the underlying spatial and spectral structure of the latent HR-HS image even only with the observed HR-RGB and LR-HS images, and it is not mandatory to prepare massive triplets of the HR-RGB, LR-HS and HR-HS images.

The main contributions of this work are three-fold:

1) We propose a novel unsupervised framework for fusing the observed LR-HS and HR-RGB (multispectral: MS) images to generate a HR-HS image, called as MS/HS fusion, in deep learning scenario.
2) We propose a deep spatial and spectral prior learning network for the MS/HS fusion, which is expected to effectively characterize the spatial structure and

the spectral attribute in the latent HR-HS image without manually analysis of the content in the under-studying scene.

3) We leverage both modality data of the observed LR-HS and HR-RGB images, and construct the loss functions of our proposed DSSP network for learning more reliable priors in the latent HR-HS image.

We validate our method on two benchmark HS image datasets, and experimental results show that our method is comparable or outperforms the state-of-the-art HS image super-resolution approaches.

The rest of this paper is organized as follows. Section 2 surveys the related work including traditional pan-sharpening and prior-promoted methods and deep learning based methods. Section 3 presents the proposed deep spatial and spectral prior learning framework for HS image reconstruction. Extensive experiments are conducted in Sect. 4 to compare our proposed framework with state-of-the-art methods on two benchmark datasets. Conclusion is given in Sect. 5.

2   Related Work

2.1   Traditional Methods

Multispectral and hyperspectral (MS/HS) image fusion is closely related multispectral (MS) image pan-sharpening which aims at merging a low-resolution MS image with a high-resolution wide-band panchromatic image [17–19]. There are many developed methods for MS pan-sharpening, which can be mainly divided into two categories: component substitution [18] and multiresolution analysis. Although MS/HS image fusion can intuitively be treated as a number of pan-sharpening sub-problems with each band of HR-MS (RGB) image as a panchromatic image, it cannot make full use of the spectral correlation and always suffers from the high spectral distortion.

Recently, many methods formulate MS/HS image fusion as an inverse optimization problem, and leverage the hand-crafted priors in the latent HR-HS image for boosting reconstruction performance. How to design the appreciate priors plays a key role in finding the feasible solutions for the optimization problem. The existing methods extensively investigated the prior knowledge for spatial and spectral representation such as physical spectral mixing, sparsity, low-rank, and manifest impressive performance. Yokoya et al. [14] proposed coupled non-negative matrix factorization (CNMF) to fuse a pair of HR-MS and LR-HS images and gave a convincing spectral recovery result. Lanaras et al. [15] exploited the coupled spectral unmixing method for HS image reconstruction, and utilized near-end alternating linearization method to optimize. The other research effort concentrated the sparsity promoting approaches via imposing sparsity constraints on the representative coefficients [20]. Grohnfeldt et al. [21] employed a joint sparse representation via firstly learning the corresponding HS and MS (RGB) patch dictionary, and then using the sparse coefficients in each individual band image to reconstruct the spatial local structure (patch). Akhtar et al. [22] conducted another sparse coefficient estimation algorithm and designed the generalized simultaneous orthogonal matching pursuit (G-SOMP) by assuming that the same atoms are used to reconstruct the spectrum of pixels in the local grid region. In order to use the prior more effectively in the inherent structure of the HR-HS image, Dong et al. [23] investigated a non-negative structured sparse representation (NSSR) method, whose principle is to use spectral similarity in local regions to limit sparse representation learning in order to restore HR-HS images closer to the real. Han et al. [24] extended to employ both local spectral and global structure similarity in the sparse-promotion scenario for further improving the robust recovery of HR-HS images. For now, although these hand-crafted prior algorithms have already achieved promising performance, seeking the suitable prior for a specific scene is still a challenging task.

2.2   Deep Learning Based Methods

Motivated by the success of deep learning in the field of nature RGB image enhancement, deep convolutional neural network has been applied for MS/HS image fusion, and does not need to model the hand-crafted prior. Han et al. [25] conducted a pilot study to use a simple 3-layer CNN for fusing the LR-HS and HR-RGB images with large difference of spatial structures, and further extended to more complex CNN for pursuing better performance. Palsson et al. [26] proposed a 3D-CNN based MS/HS fusion method by using PCA to reduce the computational cost. Dian et al. [27] proposed to combine the optimization- and CNN- based methods together, and validated promising HR image reconstruction results. All the above deep learning based methods are implemented under a fully supervised way, and require to previously prepare a lot of training triplets including the LR-HS, HR-RGB (MS) and the label HR-HS images for network training. However, large amount of training samples especially the HR-HS images in the HS image reconstruction scenario are difficult to be collected. Thus, Qu et al. [28] investigated an unsupervised encoder-decoder architecture to solve the MS/HS fusion problem which dose not need for any training by using a HS image dataset. Although the prospected applicability using a CNN-based end-to-end network in an unsupervised way, this method needs to be carefully optimized for the two subnetworks in an alternating way, and still has much potential for performance improvement. This study also aims at proposing an unsupervised MS/HS fusion network via automatically learning both the spatial and spectral priors in an end-to-end learning way.

3   Proposed Method

In this part, we firstly describe the formula expression for the problem of the MS/HS image fusion, and then investigate the proposed unsupervised MS/HS image fusion with the deep spatial and spectral priors (DSSP) including the generator network architecture, which automatically learns the underlying priors of the latent HR-HS image from the observed image pair of LR-HS and HR-RGB images only, and the constructed loss function for network training.

3.1 Problem Formulation

Given an observed image pair: a LR-HS image $\mathbf{X} \in \mathbb{R}^{w \times h \times L}$ and a HR-RGB image $\mathbf{Y} \in \mathbb{R}^{W \times H \times 3}$, where w, h and L stands for the width, height and the spectral channel number of the LR-HS image, W and H denotes the width and height of the HR-RGB image, our goal is to reconstruct HR-HS image: $\mathbf{Z} \in \mathbb{R}^{W \times H \times L}$ via merging $\mathbf{X}$ and $\mathbf{Y}$. The degraded model of the observed $\mathbf{X}$ and $\mathbf{Y}$ from the latent $\mathbf{Z}$ can be mathematically formulated as:

$$\mathbf{X} = \mathbf{ZDB} + \mathbf{n}, \mathbf{Y} = \mathbf{CZ} + \mathbf{n} \tag{1}$$

where $\mathbf{B}$ and $\mathbf{D}$ stand for the spatial blurring filter and down-sampling function to transform $\mathbf{Z}$ to $\mathbf{X}$, and $\mathbf{C}$ denotes the spectral sensitivity function (CSF) of a RGB sensor and $\mathbf{n}$ represents the observed noise. The heuristic approach to utilize the observed $\mathbf{X}$ and $\mathbf{Y}$ for estimating $\mathbf{Z}$ is usually to minimize the following reconstruction errors:

$$\mathbf{Z}^{\star} = \arg\min_{\mathbf{Z}} \|\mathbf{X} - \mathbf{ZBD}\|_F^2 + \|\mathbf{Y} - \mathbf{CZ}\|_F^2 \tag{2}$$

where $\|\cdot\|_F$ represents the Frobenius norm. Equation (2) trys to find out an optimized $\mathbf{Z}^{\star}$ which can minimize the reconstruction error of the observations. The terms in Eq. (2) rely on the observed data. According to the degradation procedure of the observed images $\mathbf{X}$ and $\mathbf{Y}$, it is known that the total number of unknown variables in $\mathbf{Z}$ is much more than the known variables in $\mathbf{X}$ and $\mathbf{Y}$, and thus results in ill-posed nature in this task. To address this problem, most existing methods popularly explores various hand-crafted priors for modeling the underlying structure of the HR-HS image to regularize the reconstruction error minimization problem, which is formulated as a regularization term:

$$\mathbf{Z}^{\star} = \arg\min_{\mathbf{Z}} \|\mathbf{X} - \mathbf{ZBD}\|_F^2 + \|\mathbf{Y} - \mathbf{CZ}\|_F^2 + \phi R(\mathbf{Z}) \tag{3}$$

where ϕ represents hyper-parameter to make a balance between the contribution of the regularization term and the reconstruction error. As we know that seeking an appropriate prior for a specific scene is difficult technically. This study advocates that a large amount of low-level image statistics can be captured by the deep network architecture itself, and it is prospected to generate a more plausible image according to the possessed low-level priors in the deep network. In the HS image scenario, we employ a deep network architecture to automatically learn the spatial and spectral priors in the latent HR-HS image, and then reconstruct a reliable HR-HS image constrained by the learned priors.

3.2 The Proposed Deep Spatial and Spectral Priors (DSSP)

The deep learning based methods such as DCGAN [29] and its variants verified that high-definition and high-quality images with a specific concept can be generated from a random noise, which means that to search the network parameter space from the initial random state can learn the inherent structure (prior) in the latent image of a specific concept. In addition, DIP [16] explored image prior possessing capability of network architecture for different restoration tasks of natural RGB images, and manifested impressive results. This study investigates the deep learned prior in the latent HR-HS image including HR spatial structure and spectral attribute, and aims at generating the HR-HS image with the observed LR-HS and HR-RGB images only. We design an hourglass network architecture consisting of encoder and decoder subnets, each with 4-blocks (levels). The network schematic in detail is shown in Fig. 1. The input of the network is a noise cube $\mathbf{n} \in \hat{\mathbb{R}}^{W \times H \times L}$ with the same size of the required HR-HS image, and we expect that the network output: $f_\theta(\mathbf{n})$ (θ: network parameters) should approach   the required HR-HS image: $\mathbf{Z}$. The goal of this work is to

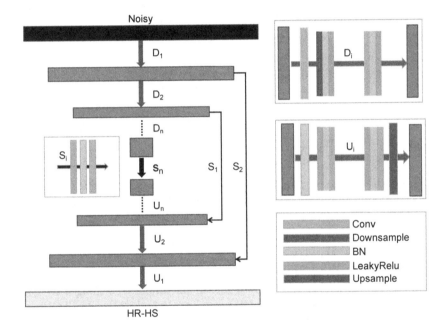

Fig. 1. Our generative network with an hourglass architecture, which generates the latent HR-HS image from a noisy input via automatically exploring the underlying spatial and spectral priors.

search the network parameter space to pursue a set of optimal parameters for satisfying the above criteria. However, due to the unknown $\mathbf{Z}$, it is impossible to construct quantitative criteria directly using $\mathbf{Z}$ for this task.

With the availability of the LR-HS and HR-RGB images, we turn to $\mathbf{X}$ and $\mathbf{Y}$ to formulate quantitative criteria (loss function) for network learning. Since, as in Eq. (1), the LR-HS image $\mathbf{X}$ is a blurred down-sampled version of $\mathbf{Z}$, and HR-RGB image $\mathbf{Y}$ is a transformed version of $\mathbf{Z}$ in channel direction using

CSF: $\mathbf{C}$, we implement the two operations as two convolutional layers with pre-defined weights (non-trainable) after the output layer of the baseline hourglass-like network. The convolutional layer for blurring/down-sampling operator has the kernel size and stride according to the spatial expanding factor W/w and the kernel weights are pre-calculated according to Lanczos2 filter. The output of this layer is denoted as $\hat{f}_{\mathbf{BD}}(f_\theta(\mathbf{n}))$, which has the same size and should be approximated to $\mathbf{X}$. Thus according to $\mathbf{X}$, the first loss function is formulated as:

$$L_1(\mathbf{n}, \mathbf{X}) = \left\| \mathbf{X} - \hat{f}_{\mathbf{BD}}(f_\theta(\mathbf{n})) \right\|_F^2 \tag{4}$$

While the spectral transformation operation (from $\mathbf{Z}$ to $\mathbf{Y}$) is implemented as the convolutional layer with 1×1 kernel size, input and output channels: L and 3, where the kernel weight is fixed as the CSF: $\mathbf{C}$ according to the used RGB camera. Then the output of this layer should be an optimal approximation of $\mathbf{Y}$. Denoting it as $\hat{f}_{\mathbf{C}}(f_\theta(\mathbf{N}))$, the second loss function is formulated as:

$$L_2(\mathbf{n}, \mathbf{Y}) = \left\| \mathbf{Y} - \hat{f}_{\mathbf{C}}(f_\theta(\mathbf{n})) \right\|_F^2 \tag{5}$$

Via combining the L_1 and L_2 loss functions, we finally minimize the following total loss for searching a set of network parameter from the initialed random state:

$$L(\mathbf{n}, \mathbf{X}, \mathbf{Y}) = \arg\min_\theta L_1(\mathbf{n}, \mathbf{X}) + L_2(\mathbf{n}, \mathbf{Y}) \tag{6}$$

From Eq. (6), it can be seen the network is learned with the available observations only without any additional training samples. After completing training, the baseline network output: $f_\theta(\mathbf{n})$ is our required HR-HS image.

4   Experiment Result

We validate our proposed DSSP network on 32 indoor HS images in CAVE dataset and 50 indoor and outdoor HS images in Harvard dataset. The images in CAVE dataset including paintings, toys, food, and so on, are captured under controlled illumination, and their dimensions are 512×512 pixels, with 31 spectral bands 10 nm wide, covering the visible spectrum from 400 to 700 nm. The Harvard dataset has 50 images under daylight illumination, both outdoors and indoors, using a commercial hyperspectral camera (Nuance FX, CRI Inc.). The images in Harvard dataset are of a wide variety of real-world materials and objects. We firstly took the top-left 1024×1024 regions from the raw HS images, and down-sampled them to size 512×512 as the ground-truth HS images. For experiment conducting, we synthesized the low-resolution HS image with the down-sampling factors of 8 and 32 using the Bicubic interpolation, and then the observed LR-HS images have sizes of $64 \times 64 \times 31$ and $16 \times 16 \times 31$, respectively. We generated the HR-RGB images via multiplying the spectral channels of the ground truth HR-HS images with the spectral response function of Nikon D700 camera.

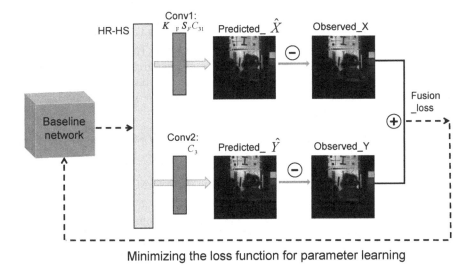

Fig. 2. The schematic concept of our proposed DSSP framework, which leverages the observed LR-HS and HR-RGB image to formulate the loss function for network training. The spatial down-sampling operation is implemented using a convolutional layer: 'Conv1: $K_{T(F)} \times S_F \times C_{31}$', with kernel size, stride and kennel number: $T(F)$, F (spatial expanding factor) and 31, respectively while the spectral linear transformation from the HR-HS image to the HR-is image, is implemented using the convolutional layer: 'Conv2: $K_1 \times S_1 \times C_3$', with the kernel size, stride and kennel number: 1, 1 and 3, respectively.

We conducted experiments with our proposed deep spatial and spectral prior (DSSP) framework using the observed LR-HS and HR-RGB images only, which means that the combined loss function in Eq. (6) is used for network parameter learning. Since our proposed method is evolved from the deep image prior for natural image restoration problems, which was further extended to enhance hyperspectral image for deep spatial prior (DSP) learning with the loss function in Eq. (4) [30], we compare the experimental results with our DSSP framework and the conventional DSP method. The experiments were conducted under the same experimental setting with 12000 iterations and learning rate 0.001 for both DSSP and DSP learning. Further, to avoid that the predicted HR-HS image drops down a local minimized point, we added a vibrated random noise with much smaller deviation to the network noise input on each iteration in the experiments. We evaluate experimental results with five commonly-used quantitative metrics: root mean square error (RMSE), peak signal to noise ration (PSNR), structure similarity (SSIM), spectral angle mapper (SAM) and relative dimensional global error (ERGAS). We calculate the mean metric values of all images in the CAVE and Harvard datasets for comparison.

The compared experimental results on CAVE dataset using our proposed DSSP and the conventional DSP methods are given in Table 1 for both expanding factors 8 and 32 in spatial domain. From the results of Table 1, it can be seen that our proposed method can greatly outperform the conventional DSP method on all five metrics. Table 2 manifests the compared results on Harvard dataset, which also demonstrates much better performance of our DSSP method.

Table 1. Quantitative comparison results of our proposed DSSP framework and the conventional DSP method [30] on the CAVE dataset.

Factor	Method	RMSE	PSNR	SSIM	SAM	ERGAS
8	DSP [30]	7.5995	31.4040	0.8708	8.2542	4.2025
	DSSP	**2.0976**	**42.5251**	**0.9780**	**5.2996**	**1.1190**
32	DSP [30]	16.0121	24.7395	0.7449	13.0761	8.5959
	DSSP	**3.1279**	**39.0291**	**0.9619**	**7.6520**	**1.6366**

Table 2. Quantitative comparison results of our proposed DSSP framework and the conventional DSP method [30] on the Harvard dataset.

Factor	Method	RMSE	PSNR	SSIM	SAM	ERGAS
8	DSP [30]	7.9449	30.8609	0.8029	3.5295	3.1509
	DSSP	**2.1472**	**42.6315**	**0.9736**	**2.3204**	**1.0089**
32	DSP [30]	13.2507	26.2299	0.7186	5.6758	5.6482
	DSSP	**2.8366**	**40.3152**	**0.9602**	**3.5171**	**1.5809**

Finally, we compare the experimental results with other state-of-the-art methods. Since our DSSP method is an unsupervised MS/HS fusion strategy, for fair comparison we provide the results of the unsupervised methods including optimization based approaches: MF [31], CMF [14], BSR [32] and unsupervised deep learning based method: uSDN [28] in Table 3 with the expanding factor 32 of spatial domain for both CAVE and Harvard datasets, which manifests the promising performance using our proposed DSSP framework. The visual examples in both CAVE and Harvard datasets with our DSSP method, the conventional DSP and the uSDN methods are shown in Fig. 3 and Fig. 4.

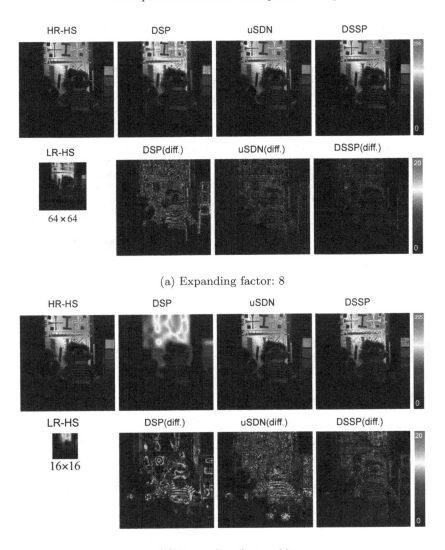

(a) Expanding factor: 8

(b) Expanding factor: 32

Fig. 3. The predicted LR-HR image of 'chart and stuffed toy' sample in the CAVE dataset for both spatial expanding factors: 8 and 32, which visualizes the 16-th band image. The first column shows the ground truth HR image and the input LR image, respectively. The second to fourth columns show results from DSP [16], uSDN [28], our proposed method, with the upper part showing the predicted images and the lower part showing the absolute difference maps w.r.t. the ground truth.

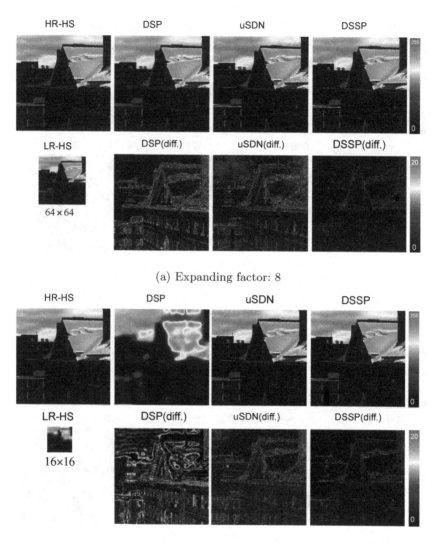

Fig. 4. The predicted LR-HR image of 'img1' sample in the Harvard dataset for both spatial expanding factors: 8 and 32, which visualizes the 16-th band image. The first column shows the ground truth HR image and the input LR image, respectively. The second to fourth columns show results from DSP [16], uSDN [28], our proposed method, with the upper part showing the predicted images and the lower part showing the absolute difference maps w.r.t. the ground truth.

Table 3. The compared average RMSE, SAM and PSNR with the state-of-the-art unsupervised methods on both CAVE and Harvard datasets.

Method	CAVE			Harvard		
	RMSE	SAM	PSNR	RMSE	SAM	PSNR
MF [31]	3.47	8.29	38.61	2.93	3.99	40.02
CMF [14]	4.23	7.71	37.98	2.86	4.46	39.97
BSR [32]	3.79	9.12	35.25	3.7	4.26	38.52
uSDN [28]	3.89	7.94	37.46	3.02	3.98	38.08
DSSP	**3.1279**	**7.652**	**39.0291**	**2.8366**	**3.5171**	**40.3152**

5 Conclusion

This study proposed a deep unsupervised prior learning network for the fusion of multispectral and hyperspectral images. Motivated that a generative network architecture itself can capture large amount of low-level image statistics, we attempted to construct a simple network for learning the spatial and spectral priors in the latent HR-HS images. The proposed prior learning network can effectively leverage the HR spatial structure in HR-RGB images and the detailed spectral properties in LR-HS images to provide more reliable HS images reconstruction without any training samples. Experimental results on both CAVE and Harvard datasets showed that the proposed method has achieved impressive performance.

Acknowledgement. This research was supported in part by the Grant-in Aid for Scientific Research from the Japanese Ministry for Education, Science, Culture and Sports (MEXT) under the Grant No. 20K11867, and ROIS NII Open Collaborative Research 2020-20FC02.

References

1. Plaza, A., et al.: Recent advances in techniques for hyperspectral image processing. Remote Sens. Environ. **113**, S110–S122 (2009)
2. Goetz, A.F.: Three decades of hyperspectral remote sensing of the earth: a personal view. Remote Sens. Environ. **113**, S5–S16 (2009)
3. Lu, G., Fei, B.: Medical hyperspectral imaging: a review. J. Biomed. Opt. **19**, 010901 (2014)
4. Manolakis, D., Shaw, G.: Detection algorithms for hyperspectral imaging applications. IEEE Sig. Process. Mag. **19**, 29–43 (2002)
5. Makantasis, K., Karantzalos, K., Doulamis, A., Doulamis, N.: Deep supervised learning for hyperspectral data classification through convolutional neural networks. In: IEEE International Geoscience and Remote Sensing Symposium (IGARSS), pp. 4959–4962. IEEE (2015)
6. Manolakis, D., Marden, D., Shaw, G.A., et al.: Hyperspectral image processing for automatic target detection applications. Lincoln Lab. J. **14**, 79–116 (2003)

7. Treado, P., Nelson, M., Gardner Jr., C.: Hyperspectral imaging sensor for tracking moving targets (2012). US Patent App. 13/199,981
8. Veganzones, M.A., Tochon, G., Dalla-Mura, M., Plaza, A.J., Chanussot, J.: Hyperspectral image segmentation using a new spectral unmixing-based binary partition tree representation. IEEE Trans. Image Process. **23**, 3574–3589 (2014)
9. Chen, Y., Nasrabadi, N.M., Tran, T.D.: Hyperspectral image classification using dictionary-based sparse representation. IEEE Trans. Geosci. Remote Sens. **49**, 3973–3985 (2011)
10. Zhao, Y.Q., Yang, J.: Hyperspectral image denoising via sparse representation and low-rank constraint. IEEE Trans. Geosci. Remote Sens. **53**, 296–308 (2014)
11. Pu, H., Chen, Z., Wang, B., Jiang, G.M.: A novel spatial-spectral similarity measure for dimensionality reduction and classification of hyperspectral imagery. IEEE Trans. Geosci. Remote Sens. **52**, 7008–7022 (2014)
12. Yu, H., Gao, L., Liao, W., Zhang, B.: Group sparse representation based on non-local spatial and local spectral similarity for hyperspectral imagery classification. Sensors **18**, 1695 (2018)
13. Dong, C., Loy, C.C., He, K., Tang, X.: Image super-resolution using deep convolutional networks. IEEE Trans. Pattern Anal. Mach. Intell. **38**, 295–307 (2015)
14. Yokoya, N., Yairi, T., Iwasaki, A.: Coupled non-negative matrix factorization (CNMF) for hyperspectral and multispectral data fusion: application to pasture classification. In: IEEE International Geoscience and Remote Sensing Symposium, pp. 1779–1782. IEEE (2011)
15. Lanaras, C., Baltsavias, E., Schindler, K.: Hyperspectral super-resolution by coupled spectral unmixing. In: Proceedings of the IEEE International Conference on Computer Vision, pp. 3586–3594 (2015)
16. Ulyanov, D., Vedaldi, A., Lempitsky, V.: Deep image prior. In: The IEEE Conference on Computer Vision and Pattern Recognition (CVPR) (2018)
17. Zhu, X.X., Bamler, R.: A sparse image fusion algorithm with application to pan-sharpening. IEEE Trans. Geosci. Remote Sens. **51**, 2827–2836 (2012)
18. Choi, J., Yu, K., Kim, Y.: A new adaptive component-substitution-based satellite image fusion by using partial replacement. IEEE Trans. Geosci. Remote Sens. **49**, 295–309 (2010)
19. Dhore, A., Veena, C.: A new pan-sharpening method using joint sparse FI image fusion algorithm. Int. J. Eng. Res. General Sci. **2**, 447–55 (2014)
20. Liang, H., Li, Q.: Hyperspectral imagery classification using sparse representations of convolutional neural network features. Remote Sens. **8**, 99 (2016)
21. Zhu, X.X., Grohnfeldt, C., Bamler, R.: Exploiting joint sparsity for pansharpening: The j-sparsefi algorithm. IEEE Trans. Geosci. Remote Sens. **54**, 2664–2681 (2015)
22. Akhtar, N., Shafait, F., Mian, A.: Sparse spatio-spectral representation for hyperspectral image super-resolution. In: Fleet, D., Pajdla, T., Schiele, B., Tuytelaars, T. (eds.) ECCV 2014. LNCS, vol. 8695, pp. 63–78. Springer, Cham (2014). https://doi.org/10.1007/978-3-319-10584-0_5
23. Meng, G., Li, G., Dong, W., Shi, G.: Non-negative structural sparse representation for high-resolution hyperspectral imaging. In: Optoelectronic Imaging and Multimedia Technology III, vol. 9273. International Society for Optics and Photonics (2014). 92730H
24. Han, X.H., Shi, B., Zheng, Y.: Self-similarity constrained sparse representation for hyperspectral image super-resolution. IEEE Trans. Image Process. **27**, 5625–5637 (2018)

25. Han, X.H., Chen, Y.W.: Deep residual network of spectral and spatial fusion for hyperspectral image super-resolution. In: 2019 IEEE Fifth International Conference on Multimedia Big Data (BigMM), pp. 266–270. IEEE (2019)
26. Palsson, F., Sveinsson, J.R., Ulfarsson, M.O.: Multispectral and hyperspectral image fusion using a 3-D-convolutional neural network. IEEE Geosci. Remote Sens. Lett. **14**, 639–643 (2017)
27. Dian, R., Li, S., Guo, A., Fang, L.: Deep hyperspectral image sharpening. IEEE Trans. Neural Netw. Learn. Syst. 1–11 (2018)
28. Qu, Y., Qi, H., Kwan, C.: Unsupervised sparse Dirichlet-net for hyperspectral image super-resolution. In: Proceedings of the IEEE Conference on Computer Vision and Pattern Recognition, pp. 2511–2520 (2018)
29. Radford, A., Metz, L., Chintala, S.: Unsupervised representation learning with deep convolutional generative adversarial networks. arXiv preprint arXiv:1511.06434 (2015)
30. Sidorov, O., Hardeberg, J.Y.: Deep hyperspectral prior: Denoising, inpainting, super-resolution. CoRR abs/1902.00301 (2019)
31. Kawakami, R., Matsushita, Y., Wright, J., Ben-Ezra, M., Tai, Y.W., Ikeuchi, K.: High-resolution hyperspectral imaging via matrix factorization. In: CVPR 2011, pp. 2329–2336. IEEE (2011)
32. Wei, Q., Bioucas-Dias, J., Dobigeon, N., Tourneret, J.Y.: Hyperspectral and multispectral image fusion based on a sparse representation. IEEE Trans. Geosci. Remote Sens. **53**, 3658–3668 (2015)

G-GCSN: Global Graph Convolution Shrinkage Network for Emotion Perception from Gait

Yuan Zhuang[1], Lanfen Lin[1(✉)], Ruofeng Tong[1], Jiaqing Liu[2], Yutaro Iwamoto[2], and Yen-Wei Chen[1,2,3(✉)]

[1] College of Computer Science and Technology, Zhejiang University,
Hangzhou 310000, China
{zhuangyuan97,llf,trf}@zju.edu.cn

[2] College of Information Science and Engineering, Ritsumeikan University,
Kyoto 525-8577, Japan
gr0302kv@ed.ritsumei.ac.jp, yiwamoto@fc.ritsumei.ac.jp,
chen@is.ritsumei.ac.jp

[3] Research Center for Healthcare Data Science, Zhejiang Lab,
Hangzhou 310000, China

Abstract. Recently, emotion recognition through gait, which is more difficult to imitate than other biological characteristics, has aroused extensive attention. Although some deep-learning studies have been conducted in this field, there are still two challenges. First, it is hard to extract the representational features of the gait from video effectively. Second, the input of body joints sequences has noise introduced during dataset collection and feature production. In this work, we propose a global link, which extends the existing skeleton graph (the natural link) to capture the overall state of gait based on spatial-temporal convolution. In addition, we use soft thresholding to reduce noise. The thresholds are learned automatically by a block called shrinkage block. Combined with the global link and shrinkage block, we further propose the global graph convolution shrinkage network (G-GCSN) to capture the emotion-related features. We validate the effectiveness of the proposed method on a public dataset (i.e., Emotion-Gait dataset). The proposed G-GCSN achieves improvements compared with state-of-the-art methods.

1 Introduction

Emotion recognition is of great value in an intelligent system to insight into human psychology. Current most studies of emotional recognition use facial expressions [1,2], speech (including words and sounds) [3,4], and physiological signals (e.g., EEG, heart rate, breathing, body temperature, etc.) [5–7]. Through the analysis and processing of these data, emotions are divided into emotional categories such as sadness, happiness, anger, etc.

Recently, some studies have shown that emotional expression is also reflected in body language. Body language includes body posture and body movement,

© Springer Nature Switzerland AG 2021
I. Sato and B. Han (Eds.): ACCV 2020 Workshops, LNCS 12628, pp. 46–57, 2021.
https://doi.org/10.1007/978-3-030-69756-3_4

in which gait is the most basic body language. Gait refers to the modalities displayed during human walking, consisting of a series of body joints in time sequence. Gait can reflect emotional information, and individuals in different emotional states may have differences in some gait characteristics, such as arm swing, speed, angle, length of steps, etc. [8–10].

Compared with traditional biological characteristics for emotion detection, such as facial expressions, speech, and physiological signals, gait is observable remotely, more difficult to imitate, and does not require a high degree of participation of the subject. In the real environment, it can be easily collected by a non-contact method, which is convenient to be applied to all kinds of scenes in real life.

So, this paper focuses on the relationship between gait and emotion. Some published studies applied models for the action recognition task, such as STEP [11]. In STEP, they applied spatial-temporal graph convolution and used the physical structure of the human skeleton as the spatial graph, which only captures the local dependencies without considering the non-local correlation of joints. Besides, the published studies ignored the noise of the input. The gait is inputted as a point cloud composed of a series of body joints in time sequence extracted from the video. External environment and extraction algorithms may introduce noise that can impact on our tasks.

In this work, we mainly solve the above two problems. First, we propose a global link, a new joint connection method of constructing the skeleton graph which is suitable for emotion recognition to perceive emotions as a whole. Second, we propose a graph convolution shrinkage (GCS) block, a new module that combines spatial graph convolution and temporal graph convolution with shrinkage block to reduce noise impacts. Based on the global links and GCS, we propose a global graph convolution shrinkage network (G-GCSN), stacked by multiple global graph convolution shrinkage blocks.

To verify the effectiveness of the proposed G-GCSN, we carry out experiments on Emotion-Gait [11], which is the same dataset as used in STEP [11]. The main contributions in this work are summarized as followed:

(1) We propose a global link that constructs a new skeleton graph to complement the original natural links in physical structures to capture the overall state of gait based on spatial-temporal convolution.
(2) We propose a graph convolution shrinkage block (GCS) to reduce the influence of the noise.
(3) We stack global graph convolution shrinkage blocks to give an outperformance network (G-GCSN) to extract emotion-related features effectively.

2   Related Work

Walking is the most basic activities of daily life and the gait displayed during walking varies from person to person. Thence, gait information can be used as a unique biological feature for identity detection [12,13] applied to security and other scenes. Moreover, some researches [14–16] used gait information to detect abnormal movements and gait patterns, which can be used as the basis for early diagnosis of mental diseases (such as cerebral palsy, Parkinson's disease, Rett syndrome, etc.) in clinical. And gait is also used in action recognition [17,18], mainly applied in video surveillance, intelligent human-computer interaction, virtual reality, etc.

Recently, the gait has been used for emotion recognition. The published studies on gait-based emotion recognition mostly adopt machine learning methods. Li et al. [19] extracted the time and frequency domain features of the six nodes on the arms and legs, and used SVM and LDA for classification; Quiroz et al. [20] adopted sliding windows to extract feature vectors, and used Random Forest for classification. Ahmed et al. [21] extracted geometric and kinematic features from an LMA framework and adopted KNN, SVM, LDA and other classifiers combined with Score-level Fusion and Rank-level Fusion for feature fusion. Zhang et al. [22] extracted 3D acceleration data from the right wrist and ankle and used Decision tree, SVM, Random Forest, Random Tree as classifiers. Venture et al. [23] extracted the joint angles and classified them based on similarity. Karg et al. [24] used PCA-based classifiers on some extracted features such as stride length, velocity and so on. Daoudi et al. [25] represented body joints' movement as symmetric positive definite matrices and performed the nearest neighbor classification. Wang et al. [26] fed low-level 3D postural features and high-level kinematic and geometrical features to a Random Forest classifier. Crenn et al. [27] computed geometric features, motion features, and Fourier features of body joints movement and used the support vector machine with a radial basis function kernel as the classifier.

There are also a few studies adopting deep learning methods. Randhavane et al. [28] used RNN-based LSTM to extract deep features and combined hand-extracted emotional features. Random Forest Classifier is used to classification. Bhattacharya et al. [11] used the features extracted by the ST-GCN network and combined with hand-extracted emotional characteristics for classification. In this work, we only use deep learning method which based on GCN (ST-GCN) [29] for feature extraction, without manually extracted features.

3   Background

ST-GCN ST-GCN [29], the spatial-temporal graph convolution network, is composed of multiple spatial-temporal graph convolution blocks. Each block consists of two parts: spatial graph convolution and temporal graph convolution, which are used to obtain the features in space and time dimensions respectively. The crucial part of spatiotemporal graph convolution is constructing the spatial-temporal graph (Fig. 1(a)). The spatial graph is the natural connection of body joints. According to the spatial configuration partition strategy in ST-GCN, it can be divided into three subgraphs (show in Fig. 1(b)): 1) the root node itself 2) centripetal group 3) centrifugal group. The neighbor relation of each subgraph is represented by an adjacency matrix. And the time graph is structed by the connection of the same node between adjacent frames. Let $\mathbf{X_{in}} \in \mathbb{R}^{c_{in}*t_{in}*v}$ be the input features of all joints in all frames and $\mathbf{X_{out}} \in \mathbb{R}^{c_{out}*t_{out}*v}$ be the output, where c_{in}, c_{out} is the dimension of input joints features and output joints features, t_{in}, t_{out} is the number of input frames and output frames, and v is the number of joints. The spatial graph convolution is formulated as:

$$X_{out} = \sum_{k=0}^{K} (M_k \odot A_k) X_{in} W_k \tag{1}$$

where K is the number of subgraphs. $\mathbf{A_k} \in \mathbb{R}^{v*v}$ is the adjacency matrix of the subgraph k. For the adjacency matrix $\mathbf{A_k}$, it has a weight matrix $\mathbf{M_k} \in \mathbb{R}^{v*v}$. $\odot$ donates element-wise product between two matrixes. $\mathbf{W_k}$ is a weight function. $\mathbf{M_k}$ and $\mathbf{W_k}$ are trainable.

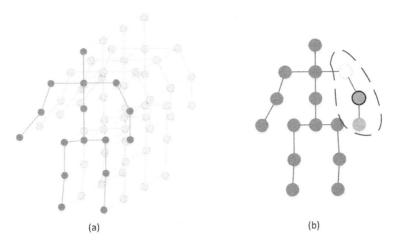

(a) (b)

Fig. 1. (a) The spatial-temporal graph used in ST-GCN. (b) Illustration of the partition strategy and different color nodes are in different subgraphs. (The green one is the root node, the yellow one and the orange one are in the centripetal group and centrifugal group respectively.) (Color figure online)

4 Proposed Method

Our work is to perceive the emotion of gait based on spatial-temporal graph convolution. The final architecture is shown in Fig. 2. We feed the 3D coordinates of body joints extracted from the walking video into the network in a time sequence. And the output is an emotion classification result of the gait. The proposed global graph convolution shrinkage network (G-GCSN) consists of three GCS blocks, followed by a global average pooling (GAP) layer, a fully connected (FC) layer, and a softmax function. The base block is the graph convolution shrinkage block GCS which comprises three components: (1) Spatial graph convolution. The original spatial graph is constructed by the natural link. The natural link only captures the local dependencies, which may miss the non-local correlation of joints. We proposed a global link to capture the overall state of gait by the non-local dependencies. The final spatial graph is constructed by our proposed global link and the natural link. (2) Temporal graph convolution. Its graph is formed by the connection of the same node between the adjacent frames. We use it to extracted features in the time dimension. (3) Shrinkage block. The input data may be mixed with noise during the collection process, and the noise may be further amplified in the network. We introduce it to reduce noise after spatial-temporal convolution. In Sects. 4.1 and 4.2, we will introduce the global link and shrinkage block in detail.

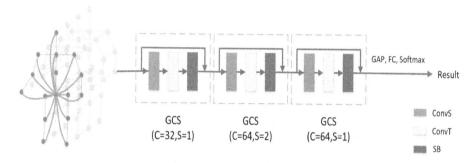

Fig. 2. Architecture Overview. "GCS", "ConvS", "ConvT" and "SB" denotes graph convolution shrinkage block, spatial graph convolution, temporal graph convolution, and shrinkage block. "C" represents the number of output channels for GCS. "S" represents the stride of temporal graph convolution. Each spatial graph convolution and temporal graph convolution is followed by a batch normalization layer and a ReLU layer which are not shown in the figure. Moreover, a residual connection is added for each GCS block.

4.1 Global Graph Convolution

Spatiotemporal graph convolution (ST-GCN) has made good progress in many fields, such as action recognition [30,31], traffic forecasting [32,33], and person re-identification [34]. Recently, ST-GCN has also been applied to emotion recognition based on gait by Bhattacharya et al. [11].

Bhattacharya et al. proposed a STEP network which is stacked by three spatiotemporal graph convolution blocks. There is no change in the spatial and temporal graph compared with ST-GCN. The spatial graph is constructed by the physical structure of the human skeleton (the natural link, shown in Fig. 3(a)). And the natural link only captures the local dependencies, which may miss the non-local correlation of joints. Besides, the difference between the different emotional gaits is not the action but the overall state. Let's consider the influence of emotion on gait in an ideal situation. When happy, the body posture is stretched overall, the steps are light, the action amplitude is slightly bigger; When sad, the body posture collapses overall, the steps are heavy, the action amplitude is slightly smaller; When angry, the body posture overall expands, the steps are strong, the action amplitude is slightly bigger. When neutral, the body is a little more stretched than when sad, the action amplitude is smaller than when happy and angry. So, it is significant to perceive gait as a whole for emotion recognition.

To perceive the emotion from the overall state of gait, we propose a global link representing the global dependencies to capture emotion-related features. We want to choose a stable center node of the skeleton as the reference joint. In this way, the overall state of gait can be simply perceived by the dependencies between the center node and other nodes. As shown in Fig. 3(b), we choose the spine joint as the reference joint and obtain the global link by connecting the joint points to the spine joint.

The natural link and the global link complement each other and cannot be replaced. We add them together to get the complete spatial graph. And the Eq. 1 can be replaced by

$$X_{out} = \sum_{k=0}^{K} \left(M_k \odot (A_n + A_g)_k \right) X_{in} W_k \qquad (2)$$

where $A_n \in \mathbb{R}^{v*v}$ is the adjacency matrix of natural link and $A_g \in \mathbb{R}^{v*v}$ is the adjacency matrix of the global link. K is the number of subgraphs, which are divided according to the spatial configuration partition strategy in ST-GCN.

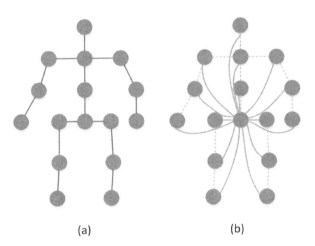

(a)   (b)

Fig. 3. The graph of body joints. (a)The natural link of body joints (b) The proposed global link of body joints (green lines) (Color figure online)

4.2   Shrinkage Block

The gait is inputted as a point cloud composed of 3D coordinates of body joints in time sequence, which is extracted from videos. Noise may be introduced in the process of gait information collection due to the environment and the accuracy of the joint coordinate extraction algorithm. In the process of the spatial-temporal graph convolution, the noise is passed while transferring the features.

When operating convolution in the spatial dimension, each node passes the feature and noise to his neighbor nodes simultaneously through the adjacency matrix, which leads to the introduction of noise in each channel to some extent. At the same time, the convolution operation makes a fusion between channels. Then the noise of each channel will be fused into the new channel after convolution. The same is true in the temporal convolution. These noises have a negative impact on the experimental results.

Inspired by DRSN [35], we introduce a subnetwork called shrinkage block in the ST-GCN block after temporal convolution to reduce noise by soft thresholding. It is crucial to set the threshold. For any two samples, their noise is different. And there are also differences in noise from channel to channel. It is difficult to set the threshold for them all. We introduce a subnet to automatically learn thresholds for each channel of each sample from the sample features. And soft thresholding is carried out according to thresholds. As the network deepens, noise decreases layer by layer, reducing the interference and negative impacts on emotion recognition tasks. The function of soft thresholding can be expressed as follows:

$$y = \begin{cases} x - \tau & x > \tau \\ 0 & \tau \le x \le \tau \\ x + \tau & x < -\tau \end{cases} \tag{3}$$

where x is the input feature, y is the output feature, and τ is the threshold. τ not only needs to be positive, but also cannot be too large to prevent the output of soft thresholding being zero.

As shown in the Fig. 4, the proposed method is similar to DRSN-CW. In the sub-network, first, perform GAP global average pooling on the absolute value of the feature map to obtain a one-dimensional vector $\mathbf{A}$. The one-dimensional vector passes through two FC layers to obtain a scale vector $\mathbf{W}$, and the elements in $\mathbf{W}$ is scaled to $(0, 1)$ through the sigmoid function. Then, an element-wise product operation is performed on $\mathbf{A}$ and $\mathbf{W}$ to get the threshold vector $\mathbf{T}$. According to $\mathbf{T}$, we use soft thresholding to reduce noise on the features map. The threshold is expressed as follows:

$$\boldsymbol{T} = \boldsymbol{W} \odot \boldsymbol{A} \tag{4}$$

where $\odot$ represents the element-wise product operation. There are c elements in the vector, corresponding to the threshold values of c channels. Every element meets the threshold requirements within the interval of $(0, \mathrm{max})$.

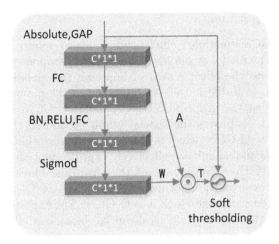

Fig. 4. The structure of shrinkage block (SB)

5   Experiments

In this section, we introduce the details of our experiments, including data sets, parameter settings, and ablation experiments.

5.1   Datasets and Implementation

Emotion-Gait (E-Gait) [11] is a public dataset, consisting of 2177 real gaits and 4000 generated gaits. Among the real gait samples, there are 342 collected from 90 participants and 1,835 from ELMD databases [36]. The 342 collected data came from the 90 participants who imaged four emotions (happy, sad, neutral, angry) while walking at a distance of 7 meters. These 2177 gaits are labeled as one of the four emotional categories by domain experts.

All experiments were performed in the PyTorch deep learning framework. For training G-GCSN, we randomly divide the data set into training set and test set according to the ratio of 9:1, and run ten times to get the average result. We use a batch size of 8 and train for 100 epochs using Adam optimizer with an initial learning rate of 0.001. The learning rate decreases to $1/10$ of its current value after 50, 75, 88 epochs. We also use a momentum of 0.9 and weight-decay of.

We quantitatively evaluate the results of our experiments by classification accuracy given by the following formula:

$$Accuracy = (TH + TS + TN + TA)/TD \tag{5}$$

where TH, TS, TN, and TA are the true positives' number of four emotions, and TD is the number of total data.

5.2   Ablation Experiments

To validate the G-GCSN module's efficiency to capture emotion-related gait features, we build up the model by adding its individual components incrementally.

First, we evaluate the effectiveness of applying the global link to capture spatial information. In Table 1, (ST-)GCN indicates the network that uses the natural link as the spatial graph in ST-GCN block. G-GCN, the global graph convolution network, improves the spatial graph by adding the global link to the natural link. The G-GCN achieves better performance than the (ST-)GCN, which shows that the global link can effectively capture emotion-related features.

Second, to verify the effectiveness of the shrinkage block, we experiment on the global graph convolution shrinkage network (G-GCSN). G-GCSN is the model that combined shrinkage block into G-GCN. The experimental results in Table 1 show that the introduction of shrinkage block can effectively improve the performance of the network.

Table 1. The ablation experiment results.

Method	Accuracy
(ST-)GCN	78.24%
G-GCN	**81.10%**
G-GCSN	**81.50%**

Besides, we try some sizes of the temporal graph convolution kernel. As Table 2 shows, the other temporal kernel sizes do not perform better than 75 which we used for all of experiments in Table 1.

Table 2. The ablation experiment results. Model accuracy with various temporal kernel size k.

Method	Accuracy
G-GCSN	
with k = 45	81.30%
with k = 65	81.35%
with k = 75	**81.50%**
with k = 85	81.36%

5.3   Comparison with State-of-the-Art Methods

In the paper of STEP, they used some prior machine learning methods [23-27] for emotion recognition on Emotion-Gait. As Table 3 shows, the accuracy of all

Table 3. Comparison with state-of-the-art methods.

Method	Accuracy
Venture et al. [23]	30.83%
Karg et al. [24]	39.85%
Daoudi et al. [25]	42.52%
Wang et al. [26]	53.73%
Crenn et al. [27]	66.22%
ST-GCN [29]	65.62%
LSTM [28]	75.10%
Base-STEP [11]	78.24%
G-GCSN	**81.50%**

is less than 70%. And the accuracy on three deep learning methods [11, 28, 29] are 65.52%, 75.10% and 78.24%. By comparison, our G-GCSN achieved 81.50% on Emotion-Gait, which exceeds state-of-the-art performance.

6   Conclusions

In this paper, we propose a novel network called global graph convolution shrinkage network (G-GCSN) for human emotion recognition based on gait. The global link extracts the emotion-related gait features from the whole. And the shrinkage block can automatically set suitable thresholds through samples features and reduce the noise of the input features by soft thresholding. We validate G-GCSN in emotion recognition using a public dataset of Emotion-Gait and the results of experiments show that G-GCSN surpasses all previous state-of-the-art approaches.

However, we did not train our network on the synthetic gaits or combine with the affective features in Emotion-Gait dataset as Bhattacharya et al. [11] did in STEP and STEP+Aug. Our work is dedicated to replacing other data processing methods with network improvements to improve performance. In current work, the performance of our network on the real gaits is not as good as that of STEP and STEP+Aug. So the next step is to further improve the network structure. Given the difference between samples, we may design a more flexible spatial-temporal graph to replace the unified one. Besides, we will also verify the performance of our network on more datasets to prove its universal applicability.

Acknowledgements. This work was supported in part by Major Scientific Research Project of Zhejiang Lab under the Grant No. 2018DG0ZX01, and in part by the Grant in Aid for Scientific Research from the Japanese Ministry for Education, Science, Culture and Sports (MEXT) under the Grant No. 20K21821.

References

1. Zhang, Y.D., et al.: Facial emotion recognition based on biorthogonal wavelet entropy, fuzzy support vector machine, and stratified cross validation. IEEE Access **4**, 8375–8385 (2016)
2. Mohammadpour, M., Khaliliardali, H., Hashemi, S.M.R., AlyanNezhadi, M.M.: Facial emotion recognition using deep convolutional networks. In: IEEE 4th International Conference on Knowledge-Based Engineering and Innovation (KBEI), pp. 0017–0021. IEEE (2017)
3. Zhao, J., Mao, X., Chen, L.: Speech emotion recognition using deep 1D & 2D CNN LSTM networks. Biomed. Sig. Process. Control **47**, 312–323 (2019)
4. Nicholson, J., Takahashi, K., Nakatsu, R.: Emotion recognition in speech using neural networks. Neural Comput. Appl. **9**, 290–296 (2000)
5. Kim, J., André, E.: Emotion recognition based on physiological changes in music listening. IEEE Trans. Pattern Anal. Mach. Intell. **30**, 2067–2083 (2008)
6. Kim, K.H., Bang, S.W., Kim, S.R.: Emotion recognition system using short-term monitoring of physiological signals. Med. Biol. Eng. Comput. **42**, 419–427 (2004)
7. Lin, Y.P., et al.: EEG-based emotion recognition in music listening. IEEE Trans. Biomed. Eng. **57**, 1798–1806 (2010)
8. Montepare, J.M., Goldstein, S.B., Clausen, A.: The identification of emotions from gait information. J. Nonverbal Behav. **11**, 33–42 (1987)
9. Halovic, S., Kroos, C.: Not all is noticed: kinematic cues of emotion-specific gait. Hum. Mov. Sci. **57**, 478–488 (2018)
10. Roether, C.L., Omlor, L., Christensen, A., Giese, M.A.: Critical features for the perception of emotion from gait. J. Vis. **9**, 15–15 (2009)
11. Bhattacharya, U., Mittal, T., Chandra, R., Randhavane, T., Bera, A., Manocha, D.: Step: spatial temporal graph convolutional networks for emotion perception from gaits. AAA I, 1342–1350 (2020)
12. Chao, H., He, Y., Zhang, J., Feng, J.: Gaitset: regarding gait as a set for cross-view gait recognition. In: Proceedings of the AAAI Conference on Artificial Intelligence, 33, pp. 8126–8133 (2019)
13. Kale, A., et al.: Identification of humans using gait. IEEE Trans. Image Process. **13**, 1163–1173 (2004)
14. Gage, J.R.: Gait analysis. an essential tool in the treatment of cerebral palsy. Clin. Orthopaedics Related Res. 126–134 (1993)
15. Jellinger, K., Armstrong, D., Zoghbi, H., Percy, A.: Neuropathology of rett syndrome. Acta Neuropathol. **76**, 142–158 (1988)
16. Jankovic, J.: Parkinson's disease: clinical features and diagnosis. J. Neurol. Neurosurg. Psychiatry **79**, 368–376 (2008)
17. Li, M., Chen, S., Chen, X., Zhang, Y., Wang, Y., Tian, Q.: Actional-structural graph convolutional networks for skeleton-based action recognition. In: Proceedings of the IEEE Conference on Computer Vision and Pattern Recognition, pp. 3595–3603 (2019)
18. Shi, L., Zhang, Y., Cheng, J., Lu, H.: Skeleton-based action recognition with directed graph neural networks. In: Proceedings of the IEEE Conference on Computer Vision and Pattern Recognition, pp. 7912–7921 (2019)
19. Li, B., Zhu, C., Li, S., Zhu, T.: Identifying emotions from non-contact gaits information based on microsoft kinects. IEEE Trans. Affect. Comput. **9**, 585–591 (2016)
20. Quiroz, J.C., Geangu, E., Yong, M.H.: Emotion recognition using smart watch sensor data: mixed-design study. JMIR Mental Health **5**, e10153 (2018)

21. Ahmed, F., Sieu, B., Gavrilova, M.L.: Score and rank-level fusion for emotion recognition using genetic algorithm. In: 2018 IEEE 17th International Conference on Cognitive Informatics & Cognitive Computing (ICCI* CC), pp. 46–53. IEEE (2018)

22. Zhang, Z., Song, Y., Cui, L., Liu, X., Zhu, T.: Emotion recognition based on customized smart bracelet with built-in accelerometer. PeerJ 4, e2258 (2016)

23. Venture, G., Kadone, H., Zhang, T., Grèzes, J., Berthoz, A., Hicheur, H.: Recognizing emotions conveyed by human gait. Int. J. Social Robot. 6, 621–632 (2014)

24. Karg, M., Kühnlenz, K., Buss, M.: Recognition of affect based on gait patterns. IEEE Trans. Syst. Man Cybern. Part B (Cybern.) 40, 1050–1061 (2010)

25. Daoudi, M., Berretti, S., Pala, P., Delevoye, Y., Del Bimbo, A.: Emotion recognition by body movement representation on the manifold of symmetric positive definite matrices. In: Battiato, S., Gallo, G., Schettini, R., Stanco, F. (eds.) ICIAP 2017. LNCS, vol. 10484, pp. 550–560. Springer, Cham (2017). https://doi.org/10.1007/978-3-319-68560-1_49

26. Wang, W., Enescu, V., Sahli, H.: Adaptive real-time emotion recognition from body movements. ACM Trans. Interactive Intell. Syst. (TiiS) 5, 1–21 (2015)

27. Crenn, A., Khan, R.A., Meyer, A., Bouakaz, S.: Body expression recognition from animated 3D skeleton. In: 2016 International Conference on 3D Imaging (IC3D), pp. 1–7. IEEE (2016)

28. Randhavane, T., Bhattacharya, U., Kapsaskis, K., Gray, K., Bera, A., Manocha, D.: Identifying emotions from walking using affective and deep features. arXiv preprint arXiv:1906.11884 (2019)

29. Yan, S., Xiong, Y., Lin, D.: Spatial temporal graph convolutional networks for skeleton-based action recognition. arXiv preprint arXiv:1801.07455 (2018)

30. Shi, L., Zhang, Y., Cheng, J., Lu, H.: Two-stream adaptive graph convolutional networks for skeleton-based action recognition. In: Proceedings of the IEEE Conference on Computer Vision and Pattern Recognition, 12026–12035 (2019)

31. Liu, Z., Zhang, H., Chen, Z., Wang, Z., Ouyang, W.: Disentangling and unifying graph convolutions for skeleton-based action recognition. In: Proceedings of the IEEE/CVF Conference on Computer Vision and Pattern Recognition, pp. 143–152 (2020)

32. Yu, B., Yin, H., Zhu, Z.: Spatio-temporal graph convolutional networks: A deep learning framework for traffic forecasting. arXiv preprint arXiv:1709.04875 (2017)

33. Diao, Z., Wang, X., Zhang, D., Liu, Y., Xie, K., He, S.: Dynamic spatial-temporal graph convolutional neural networks for traffic forecasting. In: Proceedings of the AAAI Conference on Artificial Intelligence, vol. 33, pp. 890–897 (2019)

34. Yang, J., Zheng, W.S., Yang, Q., Chen, Y.C., Tian, Q.: Spatial-temporal graph convolutional network for video-based person re-identification. In: Proceedings of the IEEE/CVF Conference on Computer Vision and Pattern Recognition, pp. 3289–3299 (2020)

35. Zhao, M., Zhong, S., Fu, X., Tang, B., Pecht, M.: Deep residual shrinkage networks for fault diagnosis. IEEE Trans. Industr. Inf. 16, 4681–4690 (2019)

36. Habibie, I., Holden, D., Schwarz, J., Yearsley, J., Komura, T.: A recurrent variational autoencoder for human motion synthesis. In: 28th British Machine Vision Conference (2017)

Cell Detection and Segmentation in Microscopy Images with Improved Mask R-CNN

Seiya Fujita$^{(\boxtimes)}$ and Xian-Hua Han$^{(\boxtimes)}$ ⓘ

Graduate School of Science and Technology for Innovation, Yamaguchi University, 1677-1 Yoshida, Yamaguchi City, Yamaguchi 753-8511, Japan
{b026vb,hanxhua}@yamaguchi-u.ac.jp

Abstract. Analyzing and elucidating the attributes of cells and tissues with an observed microscopy image is a fundamental task in both biological research and clinical practice, and automation of this task to develop computer aided system based on image processing and machine learning technique has been rapidly evolved for providing quantitative evaluation and mitigating burden and time of the biological experts. Automated cell/nuclei detection and segmentation is in general a critical step in automatic system, and is quite challenging due to the existed heterogeneous characteristics of cancer cell such as large variability in size, shape, appearance, and texture of the different cells. This study proposes a novel method for simultaneous detection and segmentation of cells based on the Mask R-CNN, which conducts multiple end-to-end learning tasks by minimizing multi task losses for generic object detection and segmentation. The conventional Mask R-CNN employs cross entropy loss for evaluating the object detection fidelity, and equally treats all training samples in learning procedure regardless to the properties of the objects such as easily or hard degree for detection, which may lead to missdetection of hard samples. To boost the detection performance of hard samples, this work integrates the focal loss for formulating detection criteria into Mask R-CNN, and investigate a feasible method for balancing the contribution of multiple task losses in network training procedure. Experiments on the benchmark dataset: DSB2018 manifest that our proposed method achieves the promising performance on both cell detection and segmentation.

1 Introduction

With the development of whole slide digital scanning technology, it is now possible to digitize and store tissue slides in digital image format. Manual analysis of these microscopy images can be very burdensome and time-consuming for professionals. Automated analysis of these types of images to provide quantitative measurements has received a lot of attention and has contributed significantly to the advancement of computer-assisted diagnostic systems. One of the key tasks in cellular image analysis is to identify certain grades (e.g., cancer) or different

I. Sato and B. Han (Eds.): ACCV 2020 Workshops, LNCS 12628, pp. 58–70, 2021.
https://doi.org/10.1007/978-3-030-69756-3_5

types of tumors related to the degree of cellular heterogeneity involved in tumor development. In this context, the recognition and detection of cell nuclei is an important step for detailed cellular analysis in computer-assisted diagnostic systems. In addition, shape recognition of cell nuclei is an important task in grade discrimination of the species or identifying whether the tumor is of a different type.

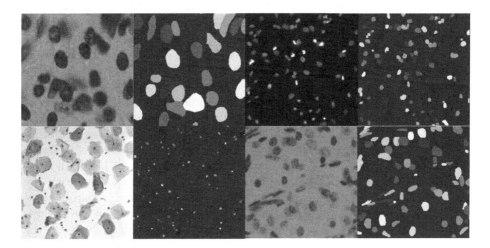

Fig. 1. Some examples of the microscopy images and their corresponding masks in DSB2018 dataset. It is obvious that the variety of the microscopy image is substantial large and would be a very challenge task for cell detection and segmentation.

Therefore, localization of different cells and pixel-wise recognition to obtain the precise shape of cell nuclear is a crucial step for most downstream tasks, and meanwhile is very difficult due to the existing heterogeneous characteristics of cancer cells, such as large variations in size, shape, appearance, color of stain, and texture of various cells. Figure 1 manifests some examples of the microscopy images and the annotated masks in DSB2018 dataset. This simultaneous detection/localization and segmentation of an object in computer vision field are well known as instance segmentation involving the assignment of instance identity to every pixel in the image. This study aims at instance segmentation of cell nuclei.

Most instance segmentation approaches follow separate detection and segmentation paradigm, which firstly employs state-of-the art object detection methods to extract the bounding box of each object and then conducts segmentation on each bounding box. For object detection, there are mainly two types of deep learning based methods: single stage detection frameworks such as SSD [8] and YOLO [9], and two stage detection frameworks [4] such as Faster R-CNN [5]. Single stage method treats object detection as a simple regression problem via simultaneously learning the class probabilities and bounding box coordinates from an input image in a single step while two stage detector firstly estimates candidate regions using a region proposal network and then performs object classification and bounding-box regression for the region proposals. Such models generally achieve higher accuracy rates, but are typically slower than single stage detector. Segmentation is implemented on the detected objects for providing the final instance segmentation results. However, such pipeline conducts object detection and the downstream segmentation independently, and may lead to sub-optimal results. He et al. [6] proposed a simple, flexible and general end-to-end learning network for instance segmentation, called as Mask R-CNN. Mask R-CNN extends Faster R-CNN by adding a prediction branch of an object mask in parallel with the bounding box regression branch in the raw faster R-CNN, and has been proven the applicability for different detection/localization and segmentation tasks [1–3].

This study adopts Mask R-CNN for simultaneously cell detection and segmentation. It is well known that the model training of Mask R-CNN involves minimization of several loss functions for the multiple task learning tasks. However, how different losses contribute to the final detection and segmentation results remains un-exploration. This work investigates the impact of different losses used in Mask R-CNN via adjusting the weights of different losses. In addition, conventional Mask R-CNN employs cross entropy loss for evaluating the object detection fidelity, and equally treats all training samples in learning procedure regardless to the properties of the objects such as easy or hard degree for detection, which may lead to miss-detection of hard samples. To boost the detection performance of hard samples, we integrate the focal loss [7] for formulating detection criteria into Mask R-CNN, and investigate a feasible method for balancing the contribution of multiple task losses in network training procedure. Experiments on the benchmark dataset: DSB2018 manifests that our proposed method achieves the promising performance on both cell detection and segmentation.

The rest of this paper is organized as follows. Section 2 surveys the related work including cell detection method and segmentation approach. Section 3 presents the strategy for exploring the effect of different losses to the detection and segmentation results and the integration of the focal loss into Mask R-CNN. Extensive experiments are conducted in Sect. 4 to compare the proposed method with the baseline Mask R-CNN on DSB2018 datasets. Conclusion is given in Sect. 5.

2 Related Work

In the past few years, cell detection and segmentation has been actively research in computer vision and medical image processing community, and substantial improvement have been witnessed. This work concentrates on simultaneously detection and segmentation of cells in microscopy images. Here, we briefly survey the related work about cell detection and segmentation, respectively.

2.1   Cell Detection Approaches

Different cell recognition and detection methods for computer-aided diagnosis systems have been explored, and many methods mainly employ traditional paradigm via extracting hand-crafted feature representation and conducting classification independently. For example, Humayun et al. [10] proposed to using morphological and multi-channel statistics features for mitosis detection. Alkofahi et al. [11] explored multiscale Laplacian-of-Gaussian filtering for nuclear seed point detect. Meanwhile Gabor filter or LBP feature [12] provides a lot of interesting texture properties and had been popularly applied for a cell detection task. Although the traditional cell detection paradigm has been widely researched, the independent procedure for hand-crafted feature extraction and classification suffer from several limitations; 1) it is difficult to select proper features for different tasks; 2) different features are needed to be designed for representing various aspects of the input; 3) the separation using of feature extraction and classification generally leads to sub-optimal results for the under-studying tasks.

Recently, motivated by the successes of the deep learning on computer vision community, deep convolutional neural network has popularly been used for cell detection and localization. [13] initially applied a fully convolutional network for cell counting via predicting a spatial density map of target cell and then estimating the cell number with an integration over the learned density map. Later, Chen et al. [14] proposed a cascaded network for cell detection which firstly uses the FCN for candidate region selection and then adopts another CNN for classifying the candidate regions and background. Meanwhile [15] investigated a CNN-based prediction method following by ad-hoc post processing, which trains CNN model to classify each pixel represented with a patch centered on the pixel and then conducts post processing on the network output. Shadi et al. [16] employed expectation maximization with deep learning framework in an end-to-end manner for cell detection, which can handle the learning task from crowds via leveraging an additional crowd-sourcing layer on the CNN architecture. More recently, Xue et al. [17] combined deep CNN with compressed sensing for cell detection and Schmidt et al. [18] proposed to localize cell nuclei via star-convex polygons for better shape representation than the conventional bounding box. In spite of the promising performance, the cell detection method cannot provide detailed shape of the cell which may be necessary for the downstream tasks.

2.2   Cell Segmentation

To analyze the characteristics of each individual cell, cell segmentation is an essential step in different microscopy image analysis systems, and many methods have been proposed. One of the most common methods for this task is to simply use intensity thresholding, and usually suffers from intensity inhomogeneity. To separate touching and overlapping cell and nuclei, watershed-based [20,21] and level-set methods [22,23] have been applied for cell segmentation. Dorini et al. [24] proposed to employ morphological operators and scale-space analysis for

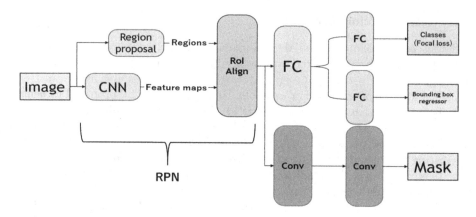

Fig. 2. The schematic concept of the Mask R-CNN for simultaneous object detection and segmentation via adding a branching subnet to Faster R-CNN to estimate the segmentation mask, which is itself a multitask learning framework with multiple loss functions.

white blood cell segmentation, which assumes a blob-like shape of the cell nucleus to conduct blob-based detection as the initialization of a graph-based method while Wang et al. explored snake algorithm for cell segmentation and tracking.

Recently, deep convolutional network has been proven to be very effective for segmentation of different types of images, and has also been applied for the segmentation of cell nuclei [25–27]. In 2015, the encoder-decoder framework: U-Net architecture was developed specifically for the segmentation of medical images, and applied on the ISBI challenge for segmentation of neuronal structures in electron microscopy stacks to produce state-of-the-art results [28]. Since then, U-Net has been used for a wide range of tasks in medical image analysis including cell segmentation and tracking on time-lapse microscopy images [29]. More recently, Mask R-CNN [6] has been proposed to extend the Faster R-CNN [5] model for simultaneous object localization and instance segmentation of natural images, and has also been adapted for cell localization and single cell segmentation. Due to the property of multi-task learning in the Mask R-CNN, it entails the use of multi-task loss functions for training the end-to-end learning network. However, how different losses contribute to the final results remains un-exploration, and balance of the multi-task losses for various applications may be a non-trivial step. This study also follows the paradigm of Mask R-CNN for segmentation of individual cells. We extensively explore the effect of different losses on the final detection and segmentation results.

3   Method

Mask R-CNN enables instance segmentation by adding mask branches to the head of the Faster R-CNN network, which allows segmentation of each detected object. In this study, we adapt Mask R-CNN to simultaneously detect and segment cell nuclei in microscopy images. The schematic concept of the Mask R-CNN is show in Fig. 2. To conduct simultaneous object detection and segmentation, Mask R-CNN is itself a multi-task learning framework, and consists of multiple losses for training the end-to-end network. However, contributions of different losses to the final results remains un-exploration, and it is still unclear how to select the proper weights (hyper-parameters) of the used multiple losses for boosting the performance of the under-studying target. This study proposes a weight-selection strategy for exploring the effect of different losses to the final prediction. In addition, conventional Mask R-CNN uses cross entropy loss to assess the fidelity of object detection and treats all training samples in the training procedure equally, regardless of object properties such as the degree of ease or difficulty of detection, and has shown high accuracy results in general object detection. However, cell nucleus detection is very difficult due to the heterogeneous properties of various images, including large variations in size, shape, appearance, staining and texture. Therefore, we propose to improve the accuracy by using focal loss instead of cross entropy loss. Next, we present the detail description of the adaptive weight-selection strategy and the focal-loss based Mask R-CNN.

3.1   Weight-Selection Strategy

To implement multiple tasks, Mask R-CNN employs multiple losses, which consisting of the losses: ($L_{Class_{RPN}}$ and $L_{Bbox_{RPN}}$) in the RPN subnet for extracting objectness regions and the final class prediction losses: class loss (L_{Class}) for classifying objectness regions into different classes, Bbox loss (L_{Bbox}) for estimating the bounding box of objects and mask loss (L_{Mask}) for segmenting individual object, to learn the shared network parameters. The loss functions of Mask R-CNN can be expressed as:

$$Loss_{total} = L_{Class_{RPN}} + L_{Bbox_{RPN}} + \alpha L_{Class} + \beta L_{Bbox} + L_{Mask} \qquad (1)$$

Mask R-CNN empirically set the hyper-parameters α and β as 1, and concurrently minimize all losses for implementing the multitask learning, where different losses may lead to different degrees of learning. For instance, the loss function with smaller value may serve little to network learning while loss with large value would give great effect to the network parameter updating. From Eq. (1), it can be seen that Mask R-CNN losses can be divided into RPN losses and prediction losses for final results. Since the RPN losses mainly aid to obtain the initial object candidates for being forwarded to the subsequent prediction procedure, it is usually considered to have no great effect on the final prediction results according to our experience and observation. This work concentrates on exploring the weight-selection strategy for the hyper-parameters α and β in Eq. (1) for adaptively selecting the weight of the prediction losses: L_{Class}, L_{Bbox} and L_{Mask}. Figure 3. (a) plots the values of different prediction losses with different epoch numbers in training procedure, which manifests the different values among the

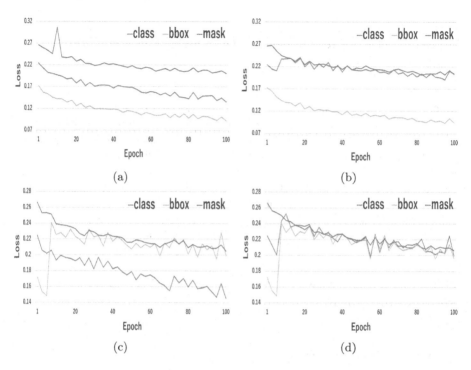

Fig. 3. The values of different predicted Losses in conventional Mask R-CNN, and the proposed models with the weight-selection strategy for updating α or β or both weights. a) Mask R-CNN; b) Weight updating for α; c) Weight updating for β; d) Weight updating for both α and β.

three prediction losses. Since the three losses contribute to various tasks: classification, segmentation and bounding box regression, respectively, smaller value of one loss may lead to not-enough learning for the corresponding task and then possibly results in adverse effect on other tasks. Thus we propose a weight-selection strategy to adaptively adjust the weights: α and β in network training procedure, and update these weights at each epoch according to the loss values of the previous epoch. The updating of the weights: α and β is formulated as the following:

$$\alpha_{t+1} = \frac{\max(L_{Class}, L_{Bbox}, L_{Mask})}{L_{Class}} \alpha_t \tag{2}$$

$$\beta_{t+1} = \frac{\max(L_{Class}, L_{Bbox}, L_{Mask})}{L_{Bbox}} \beta_t \tag{3}$$

$$Loss_{total_{t+1}} = L_{Class_{RPN}} + L_{Bbox_{RPN}} + \alpha_{t+1} L_{Class} + \beta_{t+1} L_{Bbox} + L_{Mask} \tag{4}$$

Where α_t and β_t are the weights at the t-th epoch while α_{t+1} and β_{t+1} are the updated weights at the $(t+1)$-th epoch. We firstly set the initial weights at the first epoch as $\alpha_1 = 1$, $\beta_1 = 1$, and update them at each epoch in network training procedure.

3.2 Focal-Loss Based Mask R-CNN

Due to the heterogeneous properties of microscopy images such as large variations in size, shape, appearance, staining and texture, there exist some difficult cell instances to be detected and recognized. We integrate focal loss for object classification instead of cross entropy loss into Mask R-CNN. Focal loss attenuates the effect of the losses obtained from large amount of easy samples while emphasizes the contribution of losses obtained from small proportion of hard samples that are difficult to be recognized. Thus This makes it possible to increase the loss for cell nuclei that are difficult to be distinguished in the microscopy images and decrease the loss for cell nuclei that are easy to be distinguished. Let denotes the predicted probability of a training sample as P_T on the ground truth class T, the focal loss calculated from this sample can be formulated as:

$$L_{FocalLoss} = -\delta(1 - P_T)^\gamma \log P_T \tag{5}$$

where δ, γ are hyper-parameters with δ controlling the contribution of the whole focal loss to the total loss while γ adjusting the contribution of each individual cell according to the classification difficulty. In this study, we set $\gamma = 1$. From Eq. (5), it can be seen that the value of the focal loss without considering the effect of the controlling hyper-parameter δ, would become smaller than the value of the cross-entropy loss: $-P_T \log P_T$ for most samples, which would weaken the learning degree of the object classification task compared to other tasks. Thus we propose an automatic regulating method for designing the hyper-parameter δ to balance the focal loss with other losses. The automatic regulating method for updating δ at each epoch in network training procedure is formulated as:

$$\delta_{t+1} = \frac{\max(L_{FocalLoss}, L_{Bbox}, L_{Mask})}{L_{FocalLoss}} \delta_t \tag{6}$$

where δ_t and δ_{t+1} denote the weights in the t-th and $(t+1)$-th epochs, respectively.

4 Experiments Results

4.1 Dataset

To evaluate the effectiveness of our proposed method, we conducted experiments on the 2018 Data Science Bowl dataset (DSB2018). DSB2018 dataset has in total 670 microscopy images captured in various modalities, and therein 645 images were used for training and 25 were used for testing. We also conducted data augmentation via left/right flipping, up/down flipping, rotation, Gaussian blurring and darkening operations on the raw images in training procedure.

4.2   Evaluation Metric

We adopt *F1 measure* to evaluating the performance of object detection. A detected object I_{pred} is considered as a proper match (*true positive TP_τ*) if a ground truth object I_{gt} exists whose *intersection over union*: $IoU = \frac{I_{pred} \cap I_{gt}}{I_{pred} \cup I_{gt}}$ with the prediction is greater than a given threshold $\tau \in [0, 1]$. Unmatched predicted objects are counted as *false positives* (FP_τ) while unmatched ground truth objects are as *false negatives* (FN_τ). Given the matching evaluations: TP_τ, FP_τ and FN_τ, the evaluation metrics: *Precision* for measuring prediction accuracy and *Recall* for measuring the reproducibility of forecasts are formulated as:

$$Precision = \frac{TP_\tau}{TP_\tau + FP_\tau}, Recall = \frac{TP_\tau}{TP_\tau + FN_\tau} \tag{7}$$

Then the *F1 measure* is expressed by the following equation:

$$F1measure = 2\frac{Precision * Recall}{Precision + Recall} \tag{8}$$

For segmentation evaluation, we use *Dice* metric. The segmented results are evaluated pixel by pixel to calculate TP, FP, and FN, and then $Precision_d$ and $Recall_d$ are computed based on Eq. (7). Finally the *Dice* is calculated as:

$$Dice = 2\frac{Precision_d * Recall_d}{Precision_d + Recall_d}. \tag{9}$$

4.3   Performance Comparison

We conducted experiments with different models for simultaneous cell detection and segmentation and provide the compared results.

Comparison of Mask R-CNN Models w/o the Weight-Selection Strategy: As described in Sect. 3, we explored a weight-selection strategy for adaptively adjusting the hyper-parameters of different prediction losses in Mask R-CNN. Initially, we set the hyper-parameters (weights) in Eq. (1) as $\alpha_1 = 1$, $\beta_1 = 1$, and then update the parameters according to Eq. (2) and (3). We implemented four models: Mask R-CNN without the weight-selection strategy, the other three models with the updating for only α or β or both. The values of different losses for the three improved models are shown in Fig. 3(b), (c) and (d). The compared results are given in Table 1, which manifests the updating of α for re-weighting the class loss achieves best performance. From the results in Table 1, it can be concluded that the class loss for classifying the cell candidate regions has more contribution to the final performance.

Comparison of the Focal-Loss Based Mask R-CNN: We integrated the focal loss into Mask R-CNN for evaluating cell detection and segmentation performance. Compared with the cross-entropy loss, the value of the focal loss would become smaller, and thus we explore a method for automatically designing the

Table 1. Compared cell detection and segmentation results w/o the weight-selection strategy.

	$Loss_{Class}$	$Loss_{Bbox}$	$\tau = 0.50$	0.55	0.60	0.65	0.70	0.75	0.80	0.85	0.90	$Dice$
MRCNN	–	–	0.77	0.75	0.72	0.68	0.63	0.56	0.45	0.28	0.09	0.877
Class	✓	–	0.79	0.77	0.75	0.71	0.65	0.59	0.45	0.27	0.07	0.880
Bbox	–	✓	0.77	0.75	0.74	0.70	0.65	0.57	0.46	0.26	0.08	0.878
Class_Bbox	✓	✓	0.74	0.73	0.70	0.67	0.61	0.53	0.43	0.26	0.07	0.878

contributed weight in Eq. (6). The compared results are provided with the following 4 models: 1) the conventional Mask R-CNN; 2) Mask R-CNN + FL ($\alpha = 1$) via integrating the focal loss with the weight $\alpha = 1$; 2) Mask R-CNN + FL ($\alpha = 5$) via integrating the focal loss with the weight $\alpha = 5$; 4) Mask R-CNN + FL (Balanced) via integrating the focal loss with automatically regulated weight. In all models, we set the NMS threshold as 0.3 for detecting cell candidates, and the score threshold as 0.5 for cell classification. We used the pre-trained ResNet with ImageNet dataset as the backbone network, and then perform the transfer training for cell detection and segmentation.

Table 2. Nuclei detection results, showing $F1$ *measure* for several *intersection over union* (IoU) thresholds τ, and segmentation results $Dice$.

Threshold τ	0.50	0.55	0.60	0.65	0.70	0.75	0.80	0.85	0.90	Dice
Mask R-CNN	0.77	0.75	0.72	0.68	0.63	0.56	0.45	0.28	0.09	0.877
MRCNN + FL($\alpha = 1$)	**0.81**	**0.79**	**0.76**	**0.72**	**0.67**	**0.60**	**0.48**	**0.31**	**0.11**	**0.888**
MRCNN + FL($\alpha = 5$)	0.78	0.74	0.71	0.67	0.63	0.55	0.43	0.27	0.10	0.871
MRCNN + FL(*balanced*)	0.78	0.76	0.73	0.70	0.65	0.57	0.45	0.28	0.09	0.883

The compared results with the four models are shown in Table 2. Table 2 manifests the model with the focal loss and the weight $\alpha = 1$ achieved best performance for both cell detection and segmentation. In our experiments, there are in total 1504 ground truth cells in the 25 test microscopy images, and the detected cell number with the threshold $\tau = 0.5$ by the four models: Mask R-CNN, Mask R-CNN + FL ($\alpha = 1$), Mask R-CNN + FL ($\alpha = 5$) and Mask R-CNN + FL (Balanced) are 1109, 1277, 1209 and 1128, respectively, which means that the integration of the focal loss can increase the number of detected cells. The Dice values in Table 2 are calculated for the detected cell nuclei. Finally, we give the visualization results of several microscopy images in Fig. 4, which also manifests some improvement with the integration of the focal loss in the Mask R-CNN.

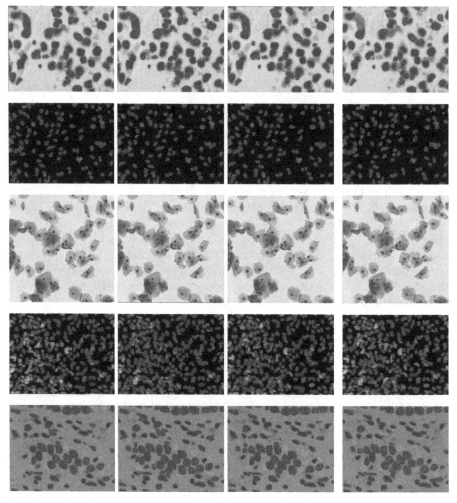

Mask R-CNN   MRCNN+FL($\alpha = 1$) MRCNN+FL($\alpha = 5$) MRCNN+FL(Balance)

Fig. 4. Compared cell detection and segmentation results using the conventional Mask R-CNN and the focal-loss based Mask R-CNN. Green color represents GT pixels, Red color represents predicted cell pixels and Brown color denotes the overlapped regions of GT and prediction. (Color figure online)

5   Conclusion

In this study, we adopted Mask R-CNN to simultaneously detect and segment cell nuclei in a microscopy image, which is the most popular deep learning-based method for instance segmentation of natural images. Specifically, due to the multi-task learning property of the Mask R-CNN, we proposed a weight-selection strategy for adaptively adjusting the hyper-parameters of different prediction losses, and evaluated the effect of different losses to the final prediction for cell detection and segmentation. Further, we integrated the focal loss into Mask R-CNN for concentrating the hard samples to be recognized and meanwhile investigated an automatic regulating method for calculating the contributed weight of the focal loss. Experimental results on DSB2018 validated that our proposed model can improve performance of both cell detection and segmentation compared with the baseline Mask R-CNN.

Acknowledgements. This research was supported in part by the Grant-in Aid for Scientific Research from the Japanese Ministry for Education, Science, Culture and Sports (MEXT) under the Grant No. 20K11867.

References

1. Anantharaman, R., Velazquez, M., Lee, Y.: Utilizing Mask R-CNN for detection and segmentation of oral diseases. In: IEEE International Conference on Bioinformatics and Biomedicine (2018)
2. Johnson, J.W.: Automatic nucleus segmentation with Mask-RCNN. In: Arai, K., Kapoor, S. (eds.) CVC 2019. AISC, vol. 944, pp. 399–407. Springer, Cham (2020). https://doi.org/10.1007/978-3-030-17798-0_32
3. Tan, C., Uddin, N., Mohammed, Y.M.: Deep learning-based crack detection using mask R-CNN technique. In: 9th International Conference on Structural Health Monitoring of Intelligent Infrastructure (2019)
4. Girshick, R.: Fast R-CNN. In: IEEE International Conference on Computer Vision (ICCV) (2015)
5. Ren, S., He, K., Girshick, R., Sun, J.: Faster R-CNN: towards real-time object detection with region proposal networks. In: Advances in Neural Information Processing Systems, pp. 91–99 (2015)
6. He, K., Gkioxari, G., Dollar, P., Girshick, R.: Mask R-CNN. In: ICCV (2017)
7. Lin, T.-Y., Goyal, P., Girshick, R., He, K., Dollar, P.: Focal loss for dense object detection. In: ICCV (2017)
8. Liu, W., et al.: SSD: single shot multibox detector. In: Leibe, B., Matas, J., Sebe, N., Welling, M. (eds.) ECCV 2016. LNCS, vol. 9905, pp. 21–37. Springer, Cham (2016). https://doi.org/10.1007/978-3-319-46448-0_2
9. Redmon, J., Divvala, S., Girshick, R., Farhadi, A.: You only look once: unified, real-time object detection. arXiv preprint arXiv:1506.02640 (2015)
10. Irshad, H.: Automated mitosis detection in histopathology using morphological and multi-channel statistics features. J. Pathol. Inform. **4**, 10 (2013)
11. Al-Kofahi, Y., Lassoued, W., Lee, W., Roysam, B.: Improved automatic detection and segmentation of cell nuclei in histopathology images. IEEE Trans. Biomed. Eng. **57**, 841–852 (2009)
12. Ojala, T., Pietikainen, M., Harwood, D.: A comparative study of texture measures with classification based on feature distributions. Pattern Recogn. **29**, 51–59 (1996)
13. Weidi, X., Noble, J.A., Zisserman, A.: Microscopy cell counting with fully convolutional regression networks. Comput. Methods Biomech. Biomed. Eng.: Imaging Vis. **6**, 283–292 (2018)
14. Chen, H., Dou, Q., Wang, X., Qin, J., Heng, P.-A.: Mitosis detection in breast cancer histology images via deep cascaded networks. In: AAAI 2016: Proceedings of the Thirtieth AAAI Conference on Artificial Intelligence, pp. 1160–1166 (2016)

15. Cireşan, D.C., Giusti, A., Gambardella, L.M., Schmidhuber, J.: Mitosis detection in breast cancer histology images with deep neural networks. In: Mori, K., Sakuma, I., Sato, Y., Barillot, C., Navab, N. (eds.) MICCAI 2013. LNCS, vol. 8150, pp. 411–418. Springer, Heidelberg (2013). https://doi.org/10.1007/978-3-642-40763-5_51

16. Albarqouni, S., Baur, C., Achilles, F., Belagiannis, V., Demirci, S., Navab, N.: AggNet: deep learning from crowds for mitosis detection in breast cancer histology images. IEEE Trans. Med. Imaging 5, 1313–1321 (2016)

17. Xue, Y., Ray, N.: Cell detection in microscopy images with deep convolutional neural network and compressed sensing. In: Computer Vision and Pattern Recognition, CVPR (2017)

18. Schmidt, U., Weigert, M., Broaddus, C., Myers, G.: Cell detection with star-convex polygons. In: Frangi, A.F., Schnabel, J.A., Davatzikos, C., Alberola-López, C., Fichtinger, G. (eds.) MICCAI 2018. LNCS, vol. 11071, pp. 265–273. Springer, Cham (2018). https://doi.org/10.1007/978-3-030-00934-2_30

19. Wahlby, C., Lindblad, J., Vondrus, M., Bengtsson, E., Bjorkesten, L.: Algorithms for cytoplasm segmentation of fluorescence labelled cells. Anal. Cell Pathol.: J. Eur. Soc. Anal. Cell Pathol. 24(2), 101–111 (2002)

20. Wang, M., Zhou, X., Li, F., Huckins, J., King, R.W., Wong, S.T.C.: Novel cell segmentation and online SVM for cell cycle phase identification in automated microscopy. Bioinformatics 24(1), 94–101 (2008)

21. Sharif, J.M., Miswan, M.F., Ngadi, M.A., Salam, M.S.H., Bin Abdul Jamil, M.M.: Red blood cell segmentation using masking and watershed algorithm: a preliminary study. In: 2012 International Conference on Biomedical Engineering (ICoBE), pp. 258–262 (2012)

22. Nath, S.K., Palaniappan, K., Bunyak, F.: Cell segmentation using coupled level sets and graph-vertex coloring. In: Larsen, R., Nielsen, M., Sporring, J. (eds.) MICCAI 2006. LNCS, vol. 4190, pp. 101–108. Springer, Heidelberg (2006). https://doi.org/10.1007/11866565_13

23. Dzyubachyk, O., Niessen, W., Meijering, E.: Advanced level-set based multiple-cell segmentation and tracking in time-lapse fluorescence microscopy images. In: 2008 5th IEEE International Symposium on Biomedical Imaging: From Nano to Macro, pp. 185–188 (2008)

24. Dorini, L.B., Minetto, R., Leite, N.J.: White blood cell segmentation using morphological operators and scale-space analysis. In: XX Brazilian Symposium on Computer Graphics and Image Processing, SIBGRAPI 2007, pp. 294–304 (2007)

25. Wang, X., He, W., Metaxas, D., Mathew, R., White, E.: Cell segmentation and tracking using texture-adaptive shakes. In: 2007 4th IEEE International Symposium on Biomedical Imaging: From Nano to Macro, pp. 101–104 (2007)

26. Van Valen, D.A., et al.: Deep learning automates the quantitative analysis of individual cells in live-cell imaging experiments. PLoS Comput. Biol. 12(11), 1–24 (2016). 1005177

27. Kraus, O.Z., et al.: Automated analysis of high-content microscopy data with deep learning. Mol. Syst. Biol. 13(4), 924 (2017)

28. Ronneberger, O., Fischer, P., Brox, T.: U-Net: convolutional networks for biomedical image segmentation. In: Navab, N., Hornegger, J., Wells, W.M., Frangi, A.F. (eds.) MICCAI 2015. LNCS, vol. 9351, pp. 234–241. Springer, Cham (2015). https://doi.org/10.1007/978-3-319-24574-4_28

29. Lugagne, J.-B., Lin, H., Dunlop, M.J.: DeLTA: automated cell segmentation, tracking, and lineage reconstruction using deep learning. PLoS Comput. Biol. 16(4), 1007673 (2020)

BdSL36: A Dataset for Bangladeshi Sign Letters Recognition

Oishee Bintey Hoque$^{(\boxtimes)}$, Mohammad Imrul Jubair, Al-Farabi Akash, and Md. Saiful Islam

Ahsanullah University of Science and Technology, Dhaka, Bangladesh
bintu3003@gmail.com, mohammadimrul.jubair@ucalgary.ca,
alfa.farabi@gmail.com, saiful.somum@gmail.com

Abstract. Bangladeshi Sign Language (BdSL) is a commonly used medium of communication for the hearing-impaired people in Bangladesh. A real-time BdSL interpreter with no controlled lab environment has a broad social impact and an interesting avenue of research as well. Also, it is a challenging task due to the variation in different subjects (age, gender, color, etc.), complex features, and similarities of signs and clustered backgrounds. However, the existing dataset for BdSL classification task is mainly built in a lab friendly setup which limits the application of powerful deep learning technology. In this paper, we introduce a dataset named BdSL36 which incorporates background augmentation to make the dataset versatile and contains over four million images belonging to 36 categories. Besides, we annotate about $40,000$ images with bounding boxes to utilize the potentiality of object detection algorithms. Furthermore, several intensive experiments are performed to establish the baseline performance of our BdSL36. Moreover, we employ beta testing of our classifiers at the user level to justify the possibilities of real-world application with this dataset. We believe our BdSL36 will expedite future research on practical sign letter classification. We make the datasets and all the pre-trained models available for further researcher.

1 Introduction

Sign language is a non-verbal form of communication used by deaf and hard of hearing people who communicate through bodily movements especially with fingers, hands and arms. Detecting the signs automatically from images or videos is an appealing task in the field of Computer Vision. Understanding what signers are trying to describe always requires recognizing of the different poses of their hands. These poses and gestures differ from region to region, language to language, i.e. for American Sign Language (ASL) [1], Chinese Sign Language (CSL) [2], etc. A considerable number of people in Bangladesh rely on BdSL [3] to communicate in their day to day life [4], and the need for a communication system as a digital interpreter between signers and non-signers is quite apparent.

© Springer Nature Switzerland AG 2021
I. Sato and B. Han (Eds.): ACCV 2020 Workshops, LNCS 12628, pp. 71–86, 2021.
https://doi.org/10.1007/978-3-030-69756-3_6

Due to the current resonance of Deep Learning, hand pose recognition [5,6] from images and videos have advanced significantly. In contrast, sign letter recognition through a real-time application has received less attention—especially when it comes to Bangladeshi Sign Language. In this work, we tend to simplify the way non-signers communicate with signers through a computer vision system for BdSL by exploiting the power of data and deep learning tools.

Most of the previous work on BdSL and other sign languages [7–10] can be described as a traditional machine learning classification framework or as a mere research as an academic purpose where less focus has been given to build a real-time recognizing system. We can generalize these researches in two modules: (1) datasets with several constraints (i.e. showing only hands, single-colored background) or (2) traditional machine learning classifiers with handcrafted features. These constrained feature-based methods are not ideal for real-life applications or to build a proper sign interpreter as these methods rely on the careful choice of features. With a real-world scenario, the classifier may fail to distinguish the signs from a clustered background.

Fig. 1. Example images of initially collected BdSL36 dataset. Each image represents different BdSL sign letter. Images are serially organized according to their class label from left to right.

In this recent era, deep learning enables the scope of overcoming these constraints and achieve a state-of-the-art performance on a variety of image classification tasks. But, to train a deep learning classifier, the role of a large dataset is unavoidable and plays a pivotal role to build a robust classifier. However, deep learning methods, so far, on BdSL letters recognition are restricted to constraint or small scale dataset [11–13], which is not useful to build a robust classifier. The collection of sign letter data is challenging due to the lack of open-source information available on the internet, human resources, the deaf community and knowledge. On the other hand, BdSL letters may have high appearance similarity, which might be confusing to human eyes as well. Hence, with handcrafted features or small scale datasets, it is a tough job to accomplish to build a robust interpreter.

To advance the BdSL letters recognition research in computer vision and to introduce a possible real-time sign interpreter to the community in need, we present the BdSL36, a new large-scale BdSL dataset in this work. As mentioned earlier, many factors hinder the process of collecting images with variation to make a large scale sign letter dataset. We organize 10 volunteers of different ages and gender to help us with the whole process of collecting the images. Initially, we receive 1200 images that are captured by the volunteers at their convenient and natural environment (see Fig. 1) followed by thorough checking by the BdSL experts to assure relevancy of the signs in the data. However, only 25 to 35 images per class for building a multi-class classifier of 36 classes are not enough. To compensate for the low data quantity issue, data augmentation has become an effective technique to improve the accuracy of modern image classifiers by increasing both the amount and diversity of data by randomly augmenting [14,15]. The most common augmentation techniques are translation by pixels, rotation, flipping, etc. Intuitively, data augmentation teaches a model about invariances, making the classifier insensitive to flips and translations. Subsequently, to incorporate potential invariances, data augmentation can be easier than hard-coding them into the model directly. In case of a dataset of hand poses, we need variation in hand shape, skin color, different postures of the sign, etc. Moreover, making the dataset insensitive to the background, it is also essential to introduce background variation with the subject being in a different position in the images. To the best of our knowledge, less attention has been paid to find better data augmentation techniques that incorporate more invariances and resolve the background variation limitation in a small scale dataset.

In our work, initially, we incorporate traditional data augmentation—rotation, translation, brightness, contrast adjustment, random cropping, zooming, shearing, cutout [16], etc.—on our raw collected dataset which we called BdSL36 version-1 (BdSL35v1). Though these augmentations improve accuracy on the validation set, when we deploy the classifier and test it with real-life users, it performs poorly. Therefore, we employ a new augmentation technique—not widely used as per our knowledge—the background augmentation to introduce second version (BdSL36v2). Here, we removed the background from our raw dataset images, perform traditional augmentation on them, and later, stack them over one million background images downloaded from the internet at random positions. After that, we perform another set of suitable traditional augmentation (perspective and symmetric warp with random probability) and build a dataset of over four million images. Our intensive experiments show that this method achieves excellent improvement in terms of both accuracy and confidence rate. We again perform another set of beta testing with two of the classifiers—trained with background augmented and non augmented data—and achieve a significant improvement in the results. This experiment shows, even with a very small scale dataset, it is possible to get the state-of-the-art performance for complicated features and surpass the limitation of the quantity of the dataset. With this dataset, we also present another version of the dataset (BdSL36v3) with bounding box labeling for object detection methods which contains over 40 thousand images labeled manually. Our intention in these experiments is to help the deaf community in real life by not limiting the sign letter recognition task to a controlled environment. To further validate the value of our proposed dataset, we also report evaluation on different deep learning networks for the state-of-the-art classification.

It is worth to note that, in some of the similar papers, the term 'fingerspelling' is used to refer to the letters of a sign language system, while many other works represent it as 'sign language'. To minimize the ambiguity, in our paper, we use the term 'sign letters' in such context; and the term 'BdSL letters' to refer the letters of Bangladeshi sign language in particular.

Our contributions are summarized as follows:

- To best of our knowledge, we build the first largest dataset of the Bangladeshi Sign Language letter—**BdSL36**—for deep learning classification and detection. Our dataset comes with four different versions: raw dataset (**BdSL36x**), augmentation on the raw dataset (**BdSL36v1**), background augmented images (**BdSL36v2**) and bounding box labelled dataset (**BdSL36v3**). We make all of these versions available to the community so that researchers can exploit them according to their requirements. We incorporate background augmentation technique for small scale dataset with the proof of significant improvement in results through extensive experiment. Dataset can found be at rb.gy/mm3yjg.
- We conduct extensive experiments on the datasets using deep learning classification and detection models to establish the baseline for future research. We also perform beta testing to identify the possibility of deploying this system in the real world. All these work and experiments are made available to the research community for further investigations.

2   Related Works

In this section, we first discuss some of the previous works and datasets in automating BdSL letters recognition, followed by reviewing some works on data augmentation.

Rahaman et al. [12] use 1800 contour templates for 18 Bangladeshi signs separately. The authors introduce a computer vision-based system that applies contour analysis and Haar-like feature-based cascaded classifier and achieve 90.11% recognition accuracy. Ahmed and Akhand [17] use 2D images to train an artificial neural network using tip-position vectors to determine the relative fingertip positions. Though they claim to have an accuracy of 98.99% in detecting the BdSL, their approach is not applicable for real-time recognition. M. A. Rahaman et al. in [11], present a real-time Bengali and Chinese numeral signs recognition system using contour matching. The system is trained and tested using a total

2000 contour templates separately for both Bengali and Chinese numeral signs from 10 signers and achieved recognition accuracy of 95.80% and 95.90% with a computational cost of 8.023 ms per frame. But these classifiers only work in a controlled lab environment. In [13], a method of recognizing Hand-Sign-Spelled Bangla language is introduced. The system is divided into two phases – hand sign classification and automatic recognition of hand-sign-spelled for BdSL using the Bangla Language Modeling Algorithm (BLMA). The system is tested for BLMA using words, composite numerals and sentences in BdSL achieving mean accuracy of 93.50%, 95.50% and 90.50% respectively. In [18], the authors use the Faster R-CNN model to develop a system that can recognize Bengali sign letters in real-time and they also propose a dataset of 10 classes. They train the system on about 1700 images and were able to successfully recognize 10 signs with an accuracy of 98.2%.

The available BdSL datasets are not sufficient enough [11,12,17–19] to develop a fully functioned real-time BdSL detection system. Half of these datasets [11,12,17,20] are also not available for further research. These datasets are further built on a controlled lab environment and the only exception is [18] but this dataset only contains 10 classes.

Recently, data augmentation in deep learning technology widely attracts the attention of researchers. In [14] introduces an automated approach to find the right set of data augmentation for any dataset through transferring learned policies from other datasets. Other auto augmentation techniques by merging two or more samples from the same class are proposed in [21,22]. Specific augmentation techniques such as flipping, rotating and adding different kinds of noise to the data samples, can increase the dataset and give better performance [23]. For generating additional data, adversarial networks have also been incorporated [24,25] to generate direct augmented data.

3   Our BdSL Dataset

3.1   Data Collection and Annotation

We collect and annotate the BdSL36 datasets with the following five stages: 1) Image collection, 2) Raw data augmentation, 3) Background removal and augmentation, 4) Background augmentation, and 5) Data Labeling with Bounding Box.

Image Collection. We establish a dataset for real-time Bangla sign letter classification and detection. Firstly, we visit a deaf school and learn about the letters they practically use in their daily life. There are total 36 Bangla sign letters in total. To build a dataset with no background constraint or controlled lab environment, we make sure to have fair variation in the BdSL36 in terms of subject and background for both classification and detection datasets. At first step we organize 10 volunteers to collect the raw images, and two experts on BdSL train them to perform this task. All of them use their phone cameras or webcam to capture the images at their convenient environment. After the collection of images from the volunteers, each image is checked by BdSL signer experts individually and they filter out the images which contain signs in the wrong style. After filtration, each class contains 25 to 35 images with a total of 1200 images altogether. We have also incorporated BdSlImset [18], containing 1700 images for 10 classes in our BdSL36 image dataset, which sums up to 2712 images in total for 36 classes (see Fig. 1).

Raw Image-Data Augmentation. For a real-time sign letter detection, the classifier must recognize the signs accurately in any form with any variation in scale, appearance, pose, viewpoint, and background. For most of the object classification dataset, it is possible to use the internet as the source of collecting the images. However, in the case of BdSL, there are not enough resources, images, or videos, available on the internet for developing a large scale dataset. Besides, no significant deaf community, awareness and privacy issues are some of the factors that hinder the collection of large scale sign datasets. We surmount this problem with data augmentation. Deep learning frameworks usually have built-in data augmentation utilities, but those can be inefficient or lack some required functionality. We have manually augmented our data with all possible variations. These include several types of transformations on each image with random probabilities, i.e., affine transformations, perspective transformations, contrast changes, noise adding, dropout of regions, cropping/padding, blurring, rotation, zoom in/out, symmetric warp, perspective warp, etc. After the augmentation process, we delete the images if the features get distorted after the augmentation. Finally, **BdSl36v1** (see Fig. 2a) has about $26, 713$ images in total, each class having 700 images on average.

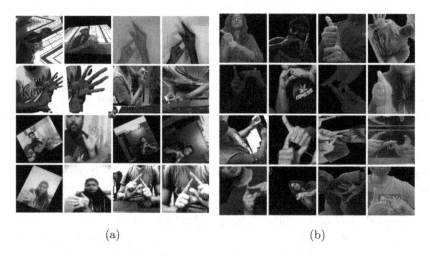

(a)   (b)

Fig. 2. (a) Examples of background augmented images from BdSL36x dataset, (b) Examples of bounding box annotated images from BdSL36v3 dataset.

Background Augmentation. As mentioned earlier, having a large dataset is crucial for the performance of the deep learning models. Recent advances in deep learning models have primarily attributed the quantity and diversity of data gathered in recent years. However, most approaches used in training these models only use basic types of augmentation; less focus has been put into discovering durable types of data augmentation and data augmentation policies that capture data invariances. In this work, we experiment with background augmentation to generate a new robust dataset. Initially, we manually remove the background from each image of the BdSL36x dataset and perform transformations, i.e. rotation ($\pm 60°$), brightness and sharpness adjustment, scaling ($\pm 10\%$), random crop, and zoom in/out, reflection padding, etc. We generate about 12 images from one image (see Fig. 2b). Each image is manually checked by our team to discard the distorted images after these transformations. We utilize the internet to collect more than one million background images of various sorts. Then each of the background-removed augmented, and non augmented images are put into five different backgrounds at random positions. After that, to ensure diversity, we employ another set of transformations—such as perspective warp, symmetric warp, random-crop with various sets of magnitudes—on these images. Finally, we have 473, 662 images in the second version of our dataset: **BdSL36v2**.

Data Labeling with Bounding Box. To utilize the features of the deep learning detection algorithm, we have also generated a dataset with bounding box labeling. Considering the difficulty and cost of labeling, we randomly select some images from BdSLv2 for each class and we appoint two volunteers to label the bounding boxes. Each class contains 1250 images on average with a total of 45, 000 images for 36 classes. The images are labeled following the Pascal VOC [26] and also a version of YOLO [27] format is available.

A visual representation of the flow of our dataset has been shown in Fig. 3.

3.2   Dataset Split

The BdSL36 dataset contains more than four million images in total. We have three versions of our dataset. The BdSL36v1 contains around 22,000 images and only split into train and validation set following 80:20 split where the train set contains approximately 17,600 and validation set 4,400 images. Subsequently, BdSL36v2 contains around 400,000 images and we follow a roughly 70:5:15 split as training, validation and testing set. Specifically, this dataset is nearly split into 300,000 training, 20,000 validation and 60,000 test images. On the other hand, for the object detection dataset, BdSL36v3 is split into 9:1 as 45,500 training and 4,500 validation images.

Fig. 3. The top left image is a raw image captured by one of the volunteers. The two rows to it's right shows the sample augmented images generated from the main image. The leftmost image under the main image has the background removed. Later, augmentation has been applied to this image shown to it's right. From those augmented images, we can see each image contain another set of 3 images with a different background at a different position. All of these images are different from the main image in terms of shape, brightness, contrast, viewpoint background, etc. And, the background augmentation helps to add more variation in a small scale dataset.

3.3   Comparison with Other Datasets

In Table 1, we compare the BdSL36 with other existing datasets related to the task of BdSL letter recognition. Most of the available BdSL [3,12,18–20,28,29] datasets have background constraint and only hand pose is shown which are not suitable for the real-time environment applications. Only BdSLImSet [18] has no such constraints but only has 10 classes. Even if we only consider BdSL36x dataset from BdSL36, the number of participants and background variation makes BdSL36x much more diverse and suitable than other available datasets for deep learning models. Besides, only half of these datasets are available. Due to all these limitations, with the most existing datasets, a real-world application is hard to achieve. Finally, BdSL36v3, is the first and only complete object detection dataset for BdSL letter detection.

Table 1. Comparison with existing BdSL datasets. The Avail, Bg. Const, BBox, Avg., 'Y' and 'N' denotes the availability of datasets to the public, Background Constraint, Bounding Box, Average, Yes and No respectively.

Dataset	Year	Class	Avail	Bg. Const	BBox Label	Sample	Avg.
Rahman et al. [28]	2014	10	N	Y	N	360	36
Rahman et al. [12]	2015	10	N	Y	N	100	10
Ahmed et al. [29]	2016	14	N	Y	N	518	37
BdSLImset [18]	2018	10	Y	N	Y	100	10
Ishara-Lipi [3]	2018	36	Y	Y	N	1,800	50
Sadik et al. [19]	2019	10	Y	Y	N	400	40
Urme et al. [20]	2019	37	N	Y	N	74,000	2,000
Our Dataset	2020	36	Y	N	Y	473,662	13,157

4   Experimental Evaluation

In this section, we empirically investigate the performance of several deep learning object detection frameworks on the BdSL36 dataset to comprehensively evaluate the performance. Our results show that applying only traditional augmentation on a small scale dataset like BdSl36v1 cannot totally overcome the overfitting problem and perform poorly in a real-time environment as well. Whereas, background augmentation yields significant improvement in real-time environment performance without adding any extra raw data, making the classifier learn the invariances more accurately and insensitive to the background.

4.1   Experiment Settings

We use deep learning model architectures - ResNet34 [30], ResNet50 [30], VGGNet_19 [31], Densenet169 [32], Densenet201 [32], Alexnet [33] and Squeezenet [34] - as our base model. We remove the last layer of the models and concatenate an AdaptiveAvgPool2d, an AdaptiveMaxPool2d, a Flatten layer followed by two blocks of [BN-Dropout-Linear-ReLU] layer. The blocks are defined by the linear filters and dropout probability (0.5) arguments. Specifically, the first block will have several inputs inferred from the backbone base architecture, and the last one will have outputs equal to the number of classes of the data. The intermediate blocks have many inputs/outputs determined by linear filters (1024->512->36), each block having inputs equal to the number of outputs of the previous block. We also add batch normalization at the end, which significantly improves the performance by scaling the output layer. We train the model in two phases: first, we freeze the base model and only train the newly added layers for two epochs to convert the base model's previously analyzed features into the prediction of our data. Next, we unfreeze the backbone layers to fine-tune the whole model with different learning rates. For primary training, we use a minibatch size of 64; the learning rate is initialized as 0.003, with a div factor of 25, a weight decay of 0.1, and a momentum of 0.9. Also, to avoid overfitting, we employ a dropout of 0.5. For the second part of the training, we only change the learning rates keeping the other parameters identical. As all these networks are pre-trained on the large scale Imagenet dataset, the earlier layers already know the basic shapes [35] and do not require much training. The deeper the network goes, the layers get more class-specific. While training the unfreezing layer, we split our model into a few sections based on the learning rate. We keep the learning rate lower for the initial layers than the deeper layers, initialized between $3e^-3$ and $3e^-4$. We use 224×224 sized images with default training time augmentation incorporated by the library. The in-depth feature-based experiments are implemented using Pytorch, a fastai library, and performed on Kaggle GPU.

4.2   Evaluation Metrics

The BdSL36 dataset has extremely common similarities among some classes. We apply several metrics evaluation on the validation set for the classification tasks, which include precision, recall, FBeta, accuracy and loss. The precision (denote as pre) quantifies the correctness of a classifier by the ability not to label a negative class as positive. The recall (denote as rec) measures the number of correctly predicted classes out of the number of the actual classes. The FBeta (denote as FB) score is the weighted harmonic mean of precision and recall. We utilize Average Precision (AP) for IoU $= [.50{:}.05{:}.95], [.50], [.75]$. We denote AP for different IoU configuration as AP, $AP^{\frac{1}{2}}$ $AP^{\frac{3}{4}}$ respectively. With higher IoU, it gets difficult to detect for the system.

4.3   Classification and Detection with Deep Learning Networks

In this section, we evaluate the performance of several deep learning model architectures—ResNet34 [30], ResNet50 [30], VGGNet_19 [31], Densenet169 [32], Densenet201 [32], Alexnet [33] and Squeezenet [34]—on BdSL36v2 dataset.

All of these networks are pre-trained on the ImageNet [36] and fined tuned on the BdSL36v2 dataset with hyper-parameters and settings mentioned in Sect. 4.1. Table 2 shows the classification performance on BdSL36v2 validation set of the deep models. The VGGNet_19 performs best compared to other models with 99.1% accuracy. All the models in our experiment are trained with the same parameters and the same number of epochs. It might be possible to use different discrete parameters for other models or train for a longer time to perform better. We can see that ResNet34, ResNet50, VGGNet_19, Densenet169, Densenet201 perform similarly in terms of all the evaluation matrices whereas Alexnet and Squeezenet perform much poorer than the others. Squeezenet has 41.5% accuracy with 44.4% precision and 42.4% recall which are very low compared to other models.

We also evaluate BdSL36v3 on several state-of-the-art object detection methods. Faster R-CNN (backbone VGG-16) [37] a two-stage based method which detects objects through first sliding the window on a feature map to identify the object. Next, it classifies and regresses the corresponding box co-ordinates. Whereas, one stage based methods, SSD300 (backbone Resnet-50) [38] and YOLOv3 (backbone DArknet-53) [27] skip the first step of FRCNN and directly regress the category and bounding box position. Table 3 shows that two-stage based FRCNN performs better over the other two networks. For the training of this network, we use the base architecture and parameters of the individual networks.

Table 2. Classification performance of the deep learning classifiers under different evaluation metrics on the BdSL36v2 dataset.

Methods	Pre	Rec	FB	Acc	Loss
ResNet34 [30]	98.29	98.28	98.28	98.17	0.0592
ResNet50 [30]	98.83	98.79	98.8	98.71	0.0421
VGG19_bn [31]	99.17	99.17	99.17	99.10	0.0284
Densenet169 [32]	98.67	98.64	98.64	98.55	0.0481
Densenet201 [32]	98.70	98.65	98.66	98.56	0.0145
Alexnet [33]	84.1	83.9	83.9	83.1	0.58
Squeezenet [34]	44.4	42.4	42.2	41.5	2.15

Table 3. Average precision performance of object detection methods under different IoU thresholds.

Method	Backbone	AP	$AP^{\frac{1}{2}}$	$AP^{\frac{1}{2}}$
FRCNN [37]	VGG16	46.8	81.4	36.59
YOLOv3 [27]	ResNet50	28.1	55.3	16.5
SSD300 [38]	VGG16	41.2	79.61	36.53

4.4 Further Analysis

As our goal is to generate a dataset that can produce an applicable real-time system with the help of a deep learning classifier, we further analyze our classifiers with beta testing. We use two of our classifiers: the first one trained on BdSL36v1 dataset (without background augmentation), the second one trained on BdSL36v2 dataset (with background augmentation), both trained on Resnet50. An evaluation on BdSL36v2 test set, between these two classifiers has been shown in Table 4. It is to be noted that, the validation accuracy shown in Table 4, is on individual validation datasets.

Table 4. A comparison between BdSL36v1 & BdSL36v2 trained classifier with Test Set.

Dataset	Val Acc.	Acc	Pre	Recall
BdSL36v1	98.6	36.7	37.2	36.9
BdSL36v2	98.83	96.1	96.8	96.2

Though classifier 1 has good accuracy on its validation set, it performs poorly on the test set whereas classier 2 performs significantly well both on the validation set and test set. As the test set is generated from BdSL36v2 dataset, there is a possibility of the result being biased on the tests. So, we run another experiment at the user level to test the robustness of these classifiers in the real-life environment. Eight signers perform this evaluation at their own home, and none of them have participated in the dataset collection process. So, the testing environments and the subjects are new to the system. We ask the users to capture the image of each sign using our system (see Fig. 4) and report the prediction values and confidence rate in the provided excel sheet. For the correct prediction

• 16: 100%   • 36: 100%   • 2: 100%   • 6: 97%

Fig. 4. Sample images from beta testing with signers with BdSLv2 classifier.

user inputs 1 or 0 otherwise and the confidence rate of the actual class predicted by the system. For a wrong prediction, we ask the user to capture a sign not more than three times and mention it in the excel sheet. From the bar chart shown in Fig. 5, even at the user level, we can see an increase of 60% in both accuracy and confidence rate. As the Fig. 5 shows, classifier 1 hardly recognizes any of the signs, and for most of the sign, the users report that they need to capture images multiple times. The confidence rate is admittedly low enough to misclassify at any time.

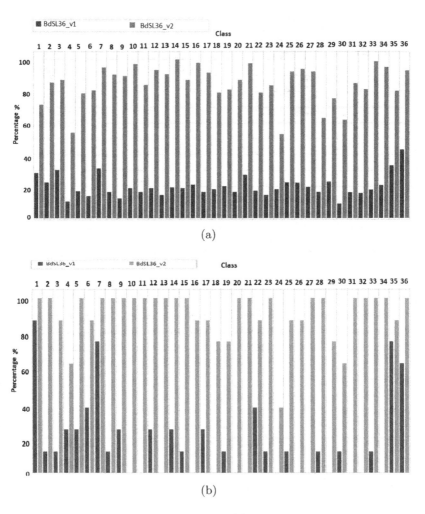

Fig. 5. Comparison of (a) confidence rate and (b) accuracy from beta testing between BdSl36v1 (without background augmentation) and BdSL36v2 (with background augmentation) classifiers

On the other hand, the user-level evaluation shows that, despite a high accuracy on the test set, classifier 2 does not perform well for six classes. Users report these classes to need multiple captures and predict with a less confidence rate. In Fig. 6, we can see that class 24, and class 14 are incredibly similar and class 24 has got the worst performance with less than 55% confidence rate and less than 40% accuracy with multiple tries. Users report shows that class 24 is mostly misclassified as 14, class 4 is misclassified as 3, and classes 29 and 30 are misclassified between each other. Consequently, as illustrated in Fig. 7, BdSL letters recognition also brings challenges to the detection task. Though the target is detected accurately, some of the signs get misclassified.

Fig. 6. Signs in BdSL36 letters with appearance similarity. We can see from the figure that class 4,6, class 14,24 and class 29,30 have high similarities in appearance. These signs are mostly misclassified by the classifiers.

Fig. 7. Sample detection results on the BdSL36v3 dataset. The top row shows the correctly classified images, where the bottom row shows the images which are correctly detected but wrongly classified.

5   Conclusion

In this work, we build a large-scale dataset, named BdSL36 with different versions, for BdSL letters recognition, detection and show the usefulness of background augmentation. Our dataset includes over four million images of 36 BdSL letters. Compared with previous datasets, all version of the BdSL36 conforms to several characteristics of real environments which is suitable for building a real-time interpreter. Moreover, we also evaluate several state-of-the-art recognition and detection methods on our dataset. The results demonstrate that it is possible to generate a classifier with a small scale dataset with proper tuning of the datasets. We hope this work will help advance future research in the field of BdSL and also for other sign languages.

References

1. Ye, Y., Tian, Y., Huenerfauth, M., Liu, J.: Recognizing American sign language gestures from within continuous videos. In: The IEEE Conference on Computer Vision and Pattern Recognition (CVPR) Workshops (2018)
2. Xue, Y., Gao, S., Sun, H., Qin, W.: A Chinese sign language recognition system using leap motion. In: 2017 International Conference on Virtual Reality and Visualization (ICVRV), pp. 180–185 (2017)
3. Sanzidul Islam, M., Sultana Sharmin Mousumi, S., Jessan, N.A., Shahariar Azad Rabby, A., Akhter Hossain, S.: Ishara-Lipi: the first complete multipurposeopen access dataset of isolated characters for Bangla sign language. In: 2018 International Conference on Bangla Speech and Language Processing (ICBSLP), pp. 1–4 (2018)
4. Tarafder, K.H., Akhtar, N., Zaman, M.M., Rasel, M.A., Bhuiyan, M.R., Datta, P.G.: Disabling hearing impairment in the Bangladeshi population. J. Laryngol. Otol. **129**, 126–135 (2015)
5. Ge, L., et al.: 3D hand shape and pose estimation from a single RGB image. In: The IEEE Conference on Computer Vision and Pattern Recognition (CVPR) (2019)

6. Yang, L., Li, S., Lee, D., Yao, A.: Aligning latent spaces for 3D hand pose estimation. In: The IEEE International Conference on Computer Vision (ICCV) (2019)
7. Camgoz, N.C., Hadfield, S., Koller, O., Bowden, R.: SubUNets: end-to-end hand shape and continuous sign language recognition. In: 2017 IEEE International Conference on Computer Vision (ICCV), pp. 3075–3084 (2017)
8. Efthimiou, E., et al.: Sign language recognition, generation, and modelling: a research effort with applications in deaf communication. In: Stephanidis, C. (ed.) UAHCI 2009. LNCS, vol. 5614, pp. 21–30. Springer, Heidelberg (2009). https://doi.org/10.1007/978-3-642-02707-9_3
9. Shivashankara, S., Srinath, S.: American sign language recognition system: an optimal approach. Int. J. Image Graph. Sig. Process. **10**, 18–30 (2018)
10. Gattupalli, S., Ghaderi, A., Athitsos, V.: Evaluation of deep learning based pose estimation for sign language recognition. In: Proceedings of the 9th ACM International Conference on Pervasive Technologies Related to Assistive Environment, p. 12 (2016)
11. Rahaman, M., Jasim, M., Ali, M., Zhang, T., Hasanuzzaman, M.: A real-time hand-signs segmentation and classification system using fuzzy rule based RGB model and grid-pattern analysis. Front. Comput. Sci. **12**, 1258–1260 (2018)
12. Rahaman, M.A., Jasim, M., Ali, M.H., Hasanuzzaman, M.: Computer vision based Bengali sign words recognition using contour analysis. In: 2015 18th International Conference on Computer and Information Technology (ICCIT), pp. 335–340 (2015)
13. Rahaman, M.A., Jasim, M., Ali, M.H., Hasanuzzaman, M.: Bangla language modeling algorithm for automatic recognition of hand-sign-spelled Bangla sign language. Front. Comput. Sci. **14**, 143302 (2019). https://doi.org/10.1007/s11704-018-7253-3
14. Cubuk, E.D., Zoph, B., Mane, D., Vasudevan, V., Le, Q.V.: AutoAugment: learning augmentation strategies from data. In: The IEEE Conference on Computer Vision and Pattern Recognition (CVPR) (2019)
15. Mun, S., Park, S., Han, D.K., Ko, H.: Generative adversarial network based acoustic scene training set augmentation and selection using SVM hyperplane. In: Detection and Classification of Acoustic Scenes and Events Workshop (2017)
16. Devries, T., Taylor, G.W.: Improved regularization of convolutional neural networks with cutout. CoRR abs/1708.04552 (2017)
17. Ahmed, S.T., Akhand, M.A.H.: Bangladeshi sign language recognition using fingertip position. In: 2016 International Conference on Medical Engineering, Health Informatics and Technology (MediTec), pp. 1–5 (2016)
18. Hoque, O.B., Jubair, M.I., Islam, M.S., Akash, A., Paulson, A.S.: Real time Bangladeshi sign language detection using faster R-CNN. In: 2018 International Conference on Innovation in Engineering and Technology (ICIET), pp. 1–6 (2018)
19. Sadik, F., Subah, M.R., Dastider, A.G., Moon, S.A., Ahbab, S.S., Fattah, S.A.: Bangla sign language recognition with skin segmentation and binary masking. In: 2019 IEEE International WIE Conference on Electrical and Computer Engineering (WIECON-ECE), pp. 1–5 (2019)
20. Urmee, P.P., Mashud, M.A.A., Akter, J., Jameel, A.S.M.M., Islam, S.: Real-time Bangla sign language detection using Xception model with augmented dataset. In: 2019 IEEE International WIE Conference on Electrical and Computer Engineering (WIECON-ECE), pp. 1–5 (2019)
21. Lemley, J., Bazrafkan, S., Corcoran, P.: Smart augmentation learning an optimal data augmentation strategy. IEEE Access **5**, 5858–5869 (2017)
22. DeVries, T., Taylor, G.: Dataset augmentation in feature space. IEEE Access (2017)

23. Perez, L., Wang, J.: The effectiveness of data augmentation in image classification using deep learning. CoRR abs/1712.04621 (2017)
24. Nielsen, C., Okoniewski, M.: GAN data augmentation through active learning inspired sample acquisition. In: The IEEE Conference on Computer Vision and Pattern Recognition (CVPR) Workshops (2019)
25. Peng, X., Tang, Z., Yang, F., Feris, R.S., Metaxas, D.N.: Jointly optimize data augmentation and network training: adversarial data augmentation in human pose estimation. CoRR abs/1805.09707 (2018)
26. Everingham, M., Van Gool, L., Williams, C.K.I., Winn, J., Zisserman, A.: The PASCAL Visual Object Classes Challenge 2012 (VOC2012) Results. http://www.pascal-network.org/challenges/VOC/voc2012/workshop/index.html (2012)
27. Redmon, J., Farhadi, A.: YOLOv3: an incremental improvement. CoRR abs/1804.02767 (2018)
28. Rahaman, M.A., Jasim, M., Ali, M.H., Hasanuzzaman, M.: Real-time computer vision-based Bengali sign language recognition. In: 2014 17th International Conference on Computer and Information Technology (ICCIT), pp. 192–197 (2014)
29. Yasir, F., Prasad, P., Alsadoon, A., Elchouemi, A., Sreedharan, S.: Bangla sign language recognition using convolutional neural network. In: Proceedings of the 2017 International Conference on Intelligent Computing, Instrumentation and Control Technologies, United States, IEEE, Institute of Electrical and Electronics Engineers, pp. 49–53 (2018). 2017 International Conference on Intelligent Computing, Instrumentation and Control Technologies: ICICICT 2017, Intelligent Systems for Smart World; Conference date: 06-07-2017 Through 07-07-2017
30. He, K., Zhang, X., Ren, S., Sun, J.: Deep residual learning for image recognition. In: 2016 IEEE Conference on Computer Vision and Pattern Recognition (CVPR), pp. 770–778 (2016)
31. Simonyan, K., Zisserman, A.: Very deep convolutional networks for large-scale image recognition. In: International Conference on Learning Representations (2015)
32. Huang, G., Liu, Z., van der Maaten, L., Weinberger, K.Q.: Densely connected convolutional networks (2016)
33. Krizhevsky, A., Sutskever, I., Hinton, G.E.: ImageNet classification with deep convolutional neural networks. Commun. ACM 60, 84–90 (2017)
34. Iandola, F.N., Moskewicz, M.W., Ashraf, K., Han, S., Dally, W.J., Keutzer, K.: SqueezeNet: Alexnet-level accuracy with 50x fewer parameters and <1 mb model size (2016)
35. Zeiler, M.D., Fergus, R.: Visualizing and understanding convolutional networks. In: Fleet, D., Pajdla, T., Schiele, B., Tuytelaars, T. (eds.) ECCV 2014. LNCS, vol. 8689, pp. 818–833. Springer, Cham (2014). https://doi.org/10.1007/978-3-319-10590-1_53
36. Deng, J., Dong, W., Socher, R., Li, L.J., Li, K., Fei-Fei, L.: ImageNet: a large-scale hierarchical image database. In: CVPR 2009 (2009)
37. Girshick, R.: Fast R-CNN. In: International Conference on Computer Vision (ICCV), pp. 1440–1448 (2015)
38. Liu, W., et al.: SSD: single shot multibox detector. In: Leibe, B., Matas, J., Sebe, N., Welling, M. (eds.) ECCV 2016. LNCS, vol. 9905, pp. 21–37. Springer, Cham (2016). https://doi.org/10.1007/978-3-319-46448-0_2

3D Semantic Segmentation
for Large-Scale Scene Understanding

Kiran Akadas$^{(\boxtimes)}$ and Shankar Gangisetty

KLE Technological University, Hubballi, India
akadask@gmail.com, shankar@kletech.ac.in

Abstract. 3D semantic segmentation is one of the most challenging events in the robotic vision tasks for detection and identification of various objects in a scene. In this paper, we solve the task of semantic segmentation to classify and assign every point in the scene with an associated label. We propose a lightweight semantic segmentation network for large-scale point clouds which consists of grid subsampling, dilated convolutions, and Gaussian error linear unit activation for gaining better performance. The dilated convolutions increase the receptive field while reducing the number of parameters, making proposed network faster and computationally more efficient with reduced number of parameters. Additionally, we use conditional random field as post processing method to boost the performance of proposed semantic segmentation network. We perform an exhaustive quantitative analysis of the proposed network on SOTA datasets, namely, SHREC 2020 street scenes dataset [1], S3DIS [2] and SemanticKITTI [3]. We show that proposed semantic segmentation network performs effectively and efficiently compared to SOTA methods.

1 Introduction

3D point clouds have attracted a lot of interest in recent years because of wide range of applications and the ability to preserve spatial information of objects and sceneries which makes point clouds efficient in capturing detailed information. With the advent of mobile 3D scanners and devices such as drones and mobile phones capable of capturing 3D information, there has been tremendous increase in the point cloud data availability.

Semantic segmentation is one of the most challenging tasks that assigns semantic labels to every point that belongs to the objects of interests. With the recent advances in deep learning, 3D semantic segmentation has become a very powerful tool with profound applicability in autonomous systems (mobile robots, autonomous driving), scene understanding, augmented reality and vegetation monitoring. The primary task of 3D semantic segmentation is to understand the constituents or the different objects present in the scene before performing further analysis. The raw point clouds acquired by 3D scanning devices are either sparse, irregularly sampled, unstructured, and unordered which makes

© Springer Nature Switzerland AG 2021
I. Sato and B. Han (Eds.): ACCV 2020 Workshops, LNCS 12628, pp. 87–102, 2021.
https://doi.org/10.1007/978-3-030-69756-3_7

Fig. 1. 3D point cloud semantic segmentation of SHREC 2020 street scenes dataset [1]. Top row: Input point cloud scene Bottom row: Segmented point cloud scene using proposed approach

segmentation task challenging. We thus need an efficient solution to accurately segment 3D point clouds.

Initial works on segmentation [4–7] employed 2D convolutional neural networks (CNN) on range images. Next, voxel-based methods [8–12] harnessed the effectiveness of 3D convolutions for segmentation. However, the voxel segmentation is computationally expensive and the sparsity of point clouds renders the methods to be non-viable for large-scale point clouds. Additionally, the conversion of point clouds to voxels results in loss of intrinsic shape details. Finally, with the introduction of PointNet [13] came a new era of point-wise feature learning considering raw point clouds as input for 3D segmentation. The point-based works like [14–19] have shown good performance in processing and segmentation. However, it's very hard for these learning-based methods to train on large-scale point clouds. In this paper, we propose a 3D point cloud semantic segmentation network for large-scale street scenes by providing effective sampling and reduced parameters, that is computationally efficient and processes the point clouds directly. In this work, we extend our proposed GRanD-Net architecture [1] from Shape Retrieval Challenge (SHREC) 2020 track on 3D point cloud semantic segmentation for street scenes.

Inspired by RandLA-Net [20], our proposed network in this paper extends and improves RandLA-Net [20]. In the proposed network, we effectively use random sampling without lose of information while sampling through the use of local feature aggregation. We then adopt dilated/atrous convolutions in the network that helps to increase the receptive field without the loss of resolution and helps in semantic segmentation. The dilated convolutions are proven to be effective on 2D semantic segmentation tasks [21]. Thus, we extend dilated convolutions use on 3D point clouds. We also use GeLU as the activation function to better learn complex functions. And optionally, use conditional random field (CRF) in post processing to boost the performance. We provide experimental analysis to demonstrate the efficiency and efficacy on various methods and datasets. The results of segmented regions like *building*, *car*, *ground*, *pole*, and *vegetation* from the large-scale outdoor scene [1] using proposed network shown in Fig. 1.

The remainder of the paper is organized as follows: Sect. 2 briefly presents related work. The proposed semantic segmentation of 3D point clouds network is described in Sect. 3. Experiments and results are presented and discussed in Sect. 4. Finally, the paper is concluded in Sect. 5.

2   Related Works

With the recent availability of large scale point cloud datasets [1,3,22–24] has motivated researcher keenness in 3D semantic segmentation tasks. Based on the input data type, the semantic segmentation tasks can be categorized to range image-based, voxel-based and point-based methods.

2.1   Range Image-Based Methods

Many works use the well-defined 2D CNNs for segmentation of range images which are a 2D representation of 3D point clouds. In SqueezeSeg [4], authors introduced FireModule and FireDeconv for efficient segmentation based on LIDAR point clouds represented as spherical range-image [25]. In Pointseg [5] and RIU-Net [6], authors used 2D CNNs for semantic segmentation on range images. In FuseSeg [7], authors extended SqueezeSeg [4] to fuse RGB features from ImageNet CNN [26]. However, the conversion of 3D objects to 2D image leads to the loss of contextual information. In 3D-MiniNet [27], a recent work, authors used a projection module to extract features from the spherical projection of point cloud for efficient segmentation of 2D image that is then projected back to 3D.

2.2   Voxel-Based Methods

The point clouds can be converted to 3D grids by voxelization and 3D CNNs are used to process these grids as in [10–12]. In 3D-FCNN [8], authors proposed to predict voxel-level semantic labels. The accuracy of segmentation depends on the resolution of voxels. In SEGCLOUD [9], authors extended 3D-FCNN [8] to obtain fine-grained results using tri-linear interpolation to point-wise labels and applied a fully connected CRF (FC-CRF), for training them jointly. These methods obtain good results for semantic segmentation, but are computationally expensive and thus, are not used for large scale point clouds.

2.3   Point-Based Methods

PointNet [13], was one of the first works to efficiently adopt convolutions for 3D point clouds using max-pooling to achieve permutation-invariance. PointNet introduced input transformations and feature transformations which ensured that the point clouds are invariant to geometric transformations. But, PointNet did not capture the local features which are essential for segmentation i.e., only global features are learned. In PointNet++ [14], authors extended PointNet [13] to capture local structure information by applying PointNet hierarchically that greatly improved segmentation scores. In PointCNN [15], authors proposed a hierarchical deep learning framework and introduced a X-Conv layer that elevated the points to a higher representation with rich features which are then propagated to pointwise feature using X-DeConv layers. But, an understanding of the operations of X-Conv are not well established. Although, all of these methods were extended to perform segmentation, they did not scale well for large-scale scene point clouds.

The graph-based methods like [16,17] made use of graph-based structure and graph CNN for processing point clouds and assign semantic labels. In [28], authors introduced PointGCR, a plug and play module which uses graph convolutions to obtain a global contextual dependency. In ASIS [29] and JSIS3D [30], authors proposed the association of instance segmentation and semantic segmentation with partnerships to jointly solve segmentation tasks. The JSIS3D additionally used a multi-valued CRF as a post processing method. In [16], authors presented a method to enrich the point representations and introduced a graph PointNet module (GPM) to update features within local structures, and spatial-wise and channel-wise attention strategy to exploit the global information to obtain pointwise labeling. Recently, in RandLA-Net [20], authors proposed to directly predict per point semantics for large point clouds efficiently with a local feature aggregation module. The dilated residual blocks, local spatial encoding and attentive pooling are used to generate informative feature vectors. However, the method is computationally expensive. In our proposed network, we extend RandLA-Net [20] and address these issues to provide a solution by improving the semantic segmentation performance.

3   3D Point Cloud Semantic Segmentation Network

In this section, we describe our network for 3D point cloud semantic segmentation for large scale scenes. The proposed network, shown in Fig. 2, is composed of the dilated residual blocks as the basic building blocks coupled with random sampling to down-sample the point cloud. We process raw point clouds as inputs, perform grid-subsampling on the large point clouds to bring it to a uniform size. We process these N points gradually by down-sampling the points using random-sampling while preserving the essential features required for segmentation through the use of dilated residual blocks that enhance the feature representation. We use dilated convolutions and GeLU as the activation function to process the point clouds in our dilated residual blocks. There are N labels

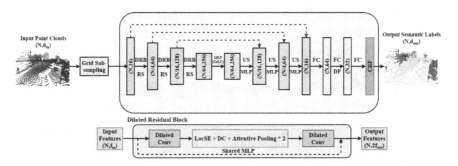

Fig. 2. The proposed 3D point cloud semantic segmentation network for large-scale scenes. DRB: Dilated Residual Block, RS: Random Sampling, US: Up-Sampling, FC: Fully Connected Layer, LocSE: Local Spatial Encoding, DC: Dilated Convolutions DP: Dropout, CRF: Conditional Random Field

obtained as output after up-sampling the results, one for each point indicating the category to which the point belongs.

3.1 Data Preparation

Let $P = \{p_i | i = 1, 2, ..., N\}$ be the point cloud with N points. To efficiently process data of large-scale 3D scenes, we sub-sample the point clouds each with N points using grid-subsampling from KPConv [18] to bring it to a uniform size. In order to get back the original number of semantic labels from the predictions, we index projections for up-sampling the point clouds, one for each point indicating the category to which the point belongs. The training dataset is augmented by scaling and rotation.

3.2 Data Loading

To load the data in batches, we generate the data flow for each batch. For a given batch size n and the steps in each epoch s, $(n \times s)$ point clouds are reserved for each epoch. To avoid ordered learning by the proposed network, we feed the data randomly. The k-Nearest Neighbours (NN) algorithm is used with a pre-defined set of k neighbours being selected of all the sub-sampled points. If the sampled points are less than the given pre-defined k points, we pick the points with replacement. To prepare a batch of point clouds, we generate the neighbour indices for every point in a point cloud. These are used to get the relative point features. We then randomly sample 25% of points to be reduced in the next phase while down-sampling and simultaneously track the indices for up-sampling. The pooling indices are obtained using k-NN search for every sampled point.

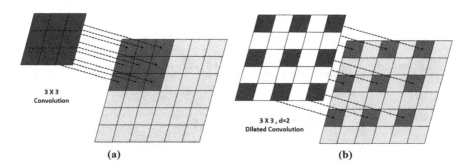

Fig. 3. Convolutions: (a) 3×3 regular convolution used in CNNs and (b) 3×3 dilated convolution with $d = 2$ covering an area of 5×5 used in our proposed model results in reduced parameters.

3.3   Background for Model Building

In our next step of model building, dilated convolutions and GeLU activation function are essential components. Let us have a brief overview before discussing on adaptation in proposed network.

Dilated Convolutions. The convolutional layer in deep learning architecture extracts low-level features in the initial layers and higher-level features deeper in the network. Dilated convolutions [31], shown in Fig. 3, brings an extra parameter d that controls the receptive area of the kernel which convolves around the input with a gap difference shown Fig. 3(b). The parameter d determines the size of the hole in the kernel. Thus, without increasing the number of parameters, it increases the receptive area of the kernel over the input making the convolutions more efficient and faster.

Consider $F : Z^2 \rightarrow R$ to be a discrete function (i.e., a region shown in Fig. 3) and $\Omega_r = [-r, r]^2 \cap Z^2$. If $k : \Omega_r \rightarrow R$ is a kernel of size $(2r + 1)^2$ (3×3 shown in Fig. 3), then the dilated convolution on an input point p with a dilation factor of d is given as,

$$(F * k)(p) = \sum_{s+dt=q} F(s)k(t) \tag{1}$$

The number of parameters remain same as we do not increase the size of units in kernel that are used to calculate the result. In our proposed network, dilated convolutions help process areas with redundant data faster while preserving the required features. Compared to normal convolutions, dilated convolutions are faster, efficient and better at semantic segmentation.

GeLU. The Gaussian error linear unit (GeLU) [32] is a nonlinear high-performing neural network activation function [33]. GeLU considers not only the sign as in ReLU [34], but the magnitude of the input and considered to be more effective than other activation functions. Instead of multiplying the input by one or zero deterministically, the GeLU determines the value stochastically based on the input and multiplies with the input. This helps in better learning of complex functions. If point p is the input then, GeLU is given as,

$$GELU(p) = 0.5p(1 + \tanh[\sqrt{\frac{2}{\pi}}(p + 0.044715p^3)]) \tag{2}$$

The GeLU activation is applied over the outputs of the dilated convolutions and others in the proposed network.

3.4 Model Building

We train the sampled point clouds over several batches of data. The loaded point clouds of dimensions (N, d_{in}), where N is the number of points in the point cloud and d_{in} is the number of features associated with each point p in the point cloud, are processed using the dilated residual blocks (DRBs) shown in Fig. 2. Each of the DRB includes multiple units of local spatial encoding (LocSE) and attentive pooling stacks. The DRBs are connected through skip-connections as proposed in RandLA-Net [20]. Unlike the convolutions used in RandLA-Net [20], we use dilated convolutions [31] to implement the DRB in order to increase the receptivity of the filters without affecting the resolution and gain better efficiency. The dilated convolutions incorporate multi-scale features, essential for semantic segmentation. These dilated convolutions make our network faster and more efficient since we are increasing the area of filter coverage without increasing the parameters and affecting the feature learning, thus reducing the number of convolutions.

The LocSE in DRB uses the centre points and their k-NN neighbours to encode the point cloud using relative positional information. At each step, we apply RS with DRB using the points we loaded earlier to reduce the size of input point cloud to 25%. The attentive pooling is used as a replacement to max-pooling in order to compute the attention score for every feature which is further aggregated to avoid loss of information and learn important local information. We use GeLU [32] as the activation layer in our proposed network for better learning of non-linear features. The GeLU prevents strong negative activations which may affect the model. The curvature and non-monotonicity of GeLU is used to learn complex functions much better compared to ReLU and leaky ReLU [34]. The output of the stacked DRBs is up-sampled and passed through multi-layer perceptrons (MLP) followed by fully connected layers. The use of skip-connections and MLP while up-sampling ensures that the labeling is accurate. Our network follows an all-inclusive up-sampling approach that refines labels gradually unlike simple interpolation, which would result in a single label for a group of points ignoring the demarcation of classes. The output of interpolation can be refined by the use of a post-processing technique (i.e., CRF).

3.5   Conditional Random Field

The CRF refines the labels based on the position of the input point and the neighboring point's label. An energy function is defined for label assignment which acts as a cost function. The minimization of the energy function leads to refinement of labels and increase in the accuracy.

Finally, the predicted semantic labels for every point are obtained as the output of the network with dimensions (N, d_{out}), where d_{out} is the number of labels (i.e., classes) in the dataset.

4   Experiments and Results

4.1   Implementation Details

We train our proposed network using the Adam optimizer with a learning rate of 0.01 and a decay rate of 0.05. A grid size of 0.06 is fixed for grid-subsampling while training and we select $k = 16$ NN to be queried. To train, we sample a fixed number (N) of $65,536$ points from each point cloud as the input and use a batch size of 4 with 500 steps per epoch. We train our proposed network for 50 epochs with a train-validation split of $3 : 1$. A four layered network is used with feature sizes of $16, 64, 128$, and 256. The network is trained on a 15 GB CPU with a single NVIDIA Tesla T4 GPU. The code of our network is released here: https://github.com/KiranAkadas/GRanDNet.

4.2   Datasets

The proposed network is experimented on three datasets, namely, SHREC 2020 street scenes [1], S3DIS [2] and SemanticKITTI [3].

SHREC 2020 Street Scenes [1] **dataset:** The dataset contains 80 large-scale 3D point clouds for street scene which are captured by a LIDAR sensor mounted on a car and manually labeled using open source software Cloud Compare [35]. Each point cloud represents a street scene and contains a group of objects labeled into 5 meaningful classes and an extra *undefined* class which is not used for evaluating the results. The distribution of points in each of

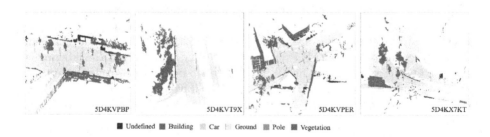

Fig. 4. Sample point clouds of SHREC 2020 Street Scenes [1] dataset.

the 6 classes, namely, *undefined, building, car, ground, pole*, and *vegetation* are $8.37\%, 17.05\%, 2.81\%, 54.64\%, 0.47\%$, and 16.64%. The 80 point clouds are randomly divided into training and testing sets with 60:20. The average number of points in training and testing dataset is approximately 2 to 4 million points per point cloud. We train our proposed network for the 5 classes leaving the *undefined* class. The sample point clouds of the dataset are visualized in Fig. 4.

S3DIS [2] **and SemanticKITTI** [3] **datasets:** The S3DIS [2] is a large-scale 3D scene dataset of indoor spaces. The dataset contains scans of 271 rooms, each provided as a separate point cloud belonging to 6 large areas. The points are classified into 13 categories of object. The SemanticKITTI dataset [3] consists of 21 sequences with 00 to 10 as training set with the sequence 08 used as validation set, and 11 to 21 as test set. There are a total of 23,201 full 3D scans for training and 20,351 scans for testing. A total of 19 categories are considered to evaluate the dataset.

4.3   Evaluation

We adopt the evaluation criteria that have been widely applied in 3D semantic segmentation tasks, Overall Accuracy (OA) and mean Intersection over Union (mIoU). Generally, OA reports the percent of points in the data set which are correctly classified. And mIoU is the average of per-class IoU. The IoU of class i is defined as,

$$IoU_i = \frac{TP_i}{GT_i + Pred_i + TP_i} \tag{3}$$

where TP_i, GT_i, $Pred_i$ denote the correctly classified number of points, the ground truth point number, and predicted point number for class i, respectively.

4.4   Results and Discussion

In this section, we evaluate the overall efficiency of our proposed network on large-scale point clouds for semantic segmentation. We compare the performance of proposed network with RandLA-Net [20]. We are the first to evaluate the performance on the SHREC 2020 street scenes [1] dataset. For a fair comparison, we use the same parameters and same number of input points in our network and RandLA-Net and train for 5 classes. The best performing model is frozen with a mIoU of 84.11%. The frozen model is used to predict segments for the 20 test point clouds that contain a total of $7, 27, 53, 747$ points. The resulting mIoU is 86.4% with an OA of 97.83% for 5 classes shown in Table 1. Our network achieves superior performance on four of the classes, except *pole*. We observe that the resulting IoU of *ground, vegetation, building*, and *car* classes are segmented accurately as the dataset distribution in these classes is high and learnt better. We also performed a qualitative analysis of our network on test set shown in Fig. 5. Visual inspection shows that our network performance is good and close to ground truth. We also compared our results with RandLA-Net for the 5 classes

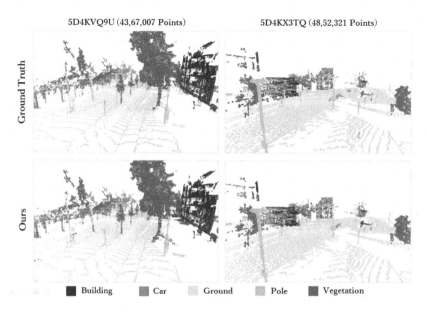

Fig. 5. Qualitative results of our proposed network on the test set (5D4KVQ9U and 5D4KX3TQ point clouds) of Street Scenes [1] dataset.

as shown in Table 1. We observe that our network outperforms RandLA-Net by a good margin.

As the *pole* class IoU is low, to estimate out the misclassification we plotted the confusion matrix for the proposed network shown in Fig. 6. Based on the confusion matrix and visual inspection, we observe that few instances of the *pole* class are mislabeled as *building* shown in Fig. 7, due to their proximity to the *building* points and also the insufficiency of the *pole* training points.

4.5   Time and Space Complexity

We compute the average time taken to complete an epoch during the training of the models and additionally calculate the total number of trainable parameters

Table 1. Quantitative results: The OA, mIoU, and IoU for each of the five classes in the test data on our proposed network.

Methods	OA (%)	mIoU (%)	Building	Car	Ground	Pole	Vegetation
RandLA-Net [20]	95.92	84.3	91.76	80.72	96.31	59.80	93.23
Ours	**97.83**	**86.40**	**93.66**	**83.92**	**98.10**	**61.79**	**94.55**

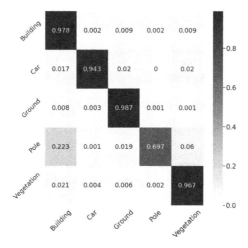

Fig. 6. Confusion matrix for 5 classes of Street Scenes dataset [1] using our model.

to estimate the memory consumption shown in Table 2. We observe that there is a significant decrease in the number of trainable parameters and the average training time in our network. Unlike RandLA-Net, the use of dilated convolutions in our network helps us increase the receptive area across every input resulting in faster training and lesser number of trainable parameters.

4.6 Comparison with Other Datasets

In this section, we compare the results of our network with existing segmentation methods on other datasets.

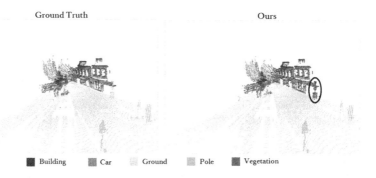

Fig. 7. Qualitative results of our proposed network on the test dataset of Street Scenes [1]. The black circle shows the *pole* mislabeled as *building* class.

Table 2. Time and space complexity of our network and RandLA-Net [20] on Street Scenes [1] dataset.

	Average training time per epoch (seconds)	# Trainable parameters ('M' stands for Million)
RandLA-Net [20]	18,070	1.24
Ours	**15,960**	**0.99**

S3DIS [2]. The proposed network achieves comparably better performance to the SOTA methods on S3DIS [2] dataset shown in Table 3. Most of the SOTA methods are computationally expensive and operate on blocks of point clouds. Our network takes the entire large-scale scene as input and processes the output labels for every point in a single pass while being more efficient and faster. The qualitative results are shown in Fig. 8.

SemanticKITTI [3]. The quantitative results of our network compared to SOTA methods shown in Table 4. We observe that our network achieves the best mIoU over other SOTA methods on SemanticKITTI [3] dataset.

4.7 Proposed Network with CRF

A CRF explicitly designed for point clouds is used after we get the pointwise labels from our network. The parameters for the CRF are selected using grid search to obtain best set of parameters. The comparison results of our proposed network with and without CRF on the street scenes [1] dataset are shown in Table 5. We observe that there is a incremental boost in the classwise IoU performance of all 5 classes. This increase in the IoU is attributed to the correction of mislabeled points near the demarcation of two classes. The CRF based post-processing takes around 30 s per point cloud (with approximately 3 million points) and is hence very efficient. Considering the scale of the dataset, we state that our CRF is able to refine large set of points and gives a performance which is much better.

Table 3. Quantitative results of our network and SOTA methods on S3DIS [2] dataset.

	OA(%)	mAcc(%)	mIoU(%)	ceil.	floor	wall	beam	col.	wind.	door	table	chair	sofa	book.	board	clut.
PointNet [13]	78.6	66.2	47.6	88.0	88.7	69.3	42.4	23.1	47.5	51.6	54.1	42.0	9.6	38.2	29.4	35.2
RSNet [36]	-	66.5	56.5	92.5	92.8	78.6	32.8	34.4	51.6	68.1	59.7	60.1	16.4	50.2	44.9	52.0
3P-RNN [37]	86.9	-	56.3	92.9	93.8	73.1	42.5	25.9	47.6	59.2	60.4	66.7	24.8	57.0	36.7	51.6
SPG [19]	86.4	73.0	62.1	89.9	95.1	76.4	62.8	47.1	55.3	68.4	**73.5**	69.2	63.2	45.9	8.7	52.9
PointCNN [15]	88.1	75.6	65.4	**94.8**	97.3	75.8	63.3	51.7	58.4	57.2	71.6	69.1	39.1	61.2	52.2	58.6
PointWeb [38]	87.3	76.2	66.7	93.5	94.2	80.8	52.4	41.3	64.9	68.1	71.4	67.1	50.3	62.7	62.2	58.5
ShellNet [39]	87.1	-	66.8	90.2	93.6	79.9	60.4	44.1	64.9	52.9	71.6	**84.7**	53.8	64.6	48.6	59.4
KPConv [18]	-	79.1	70.6	93.6	92.4	**83.1**	**63.9**	**54.3**	**66.1**	**76.6**	57.8	64.0	**69.3**	**74.9**	61.3	60.3
RandLA-Net [20]	88.0	82.0	70.0	93.1	96.1	80.6	62.4	48.0	64.4	69.4	69.4	76.4	60.0	64.2	65.9	60.1
Ours	**88.3**	**82.3**	**71.0**	94.5	**97.7**	80.7	59.8	51.5	64.8	69.9	70.4	75.4	64.2	66.1	**67.7**	**60.5**

Fig. 8. Qualitative results of our network on the test set of S3DIS [2] dataset.

4.8 Ablation Study

To verify the effectiveness of dilated convolutions and the GeLU activation layer in DRBs, we conduct the ablation studies on street scenes [1] dataset. Using normal 2D convolution in proposed network instead of dilated convolutions within the DRBs gave an mIoU of 87.8% which is slightly better but on S3DIS we get an mIoU of 68.3%, which is 3% less. Moreover, the network without dilated convolution takes 20% more time and space. Further, when the GeLU activation layer is replaced with it's predecessor leaky ReLU in the DRBs and also in the layers preceding the encoding layer, we obtain a lower mIoU of 86.1%. Thus, we observe that our proposed network architecture is effective and efficient for 3D point cloud semantic segmentation of large-scale scene understanding.

Table 4. Quantitative results of our network and SOTA methods on SemanticKITTI [3] dataset.

Methods	Size	mIoU(%)	road	sidewalk	parking	other-ground	building	car	truck	bicycle	motorcycle	other-vehicle	vegetation	trunk	terrain	person	bicyclist	motorcyclist	fence	pole	traffic-sign
PointNet [13]		14.6	61.6	35.7	15.8	1.4	41.4	46.3	0.1	1.3	0.3	0.8	31.0	4.6	17.6	0.2	0.2	0.0	12.9	2.4	3.7
SPG [19]		17.4	45.0	28.5	0.6	0.6	64.3	49.3	0.1	0.2	0.2	0.8	48.9	27.2	24.6	0.3	2.7	0.1	20.8	15.9	0.8
SPLATNet [40]	50K pts	18.4	64.6	39.1	0.4	0.0	58.3	58.2	0.0	0.0	0.0	0.0	71.1	9.9	19.3	0.0	0.0	0.0	23.1	5.6	0.0
PointNet++ [14]		20.1	72.0	41.8	18.7	5.6	62.3	53.7	0.9	1.9	0.2	0.2	46.5	13.8	30.0	0.9	1.0	0.0	16.9	6.0	8.9
TangentConv [41]		40.9	83.9	63.9	33.4	15.4	83.4	90.8	15.2	2.7	16.5	12.1	79.5	49.3	58.1	23.0	28.4	8.1	49.0	35.8	28.5
SqueezeSeg [4]		29.5	85.4	54.3	26.9	4.5	57.4	68.8	3.3	16.0	4.1	3.6	60.0	24.3	53.7	12.9	13.1	0.9	29.0	17.5	24.5
SqueezeSegV2 [42]		39.7	88.6	67.6	45.8	17.7	73.7	81.8	13.4	18.5	17.9	14.0	71.8	35.8	60.2	20.1	25.1	3.9	41.1	20.2	36.3
DarkNet21Seg [3]		47.4	91.4	74.0	57.0	26.4	81.9	85.4	18.6	26.2	26.5	15.6	77.6	48.4	63.6	31.8	33.6	4.0	52.3	36.0	50.0
DarkNet53Seg [3]	64*2048 pixels	49.9	**91.8**	74.6	64.8	**27.9**	84.1	86.4	25.5	24.5	32.7	22.6	78.3	50.1	64.0	36.2	33.6	4.7	55.0	38.9	52.2
RangeNet53++ [43]		52.2	**91.8**	**75.2**	**65.0**	27.8	87.4	91.4	25.7	25.7	**34.4**	23.0	80.5	55.1	64.6	38.3	38.8	4.8	58.6	47.9	55.9
LatticeNet [44]		52.2	88.8	73.8	64.6	25.6	86.9	88.6	43.3	12.0	20.8	24.8	76.4	57.9	54.7	34.2	39.9	**60.9**	55.2	41.5	42.7
SalsaNext [45]		54.5	90.9	74.0	58.1	27.8	87.9	90.9	21.7	36.4	29.5	19.9	81.8	61.7	66.3	**52.0**	**52.7**	16.0	58.2	**51.7**	**58.0**
SqueezeSegV3 [46]		54.5	90.9	74.0	58.1	27.8	87.9	90.9	21.7	36.4	29.5	19.9	81.8	61.7	66.3	**52.0**	**52.7**	16.0	58.2	**51.7**	**58.0**
RandLA-Net [20]	50K pts	55.9	90.5	74.0	61.8	24.5	89.7	94.2	43.9	**47.4**	32.2	39.1	**83.8**	63.6	**68.6**	48.4	47.4	9.4	60.4	51.0	50.7
Ours	50K pts	**56.0**	90.6	74.0	61.4	24.1	**89.8**	**94.5**	**44.6**	30.9	29.6	**40.3**	83.2	**63.9**	**68.6**	48.7	47.8	9.9	**60.7**	51.5	50.0

Table 5. Comparison of results for our model with and without CRF on Street Scenes dataset [1].

Methods	OA (%)	mIoU (%)	Building	Car	Ground	Pole	Vegetation
Ours (without CRF)	97.83	86.41	93.66	83.92	98.10	61.79	94.55
Ours (with CRF)	97.91	86.53	93.78	84.04	98.21	61.93	94.67

5   Conclusions and Future Work

In this paper, we proposed a 3D semantic segmentation network for assigning pointwise labels to large-scale 3D scenes. We use dilated convolutions as an essential unit to our building blocks of DRBs which coupled with random sampling unlike other sampling strategies helps our network to reduce the computational cost and preserve important features. We used GeLU as our activation function to learn complex functions. We also used an optional post processing module, CRF that helps refine labels assigned to the points at the boundaries of different classes. The resulting mIoU of our proposed network is 86.41% with an OA of 97.83% for 5 classes on street scenes dataset [1]. Additionally, our network achieves superior performance compared to SOTA methods on other large scale point cloud datasets, namely, S3DIS [2] and SemanticKITTI [3]. In the future, we plan to extend our network to perform instance and hierarchical semantic segmentation for scene understanding.

Acknowledgement. This research work is partly supported (DST/ICPS/IHDS/ 2018) under the Indian Heritage in Digital Space (IHDS) of Interdisciplinary Cyber Physical Systems (ICPS) Programme of the Department of Science and Technology (DST), Government of India.

References

1. Ku, T., et al.: Shrec 2020: 3D point cloud semantic segmentation for street scenes. Comput. Graphics **93**(2020), 13–24 (2020)
2. Armeni, I., Sax, S., Zamir, A.R., Savarese, S.: Joint 2D–3D-semantic data for indoor scene understanding. CoRR abs/1702.01105 (2017)
3. Behley, J., et al.: Semantickitti: a dataset for semantic scene understanding of lidar sequences. In: IEEE ICCV, pp. 9296–9306 (2019)
4. Wu, B., Wan, A., Yue, X., Keutzer, K.: Squeezeseg: convolutional neural nets with recurrent CRF for real-time road-object segmentation from 3D lidar point cloud. In: IEEE ICRA, pp. 1887–1893 (2018)
5. Wang, Y., Shi, T., Yun, P., Tai, L., Liu, M.: Pointseg: real-time semantic segmentation based on 3D lidar point cloud. CoRR abs/1807.06288 (2018)

6. Biasutti, P., Bugeau, A., Aujol, J.F., Brédif, M.: Riu-net: embarrassingly simple semantic segmentation of 3d lidar point cloud. ArXiv abs/1905.08748 (2019)
7. Krispel, G., Opitz, M., Waltner, G., Possegger, H., Bischof, H.: Fuseseg: lidar point cloud segmentation fusing multi-modal data. In: IEEE WACV, pp. 1863–1872 (2020)
8. Huang, J., You, S.: Point cloud labeling using 3D convolutional neural network. In: ICPR, pp. 2670–2675 (2016)
9. Tchapmi, L.P., Choy, C.B., Armeni, I., Gwak, J., Savarese, S.: Segcloud: semantic segmentation of 3D point clouds. In: 3DV, pp. 537–547 (2017)
10. Choy, C.B., Gwak, J., Savarese, S.: 4D spatio-temporal convnets: Minkowski convolutional neural networks. In: IEEE CVPR, pp. 3070–3079 (2019)
11. Graham, B., Engelcke, M., van der Maaten, L.: 3D semantic segmentation with submanifold sparse convolutional networks. In: IEEE CVPR, pp. 9224–9232 (2018)
12. Meng, H.Y., Gao, L., Lai, Y.K., Manocha, D.: Vv-net: Voxel vae net with group convolutions for point cloud segmentation. In: IEEE ICCV, pp. 8499–8507 (2019)
13. Qi, C.R., Su, H., Mo, K., Guibas, L.J.: Pointnet: deep learning on point sets for 3D classification and segmentation. In: IEEE CVPR, pp. 77–85 (2017)
14. Qi, C.R., Yi, L., Su, H., Guibas, L.J.: Pointnet++: deep hierarchical feature learning on point sets in a metric space, pp. 5099–5108 (2017)
15. Li, Y., Bu, R., Sun, M., Wu, W., Di, X., Chen, B.: Pointcnn: convolution on x-transformed points. In: NeurIPS, pp. 828–838 (2018)
16. Wang, L., Huang, Y., Hou, Y., Zhang, S., Shan, J.: Graph attention convolution for point cloud semantic segmentation. In: IEEE CVPR, pp. 10296–10305 (2019)
17. Wang, C., Samari, B., Siddiqi, K.: Local spectral graph convolution for point set feature learning. In: Ferrari, V., Hebert, M., Sminchisescu, C., Weiss, Y. (eds.) ECCV 2018. LNCS, vol. 11208, pp. 56–71. Springer, Cham (2018). https://doi.org/10.1007/978-3-030-01225-0_4
18. Thomas, H., Qi, C.R., Deschaud, J.E., Marcotegui, B., Goulette, F., Guibas, L.J.: Kpconv: flexible and deformable convolution for point clouds. In: IEEE ICCV, pp. 6410–6419 (2019)
19. Landrieu, L., Simonovsky, M.: Large-scale point cloud semantic segmentation with superpoint graphs. In: IEEE CVPR, pp. 4558–4567 (2018)
20. Hu, Q., et al.: Randla-net: efficient semantic segmentation of large-scale point clouds. In: IEEE CVPR, pp. 11105–11114 (2020)
21. Hamaguchi, R., Fujita, A., Nemoto, K., Imaizumi, T., Hikosaka, S.: Effective use of dilated convolutions for segmenting small object instances in remote sensing imagery. In: IEEE WACV, pp. 1442–1450 (2018)
22. Hackel, T., Savinov, N., Ladicky, L., Wegner, J.D., Schindler, K., Pollefeys, M.: Semantic3d.net: a new large-scale point cloud classification benchmark. CoRR abs/1704.03847 (2017)
23. Roynard, X., Deschaud, J., Goulette, F.: Paris-lille-3D: a point cloud dataset for urban scene segmentation and classification. In: CVPR Workshops, pp. 2027–2030 (2018)
24. Zolanvari, S.M.I., et al.: Dublincity: annotated lidar point cloud and its applications. In: BMVC, vol. 44. BMVA Press (2019)
25. Biasutti, P., Aujol, J.F., Brédif, M., Bugeau, A.: Range-image: incorporating sensor topology for lidar point cloud processing. Photogram. Eng. Remote Sensing **84**, 367–375 (2018)
26. Krizhevsky, A., Sutskever, I., Hinton, G.E.: Imagenet classification with deep convolutional neural networks. Commun. ACM **60**, 84–90 (2017)

27. Alonso, I., Riazuelo, L., Montesano, L., Murillo, A.C.: 3D-mininet: Learning a 2D representation from point clouds for fast and efficient 3D lidar semantic segmentation (2020)
28. Ma, Y., Guo, Y., Liu, H., Lei, Y., Wen, G.: Global context reasoning for semantic segmentation of 3D point clouds. In: IEEE WACV, pp. 2920–2929 (2020)
29. Wang, X., Liu, S., Shen, X., Shen, C., Jia, J.: Associatively segmenting instances and semantics in point clouds. In: IEEE CVPR, pp. 4091–4100 (2019)
30. Pham, Q.H., Nguyen, T., Hua, B.S., Roig, G., Yeung, S.K.: Jsis3d: joint semantic-instance segmentation of 3D point clouds with multi-task pointwise networks and multi-value conditional random fields. In: IEEE CVPR, pp. 8827–8836 (2019)
31. Yu, F., Koltun, V.: Multi-scale context aggregation by dilated convolutions. In: ICLR (Poster) (2016)
32. Hendrycks, D., Gimpel, K.: Bridging nonlinearities and stochastic regularizers with gaussian error linear units. CoRR abs/1606.08415 (2016)
33. Lin, M., Chen, Q., Yan, S.: Network in network. CoRR abs/1312.4400 (2014)
34. Agarap, A.F.: Deep learning using rectified linear units (relu). CoRR abs/1803.08375 (2018)
35. CloudCompare: 3D point cloud and mesh processing software open source project (2020)
36. Huang, Q., Wang, W., Neumann, U.: Recurrent slice networks for 3D segmentation of point clouds. In: IEEE CVPR, pp. 2626–2635 (2018)
37. Ye, X., Li, J., Huang, H., Du, L., Zhang, X.: 3D recurrent neural networks with context fusion for point cloud semantic segmentation. In: Ferrari, V., Hebert, M., Sminchisescu, C., Weiss, Y. (eds.) ECCV 2018. LNCS, vol. 11211, pp. 415–430. Springer, Cham (2018). https://doi.org/10.1007/978-3-030-01234-2_25
38. Zhao, H., Jiang, L., Fu, C.W., Jia, J.: Pointweb: enhancing local neighborhood features for point cloud processing. In: IEEE CVPR, pp. 5560–5568 (2019)
39. Zhang, Z., Hua, B.S., Yeung, S.K.: Shellnet: Efficient point cloud convolutional neural networks using concentric shells statistics. In: IEEE ICCV, pp. 1607–1616 (2019)
40. Su, H., et al.: Splatnet: sparse lattice networks for point cloud processing. In: IEEE CVPR, pp. 2530–2539 (2018)
41. Tatarchenko, M., Park, J., Koltun, V., Zhou, Q.Y.: Tangent convolutions for dense prediction in 3D. In: IEEE CVPR, pp. 3887–3896 (2018)
42. Wu, B., Zhou, X., Zhao, S., Yue, X., Keutzer, K.: Squeezesegv 2: improved model structure and unsupervised domain adaptation for road-object segmentation from a lidar point cloud. In: ICRA, pp. 4376–4382 (2019)
43. Milioto, A., Vizzo, I., Behley, J., Stachniss, C.: Rangenet ++: fast and accurate lidar semantic segmentation. In: IEEE IROS, pp. 4213–4220 (2019)
44. Rosu, R.A., Schütt, P., Quenzel, J., Behnke, S.: Latticenet: fast point cloud segmentation using permutohedral lattices. CoRR abs/1912.05905 (2019)
45. Cortinhal, T., Tzelepis, G., Aksoy, E.E.: Salsanext: fast, uncertainty-aware semantic segmentation of lidar point clouds for autonomous driving (2020)
46. Xu, C., et al.: Squeezesegv3: spatially-adaptive convolution for efficient point-cloud segmentation. CoRR abs/2004.01803 (2020)

A Weakly Supervised Convolutional Network for Change Segmentation and Classification

Philipp Andermatt$^{(\boxtimes)}$ and Radu Timofte

Computer Vision Lab, ETH Zürich, Zürich, Switzerland
{anphilip,timofter}@ethz.ch

Abstract. Fully supervised change detection methods require difficult to procure pixel-level labels, while weakly supervised approaches can be trained with image-level labels. However, most of these approaches require a combination of changed and unchanged image pairs for training. Thus, these methods can not directly be used for datasets where only changed image pairs are available. We present W-CDNet, a novel weakly supervised change detection network that can be trained with image-level semantic labels. Additionally, W-CDNet can be trained with two different types of datasets, either containing changed image pairs only or a mixture of changed and unchanged image pairs. Since we use image-level semantic labels for training, we simultaneously create a change mask and label the changed object for single-label images. W-CDNet employs a W-shaped siamese U-net to extract feature maps from an image pair which then get compared in order to create a raw change mask. The core part of our model, the Change Segmentation and Classification (CSC) module, learns an accurate change mask at a hidden layer by using a custom Remapping Block and then segmenting the current input image with the change mask. The segmented image is used to predict the image-level semantic label. The correct label can only be predicted if the change mask actually marks relevant change. This forces the model to learn an accurate change mask. We demonstrate the segmentation and classification performance of our approach and achieve top results on AICD and HRSCD, two public aerial imaging change detection datasets as well as on a Food Waste change detection dataset. Our code is available at: https://github.com/PhiAbs/W-CDNet.

1 Introduction

Change detection [1,2] is an important computer vision task. It has applications in remote sensing [3,4], video surveillance [5] and street view imaging [6,7], amongst others. It is a challenging task since one has to distinguish relevant changes between two temporally different images from noise as well as from irrelevant semantic changes. An image pair can belong to one of two classes: *Changed* which means that there are relevant changes between the two images, or

© Springer Nature Switzerland AG 2021
I. Sato and B. Han (Eds.): ACCV 2020 Workshops, LNCS 12628, pp. 103–119, 2021.
https://doi.org/10.1007/978-3-030-69756-3_8

unchanged which means that there are either no changes at all or only irrelevant ones. The user has to define in advance what counts as relevant change.

Many data-driven change detection methods are trained with pixel-level labels [6–8]. However, creating a pixel-level change detection dataset is costly and time-consuming since two images have to be compared by hand and labeled on pixel-level. As a result, there is a need for change detection approaches which can be trained with simpler labels, for example image-level labels or bounding boxes. Additionally, many weakly supervised change detection approaches need both changed and unchanged images for training. This reduces their usability to datasets where unchanged images are actually available or can be generated with image augmentation.

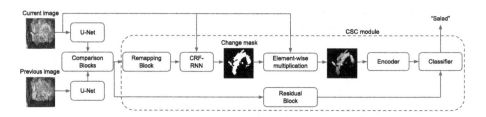

Fig. 1. Overview of the proposed W-CDNet solution.

In this work, we propose W-CDNet, a data-driven change detection network that can be trained with image-level semantic labels. By image-level semantic labels we mean that the labels describe the changed object and not only the binary state of the image pair (*changed* or *unchanged*, as used in other works [9–11]). Thus, the label *changed* is further split up into several semantic labels like *apple* or *bread* in case of a Food Waste dataset.

In contrast to other approaches [9–11], our method can be trained in one of two ways: (i) With changed image pairs only, meaning that every image pair in the dataset contains at least some relevant change; (ii) With a mix of *changed* and *unchanged* image pairs.

Figure 1 shows a high-level overview of our W-CDNet model. We use a W-shaped siamese network [12] based on two U-Nets [13] with shared weights for feature extraction. A group of custom Comparison Blocks compares the feature maps from the siamese network and creates a high-resolution feature map containing information about the differences between the two images. Our custom Change Segmentation and Classification (CSC) module remaps these features to create a meaningful change mask which is then used to segment the current input image. The segmented image gets encoded and, together with the feature vector from the Residual Block, gets fed to a classifier which predicts an image-level label.

If the change mask created within the CSC module does not contain relevant change, the classifier is not able to predict the correct image-level label. At the same time, the model can not simply focus on the complete image thanks to our remapping function (part of the CSC module). Thus, the model is forced to learn a change mask which marks relevant changes and suppresses irrelevant changes, with weak supervision. Moreover, we integrate a CRF-RNN layer [14] to refine the change mask created within the CSC module. Our approach works for single-label images. Since it is trained with image-level semantic labels, we can directly classify the changed object.

The key contributions of our work include:

(i) W-CDNet, a novel change detection network which can be trained with weak supervision using image-level semantic labels. To the best of our knowledge we are the first ones to use image-level *semantic* labels instead of binary labels for weak supervision.

(ii) CSC, a novel Change Segmentation and Classification module that creates a high-resolution change mask at a hidden layer and encodes the segmented current input image. The CSC module is crucial for W-CDNet's performance.

(iii) We show that our W-CDNet improves the state-of-the-art for weakly supervised change detection on the AICD dataset [15]. Additionally, we are the first ones to report weakly supervised change detection results on the HRSCD [16] dataset. We also report performance on the Food Waste dataset.

(iv) We make newly collected image-level semantic labels for the AICD dataset publicly available.

2   Related Work

Change detection plays an important role in remote sensing [2,16–18] and in street view imagery [6,7,19]. Today, with the advent of deep learning [20,21], data-driven approaches are used most often as they lead to better performance than previous approaches [22–24]. These related works can be categorized into fully supervised, weakly supervised and unsupervised change detection data-driven methods.

2.1   Fully Supervised Change Detection

Many methods are trained in full supervision with pixel-level labels to obtain a good segmentation performance. Depending on the exact task, either binary change masks or semantic change masks are used.

Guo *et al.* [19] proposed a siamese fully convolutional network. They subtracted the features from three hidden layers, used the result to create a change mask and proposed a new loss to punish noisy changes. Jiang *et al.* [25] introduced a pyramid feature-based attention-guided siamese network using a global co-attention mechanism to emphasize correlations between input feature pairs. Daudt *et al.* [8] presented three fully convolutional networks for change detection. Two use a siamese architecture with shared weights as an encoder. A decoder uses features from different hidden layers from the encoder to create a change mask. Lebedev *et al.* [18] created a conditional adversarial network for fully supervised change detection.

Bu *et al.* [26] proposed a method for change detection in unregistered images. A first module roughly predicts change areas and matching information for an image pair and a second one refines the change areas. Daudt *et al.* [16] proposed four methods to perform semantic change detection, all of which use the same encoder-decoder structure with residual connections. They either directly predict a semantic change mask or an individual change mask and semantic labels which are then combined in a second step.

2.2   Weakly Supervised and Unsupervised Change Detection

Sakurada *et al.* [27] proposed a siamese network which first creates a change mask and then performs semantic segmentation of the changed regions. Both model parts are trained with pixel-level labels. They use separate change detection and semantic segmentation datasets for training. Jiang *et al.* [10] used a siamese network in combination with a conditional random field (CRF) [28]. They only use image-level labels for training. Additionally, they proposed a weighted global average pooling layer (WGAP) which allows them to jointly predict pixel-level and image-level labels.

Yu *et al.* [17] used active learning and markov random fields to reduce the number of needed ground truth change masks. Jong *et al.* [29] trained their model on a standard segmentation dataset. They then compared extracted features of two images in order to create a difference image.

Minematsu *et al.* [11] proposed a convolutional neural network (CNN) which uses a simple pixel-wise subtraction of the two input images as an additional constraint. Their model is trained with image-level labels only. Chianucci *et al.* [30] used spatial transformer networks [31] and a sliding window to detect changes between two images. They did not perform change segmentation but rather simple change detection with bounding boxes. Khan *et al.* [9] used a CNN in combination with a CRF in order to simultaneously perform binary classification and create a change mask. They use a CNN to predict a first change mask and a CRF to refine the change mask. They trained their model with image-level binary labels.

In contrast to the existing weakly supervised change detection approaches, our method can be trained with image-level *semantic* labels which describe the changed object. Our proposed Change Segmentation and Classification (CSC) module allows us to create a change mask and simultaneously label the changed object for single-label images. As a result, our method can be trained with datasets which contain *changed* image pairs only or with datasets which contain a mix of *changed* and *unchanged* image pairs. Additionally, in contrast to other works [9–11], our model creates a change mask and segments the image containing change at a hidden layer. The resulting segmented image is then refined using a CRF-RNN [14] layer and used to predict an image-level semantic label. Akin to [8,10,19,25,27], we too employ a siamese network to extract feature maps from an image pair. However, we propose a W-shaped siamese network based on two U-Nets [13] and introduce a custom Comparison Block to compare these feature maps before our novel CSC module to jointly segment and classify the change.

3   Proposed Method

In this section we introduce our proposed W-CDNet. We start by providing an overview of the processing pipeline and architecture, then we provide the details for each of the major components. We also explain how the Change Segmentation and Classification (CSC) module lets the model learn an accurate change mask at a hidden layer.

3.1   W-CDNet Overview

We introduce W-CDNet (see Fig. 2), a weakly supervised convolutional network which detects and segments relevant pixel-level changes in an image pair. The proposed method was trained with image-level semantic labels, as explained in introductory Sect. 1. The model takes two temporally different, co-registered RGB images as input (called *previous image* and *current image*). If the image pairs were not yet co-registered, we aligned them in a pre-processing step.

A siamese model (shared weights), which consists of two U-Nets [13], extracts feature maps from the image pair. These feature maps get compared by a chain of Comparison Blocks. By comparing features from several hidden layers, we leveraged both high-level and low-level information which allowed us to filter out unwanted changes while still creating an accurate high-resolution change mask.

The output of the last Comparison Block is a raw change mask, which gets processed by the CSC module. The CSC module is the core of W-CDNet: It lets the model learn a change mask at a hidden layer. The CSC module and the individual blocks are described in more detail in the following sections.

3.2   Siamese Network

The Siamese Network is based on U-Net [13] which uses a VGG16 [32] model as feature extractor. An image pair is used as model input. The U-Nets extract high-level and low-level feature maps from the two images. The feature maps generated before every up-sampling layer are passed on to the Comparison Blocks.

3.3   Comparison Block

This block compares feature maps from the two U-Nets. It highlight differences of relevant features between the two images. Figure 3 shows the different layers of a single Comparison Block. We used a total of six Comparison Blocks, each of which compares features from a different U-Net layer. This allows the model

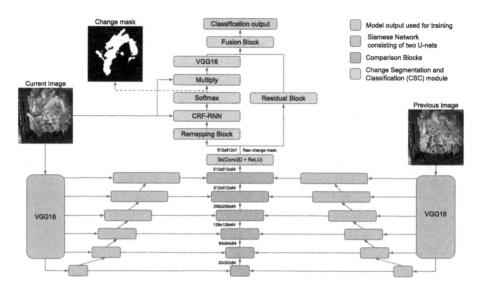

Fig. 2. W-CDNet model architecture.

to use both high-level and low-level information to create a change mask. The feature maps created by one Comparison Block get up-sampled and are fed to the next Comparison Block. The feature maps from the last block get processed by three convolutional layers with ReLU [33] activation, which then output a single-channel raw change mask.

3.4 CSC Module

The CSC module is the core of W-CDNet. It is split up into two independent branches. One branch, consisting only of a Residual Block, extracts features which help to decide whether the image pair contains any relevant change at all.

The other branch further processes the raw change mask in the Remapping Block which assumes that the highest mask activations always correspond to relevant change, independent of whether there actually is relevant change in the image pair or not. The Remapping Block creates a change mask which gets refined by the CRF-RNN [14] layer. The resulting final change mask is used to segment the current input image. The segmented image then gets encoded by the VGG16 [32] model. The Fusion Block concatenates the feature vectors from the two branches and predicts an image-level label. The model has to highlight relevant changes, else the Fusion Block will not be able to predict the correct image-level label. We now describe the blocks from the CSC module in more detail.

Remapping Block. The Remapping Block receives the raw change mask from the Comparison Blocks. The change mask pixels with a high activation (relative to the other pixels) are assumed to mark relevant change. This is enforced by the following formulas:

$$\hat{X}_{map} = \left(\frac{\hat{X} - min(\hat{X})}{max(\hat{X}) - min(\hat{X})} \cdot \alpha \right) - \frac{\alpha}{2} \tag{1}$$

$$\hat{Y} = sig\left(\hat{X}_{map}\right) \tag{2}$$

where $\hat{X}$ is the raw change mask which can contain values from the interval $[0, \infty]$, α is a hyper-parameter, $sig()$ is the sigmoid function and $\hat{Y}$ is the intermediate predicted change mask which now contains values from the interval $[0, 1]$.

Equation (1) shows the intermediate result of the remapping process. Independent of the input range, the values of $\hat{X}_{map}$ lie in the interval $\left[-\frac{\alpha}{2}, \frac{\alpha}{2}\right]$ where $min(\hat{X})$ gets mapped to $-\frac{\alpha}{2}$ and $max(\hat{X})$ gets mapped to $\frac{\alpha}{2}$ (Exception: All features in $\hat{X}$ have the exact same value). Since these values are then fed into a sigmoid function, the hyper-parameter α influences how strongly the values marking relevant change get separated from the values marking irrelevant change. The smaller α is, the smoother the distribution of the change mask values will be. We set α to 32 for training (without CRF-RNN layer) and to 16 for finetuning (including CRF-RNN layer).

The intermediate change mask can now be further refined with a CRF-RNN [14] layer. The final change mask then gets multiplied element-wise with the current input image, which results in an image where only regions with relevant change are visible. This step, combined with the remapping explained above, forces the model to learn an accurate change mask. The segmented image is then fed to a VGG16 [32] model which creates a feature vector describing the region marked by the change mask.

Residual Block. While the Remapping Block assumes that there is always *some* relevant change between the two input images, the Residual Block helps to decide if this is actually true or not. To this end the Residual Block takes the raw change mask as input and creates a feature vector which helps the model to distinguish between changed and unchanged image pairs. Without the Residual Block, the model is not able to do this distinction due to the Remapping Block. It can, however, still learn to segment changes when trained on changed images only. Figure 3 shows the different layers of the Residual Block.

Fusion Block. The Fusion Block concatenates the feature vectors created by the VGG16 model and the Residual Block and classifies them into N classes, from which $N - 1$ describe the changed object and one is the unchanged class. Figure 3 shows the different layers of the Fusion Block.

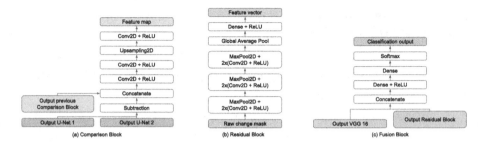

Fig. 3. Comparison Block, Residual Block and Fusion Block in more detail. The colors of the block inputs and outputs refer to the ones in Fig. 2. (Color figure online)

3.5   Model Variations

W-CDNet can be trained with a combination of changed and unchanged image pairs. By removing the Residual Block from the CSC module, the model can be trained with changed image pairs only. In this case, the Fusion Block has only one input and simply serves as a classifier. It is also possible to train our model with full supervision in a multitask learning setting [34]. In this case, one uses both the change mask and the image-level label as model outputs.

3.6   Training

In order to speed up training, we leveraged transfer learning and used publicly available pre-trained weights for U-Net [35]. For the VGG16 [32] model we used publicly available pre-trained weights from a training on ImageNet [36]. All other weights were initialized by sampling from a normal distribution.

The model has to be trained in two steps:

(1) Training: The CRF-RNN layer [14] is removed from the model. The model has to learn to correctly label the image pairs (image-level labels). During this process, it learns to create an unrefined change mask at a hidden layer. The boundaries of change objects are not accurately segmented yet, as one can see in Fig. 4.

(2) Finetuning: In a second step, the CRF-RNN layer is inserted into the model and the weights from step 1 for all other layers are loaded. The model is then trained again end-to-end, but with a reduced learning rate. After this training step, the changed objects get segmented more accurately thanks to the segmentation refinement by the CRF-RNN layer, as one can see in Fig. 4.

Loss Function. We used categorical crossentropy loss to train our weakly supervised model. For fully supervised training we combined two losses: Categorical crossentropy loss for image-level semantic labels $\mathcal{L}_{IL}$ and a custom Conditional Loss $\mathcal{L}_{CM}$ for the pixel-level change mask. $\mathcal{L}_{CM}$ takes on the form of a standard binary crossentropy loss if $max(Y) > 0$, else it is set to 0. Y is the ground truth

Fig. 4. Influence of CRF-RNN layer on change segmentation performance, shown for an image pair from the AICD dataset. From left to right: previous image, current image with change object, change mask without refinement, change mask with refinement by CRF-RNN layer, ground truth change mask.

change mask. This Conditional Loss is needed since the model branch, which predicts the change mask, assumes that there is always at least some relevant change in the image pair. Thus, if the image pair does not contain any change, we do not want to induce any loss for the change mask, but only for the image-level semantic label. $\mathcal{L}_{IL}$ and $\mathcal{L}_{CM}$ are summed up to the final loss $\mathcal{L}$.

4 Experiments and Results

In this section we describe the experimental benchmark (datasets and performance measures), the conducted experiments, and discuss the achieved results in relation to the reported results from the literature. There is only a very limited number of weakly supervised change detection methods which report their results on publicly available datasets. Since the code for these methods is often not publicly available, we compare our results to the ones provided by the authors, by using the performance measures also used by them.

4.1 Datasets

Most change detection datasets contain pixel-level binary labels [6,15,37,38]. In our work, however, we used image-level semantic labels. We could also extract them from pixel-level semantic labels. HRSCD [16], PSCD [27] and SCPA-WC [39] contain pixel-level labels for semantic change detection, but only HRSCD is publicly available. We refer to [1] for an extended review of datasets and related literature. In this work we validated our approach on HRSCD, AICD [15] for which we collected image-level semantic labels, and on the Food Waste dataset.

Food Waste Dataset. The Food Waste dataset contains 57,674 image pairs of which 3,447 pairs have the image-level label *unchanged*. The changed image pairs are spread over 20 classes, which results in a dataset with 21 classes, including the *unchanged* class. Since the Food Waste dataset is very new, most images only contain image-level labels. A total of 145 images also contain pixel-level binary labels. They were used to evaluate segmentation performance. The image-level labels of 1,050 image pairs was double-checked by hand. These pairs were used to evaluate semantic and binary classification performance (50 of which belonged to the *unchanged* class).

The images were resized from 3,280 × 2,464 pixels to 512 × 512 pixels for training and testing. The model was trained with image augmentation.

AICD Dataset. The *Aerial Image Change Detection* (AICD) dataset [15] is a synthetic dataset consisting of 1,000 image pairs (600 × 800 pixels), 500 of which include hard shadows. For our experiments we only used the image pairs with hard shadows. For each image pair, there is only one object which is considered as relevant change. Since these objects are very small, we split up the images into 48 patches of size 122 × 122 pixels with minimal overlap, which results in 24,000 image pairs. The patches were resized to 128 × 128 pixels for training. We manually annotated the image pairs with image-level semantic labels. We will make the labels publicly available for further research.

HRSCD Dataset. The *High Resolution Semantic Change Detection* (HRSCD) dataset [16] is a very challenging dataset that contains 291 high-resolution aerial images pairs (10,000 × 10,000 pixels). The dataset contains pixel-level semantic labels for 5 classes (Artificial surfaces, Agricultural surfaces, Forests, Wetlands, Water). Additionally, there is a ground truth change mask available for every image pair. We extracted image-level semantic labels from pixel-level semantic labels for the changed regions.

We used 146 image pairs for training and 145 image pairs for testing. We work on image crops of size 1,000 × 1,000 pixels which were further resized to 512 × 512 pixels for training and testing. The original images were cropped without any overlap, which resulted in 29,100 image pairs.

Since our model only works with single-label image pairs but HRSCD contains multi-labels, we created one label for each possible combination of the 5 semantic labels. This resulted in 31 unique semantic labels, plus the additional unchanged label. We oversampled the underrepresented classes and made sure that every class had at least 600 training samples.

4.2   Performance Measures

For assessing the performance we use standard measures from the literature. For classification performance we employ:

$$average\,precision\,(AP) = \sum_n (R_n - R_{n-1})P_n, \quad accuracy = \frac{T}{N}$$

where P_n and R_n are precision and recall at the n-th threshold, T is the number of all true predictions and N is the total number of samples.

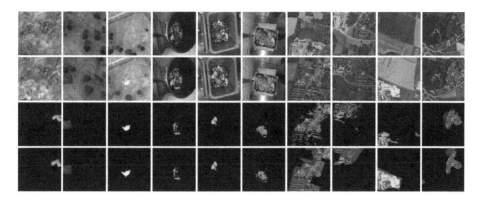

Fig. 5. Qualitative results of the predicted change masks. Row 1: previous image. Row 2: current image. Row 3: Predicted change mask. Row 4: ground truth change mask. Columns 1–3: AICD dataset. Columns 4–6: food Waste dataset. Columns 7–10: HRSCD dataset.

For change segmentation performance we use the standard:

$$mIoU = mean(\frac{TP}{TP + FP + FN}), \qquad Kappa = \frac{p_o - p_e}{1 - p_e},$$

$$Dice = \frac{2 \cdot TP}{2 \cdot TP + FP + FN}, \qquad Total\ accuracy = \frac{TP + TN}{TP + TN + FP + FN}$$

where TP - true positive, TN - true negative, FP - false positive, FN - false negative, p_o - observed agreement between ground truth and predictions, p_e - expected agreement between ground truth and predictions given class distributions. Cohen's Kappa [40], the Sørensen-Dice coefficient [41] and Total accuracy are defined as in [16].

4.3   Influence of Residual and Comparison Blocks on Performance

We study the importance of the Residual Block in our CSC module by training our W-CDNet with and without that Block. Since the Residual Block is needed to decide whether an image pair contains any relevant change at all, the model without this block must be trained with changed images only. Thus, we compare the change detection and segmentation performance of the full model (dataset contains also unchanged image pairs) to the model without a Residual Block (trained with changed images only). Additionally, we studied the influence on performance of different numbers of filters in the Comparison Blocks. We compare two models where the number of filters was kept constant at either 64 or 256 and a model where the number of filters decreased (256, 128, 64, 32, 16, 16 filters, from first to last Comparison Block).

We show numerical results for tests on the Food Waste dataset in Table 1. The models without a Residual Block were trained on changed images only. The models with a Residual Block were trained on unchanged images plus the same changed images as the models without a Residual Block. We show that both models, with and without Residual Block, learn to create a change mask. They achieve similar segmentation performances. However, the influence on performance of the number of filters is very different for the two models. The model with a Residual Block shows the best segmentation results for 64 filters while the model without a Residual Block performs best with a decaying number of filters.

Additionally, the model with a Residual Block and 256 filters did not learn to segment any changes at all. We argue that while the Residual Block is crucial for the model to distinguish between changed and unchanged images, it increases the model complexity which made training unstable for too many filters in the Comparison Blocks.

We also show that change segmentation performance for the model without the Residual Block (and thus for a dataset without unchanged images) is on par with the performance for the model with the Residual Block. This shows that our model learns to distinguish relevant from irrelevant changes already from changed images only.

Table 1. Results on Food Waste dataset for training a model with or without the Residual Block and with different numbers of filters in the Comparison Blocks.

	With Residual Block				Without Residual Block			
Number of filters	mIoU	AP	Top-1- acc.	Top-5- acc.	mIoU	AP	Top-1- acc.	Top-5- acc.
64	**46.5**	**74.9**	**68.2**	**91.7**	45.5	77.7	72.2	93.0
256	0.0	14.3	16.9	49.9	47.4	**81.9**	**74.4**	**95.5**
Decaying	43.2	68.9	63.9	89.3	**47.7**	79.4	72.4	94.6

4.4   Influence of CRF Refinement on Performance

In Table 2 we compare the change segmentation performance and the binary classification performance of our W-CDNet model without any refinement to a model with a standard CRF [42] as post-processing step and to a model with an integrated CRF-RNN layer [14] for segmentation refinement. The standard CRF was only applied after training the model without any refinement. The CRF-RNN layer was included in the training process.

We observe a significant segmentation performance increase for our model with CRF-RNN layer. The standard CRF (without parameter optimization) applied as post-processing shows only a marginal performance improvement on the AICD dataset and even significantly decreases performance on the Food Waste and HRSCD datasets. This was to be expected, as the CRF-RNN layer learns its parameters during training and adapts to each dataset individually.

Table 2. Influence on segmentation and classification performance of refining the change mask with a standard CRF or with a CRF-RNN layer.

	AICD			Food waste			HRSCD		
	mIoU	AP	Acc.	mIoU	AP	Acc.	mIoU	AP	Acc.
No refinement	51.6	**98.8**	**99.2**	43.3	**97.3**	**98.2**	8.4	**75.9**	**81.7**
Post-processing with CRF	52.5	**98.8**	**99.2**	30.3	**97.3**	**98.2**	4.5	**75.9**	**81.7**
Integration of a CRF-RNN layer	**66.2**	98.7	**99.2**	**46.5**	89.8	92.9	**9.5**	75.1	81.0

4.5   Comparison Results on AICD Dataset

In Table 3 and Fig. 5 we report change segmentation and binary as well as semantic change classification results on the AICD dataset [15]. We directly compare our results to the ones reported by Khan *et al.* [9] and Chianucci *et al.* [30]. Additionally, we trained our W-CDNet model with full supervision in a multi-task learning setting as described in Sect. 3.5.

On AICD, we improved the state-of-the-art for weakly supervised change segmentation. However, the model from Khan *et al.* performs slightly better for full supervision. The qualitative results show that our model successfully suppresses irrelevant changes while highlighting relevant change.

Our model had the most difficulties with objects at the edge of the images. Also, our weakly supervised model interpreted hard shadows from changed objects as part of the object itself while the ground truth masks excluded these shadows.

Table 3. Change segmentation and classification results on the AICD dataset [15].

	Weak supervision						Full supervision
	Semantic classification			Binary classification		Segmentation	Segmentation
	AP	Top-1 acc.	Top-5 acc.	AP	Acc.	mIoU	mIoU
Khan *et al.* [9]	-	-	-	97.3	99.1	64.9	**71.0**
Bu *et al.* [26]	-	-	-	-	-	-	64.9
Chianucci *et al.* [30]	-	-	-	-	-	57.0	-
W-CDNet (ours)	99.5	98.9	99.8	**98.7**	**99.2**	**66.2**	70.3

4.6   Comparison Results on HRSCD Dataset

In Table 4 and Fig. 5 we report change segmentation and classification results on the HRSCD dataset [16]. We are the first ones to report weakly supervised change detection performance on HRSCD.

For full supervision we compare our results to the ones from Daudt *et al.* [16]. We compare to the performance of the change detector from their *strategy 3* which is trained with pixel-level binary labels. Our fully supervised model shows better performance than *strategy 3* and our weakly supervised model's performance is slightly better. Daudt *et al.* reported better results than us for their *strategy 4.2*, but it was additionally trained with pixel-level semantic labels and thus was stronger supervised than our method. We refer to their work [16] for the results of all strategies trained by Daudt *et al.*

The change segmentation results on HRSCD are significantly lower than the ones on Food Waste or AICD. There are three main reasons for that: (i) The HRSCD ground truth change masks are generally too large: they not only contain the changed objects but they mark complete building zones; (ii) HRSCD is highly imbalanced, even more so than the AICD dataset; (iii) A part of the classes are visually very similar, which makes classification, in combination with the high class imbalance, very difficult.

Table 4. Change segmentation and classification results on the HRSCD dataset [16].

	Weak supervision								Full supervision		
	Semantic classification			Binary classification		Segmentation			Segmentation		
	AP	Top-1 acc.	Top-5 acc.	AP	Acc.	Kappa	Dice	Total acc.	Kappa	Dice	Total acc.
Daudt *et al.* [16], strategy 3	-	-	-	-	-	-	-	-	12.5	13.8	94.7
W-CDNet (ours)	83.0	79.9	98.0	75.1	81.0	13.3	14.1	98.4	**15.9**	**16.8**	**98.0**

5 Conclusion

This paper presented W-CDNet, a novel data-driven convolutional network for change detection which can be trained with weak supervision using image-level semantic labels. The proposed Change Segmentation and Classification (CSC) module enables W-CDNet to learn a change mask at a hidden layer by using the custom Remapping Block and then segmenting the current input image with the predicted change mask. The segmented image is then used to predict the image-level semantic label which is used for training. In ablative studies we showed the importance of our Residual Block and of the integrated CRF-RNN layer and their impact on the W-CDNet overall performance.

We improved the state-of-the-art for weakly supervised change detection on AICD and are the first to report weakly supervised change detection results on the HRSCD dataset. On HRSCD the performance of our weakly supervised approach is on par with a related work using full supervision.

For future work we propose to try multi-label change detection. Since our model uses image-level semantic labels for training, one could predict an individual change mask for each label. One could also try to improve information sharing within the model to improve performance. Another interesting task would be to perform change detection on unregistered images. Additionally, we hope that the fact that our model can be trained with or without unchanged image pairs opens new applications for weakly supervised change detection methods.

References

1. Shi, W., Min, Z., Zhang, R., Chen, S., Zhan, Z.: Change detection based on artificial intelligence: state-of-the-art and challenges. Remote Sens. **12**, 1688 (2020)
2. Ban, Y., Yousif, O.: Change detection techniques: a review. In: Ban, Y. (eds.) Multitemporal Remote Sensing. Remote Sensing and Digital Image Processing, vol. 20. Springer, Cham (2016). https://doi.org/10.1007/978-3-319-47037-5_2
3. Liu, Z., Li, G., Mercier, G., He, Y., Pan, Q.: Change detection in heterogenous remote sensing images via homogeneous pixel transformation. IEEE Trans. Image Process. **27**, 1822–1834 (2018)
4. Zhang, P., Gong, M., Su, L., Liu, J., Li, Z.: Change detection based on deep feature representation and mapping transformation for multi-spatial-resolution remote sensing images. ISPRS J. Photogramm. Remote Sens. **116**, 24–41 (2016)
5. Wang, K., Gou, C.: M4CD: a robust change detection method for intelligent visual surveillance. IEEE Access **6**, 15505–15520 (2018)
6. Sakurada, K., Okatani, T.: Change detection from a street image pair using CNN features and superpixel segmentation. BMVC **61**, 1–12 (2015)
7. Alcantarilla, P.F., Stent, S., Ros, G., Arroyo, R., Gherardi, R.: Street-view change detection with deconvolutional networks. Auton. Robots **42**, 1301–1322 (2018)
8. Daudt, R.C., Le Saux, B., Boulch, A.: Fully convolutional Siamese networks for change detection. In: 2018 25th IEEE International Conference on Image Processing (ICIP), pp. 4063–4067. IEEE (2018)
9. Khan, S.H., He, X., Porikli, F.M., Bennamoun, M., Sohel, F., Togneri, R.: Learning deep structured network for weakly supervised change detection. In: IJCAI (2017)
10. Jiang, X., Tang, H.: Dense high-resolution Siamese network for weakly-supervised change detection. In: 2019 6th International Conference on Systems and Informatics (ICSAI), pp. 547–552 (2019)
11. Minematsu, T., Shimada, A., Taniguchi, R.I.: Simple background subtraction constraint for weakly supervised background subtraction network. In: 2019 16th IEEE International Conference on Advanced Video and Signal Based Surveillance (AVSS), pp. 1–8. IEEE (2019)
12. Bromley, J., et al.: Signature verification using a "Siamese" time delay neural network. Int. J. Pattern Recognit. Artif. Intell. **7**, 25 (1993)
13. Ronneberger, O., Fischer, P., Brox, T.: U-Net: convolutional networks for biomedical image segmentation. In: Navab, N., Hornegger, J., Wells, W.M., Frangi, A.F. (eds.) MICCAI 2015. LNCS, vol. 9351, pp. 234–241. Springer, Cham (2015). https://doi.org/10.1007/978-3-319-24574-4_28
14. Zheng, S., et al.: Conditional random fields as recurrent neural networks. In: International Conference on Computer Vision (ICCV) (2015)
15. Bourdis, N., Marraud, D., Sahbi, H.: Constrained optical flow for aerial image change detection. In: 2011 IEEE International Geoscience and Remote Sensing Symposium, pp. 4176–4179. IEEE (2011)
16. Daudt, R., Le Saux, B., Boulch, A., Gousseau, Y.: Multitask learning for large-scale semantic change detection. Comput. Vis. Image Underst. **187**, 102783 (2019)

17. Yu, H., Yang, W., Hua, G., Ru, H., Huang, P.: Change detection using high resolution remote sensing images based on active learning and Markov random fields. Remote Sens. **9**, 1233 (2017)
18. Lebedev, M., Vizilter, Y., Vygolov, O., Knyaz, V., Rubis, A.: Change detection in remote sensing images using conditional adversarial networks. ISPRS - Int. Arch. Photogramm. Remote Sens. Spat. Inf. Sci. **XLII**(2), 565–571 (2018)
19. Guo, E., et al.: Learning to measure change: fully convolutional Siamese metric networks for scene change detection. CoRR abs/1810.09111 (2018)
20. Lecun, Y., Bottou, L., Bengio, Y., Haffner, P.: Gradient-based learning applied to document recognition. Proc. IEEE **86**, 2278–2324 (1998)
21. LeCun, Y., Bengio, Y., Hinton, G.: Deep learning. Nature **521**, 436–444 (2015)
22. Muchoney, D.M., Haack, B.N.: Change detection for monitoring forest defoliation. Photogramm. Eng. Remote Sens. **60**, 1243–1252 (1994)
23. Lambin, E.F.: Change detection at multiple temporal scales: seasonal and annual variations in landscape variables. Photogramm. Eng. Remote Sens. **62**, 931–938 (1996)
24. Collins, J.B., Woodcock, C.E.: Change detection using the Gramm-Schmidt transformation applied to mapping forest mortality. Remote Sens. Environ. **50**(3), 267–279 (1994)
25. Jiang, H., Hu, X., Li, K., Zhang, J., Gong, J., Zhang, M.: PGA-SiamNet: pyramid feature-based attention-guided Siamese network for remote sensing orthoimagery building change detection. Remote Sens. **12**, 484 (2020)
26. Bu, S., Li, Q., Han, P., Leng, P., Li, K.: Mask-CDNet: a mask based pixel change detection network. Neurocomputing **378**, 166–178 (2019)
27. Sakurada, K., Shibuya, M., Weimin, W.: Weakly supervised silhouette-based semantic scene change detection. In: Proceedings of the IEEE International Conference on Robotics and Automation (ICRA) (2020)
28. Lafferty, J.D., McCallum, A., Pereira, F.C.: Conditional random fields: probabilistic models for segmenting and labeling sequence data. In: Proceedings of the Eighteenth International Conference on Machine Learning, pp. 282–289 (2001)
29. de Jong, K.L., Bosman, A.S.: Unsupervised change detection in satellite images using convolutional neural networks. In: 2019 International Joint Conference on Neural Networks (IJCNN), pp. 1–8. IEEE (2019)
30. Chianucci, D., Savakis, A.: Unsupervised change detection using spatial transformer networks. In: 2016 IEEE Western New York Image and Signal Processing Workshop (WNYISPW), pp. 1–5. IEEE (2016)
31. Jaderberg, M., Simonyan, K., Zisserman, A., Kavukcuoglu, K.: Spatial transformer networks. In: Advances in Neural Information Processing Systems (NIPS 2015), vol. 28 (2015)
32. Simonyan, K., Zisserman, A.: Very deep convolutional networks for large-scale image recognition. CoRR abs/1409.1556 (2014)
33. Hahnloser, R., Sarpeshkar, R., Mahowald, M., Douglas, R., Seung, H.: Digital selection and analogue amplification coexist in a cortex-inspired silicon circuit. Nature **405**, 947–51 (2000)
34. Caruana, R.: Multitask learning. In: Thrun, S., Pratt, L. (eds.) Learning to Learn. Springer, Boston (1998). https://doi.org/10.1007/978-1-4615-5529-2_5
35. Yakubovskiy, P.: Segmentation models (2019). https://github.com/qubvel/segmentation_models
36. Deng, J., Dong, W., Socher, R., Li, L.J., Li, K., Fei-Fei, L.: ImageNet: a large-scale hierarchical image database. In: CVPR 2009 (2009)

37. Ji, S., Wei, S., Lu, M.: Fully convolutional networks for multisource building extraction from an open aerial and satellite imagery data set. IEEE Trans. Geosci. Remote Sens. **57**, 574–586 (2019)
38. Wang, Y., Jodoin, P.M., Porikli, F., Konrad, J., Benezeth, Y., Ishwar, P.: CDNet 2014: an expanded change detection benchmark dataset. In: IEEE Computer Society Conference on Computer Vision and Pattern Recognition Workshops (2014)
39. Cheng, W., Zhang, Y., Lei, X., Yang, W., Xia, G.: Semantic change pattern analysis (2020)
40. Cohen, J.: A coefficient of agreement for nominal scales. Educ. Psychol. Meas. **20**, 37–46 (1960)
41. Sørensen, T.: A method of establishing groups of equal amplitude in plant sociology based on similarity of species content and its application to analyses of the vegetation on Danish commons. Biologiske skrifter. I kommission hos E, Munksgaard (1948)
42. Krähenbühl, P., Koltun, V.: Efficient inference in fully connected CRFs with Gaussian edge potentials. In: Shawe-Taylor, J., Zemel, R.S., Bartlett, P.L., Pereira, F., Weinberger, K.Q. (eds.) Advances in Neural Information Processing Systems, vol. 24, pp. 109–117. Curran Associates, Inc. (2011)

Multi-Visual-Modality Human Activity Understanding (MMHAU)

Visible and Thermal Camera-Based Jaywalking Estimation Using a Hierarchical Deep Learning Framework

Vijay John[1(✉)], Ali Boyali[2], Simon Thompson[2], Annamalai Lakshmanan[1], and Seiichi Mita[1]

[1] Toyota Technological Institute, Nagoya, Japan
{vijayjohn,smita}@toyota-ti.ac.jp,
lakshmanan.annamalai@outlook.com
[2] Tier IV, Tokyo, Japan
{ali.boyali,simon.thompson}@tier4.jp

Abstract. Jaywalking is an abnormal pedestrian behavior which significantly increases the risk of road accidents. Owing to this risk, autonomous driving applications should robustly estimate the jaywalking pedestrians. However, the task of robustly estimating jaywalking is not trivial, especially in the case of visible camera-based estimation. In this work, a two-step hierarchical deep learning formulation using visible and thermal camera is proposed to address these challenges. The two steps are comprised of a deep learning-based scene classifier and two scene-specific semantic segmentation frameworks. The scene classifier classifies the visible-thermal image into legal pedestrian crossing and illegal pedestrian crossing scenes. The two scene-specific segmentation frameworks estimate the normal pedestrians and jaywalking pedestrians. The two segmentation frameworks are individually trained on the legal or illegal crossing scenes. The proposed framework is validated on the FLIR public dataset and compared with baseline algorithms. The experimental results show that the proposed hierarchical strategy reports better accuracy than baseline algorithms in real-time.

1 Introduction

Autonomous driving and ADAS applications, which aim to increase the safety of road users, have received significant attention from the research community [1–3]. Environment perception is a key task for autonomous driving. Examples of environment perception include pedestrian detection [4], road surface segmentation [3], pedestrian behavior estimation [5] etc. Jaywalking is an example of abnormal pedestrian behavior which occurs when pedestrians walk or cross the road at locations, disregarding traffic rules.

Owing to the risk of accidents associated with this behavior, autonomous driving applications should robustly estimate jaywalking pedestrians. However,

© Springer Nature Switzerland AG 2021
I. Sato and B. Han (Eds.): ACCV 2020 Workshops, LNCS 12628, pp. 123–135, 2021.
https://doi.org/10.1007/978-3-030-69756-3_9

jaywalking estimation is not a trivial task with several challenges, especially when the visible camera is used. The challenges include variations in illumination, appearance similarity between *normal* pedestrian behavior and *abnormal* pedestrian behavior (Fig. 1), appearance variations in *legal* pedestrian crossing points or scenes (Fig. 2), environmental noise etc.

(a) Normal Behavior: Legal Pedestrian Cross- (b) Jaywalking: Illegal Pedestrian Crossing
ing Scene   Scene

Fig. 1. Appearance similarity in legal and illegal crossing scene.

A naive vision-based approach to solving this problem involves segmenting or detecting pedestrians and legal-illegal crossing image regions, and using the segmentation results to estimate the pedestrian behavior. However, such an approach is limited by the appearance similarity between the *normal* and *abnormal* pedestrian behavior in certain scenes (Fig. 1). In such scenes, the pedestrian crossing segmentation can be used to classify the pedestrian behavior. But as shown in Fig. 2, the pedestrian crossing estimation is by itself a challenging problem owing to varying pedestrian crossing regions.

Fig. 2. Challenges in jaywalking estimation due to variations in the pedestrian crossing markers.

To address these challenges, a two-step hierarchical framework is proposed using the visible and thermal camera. The sensor fusion of the thermal and visible camera address the challenges associated with the visible camera such as illumination variations and sensor noise [6]. The other challenges are addressed by the hierarchical framework.

The hierarchical framework is comprised of a classification step and a semantic segmentation step. The classification step is formulated using a single deep learning-based scene classifier which classifies the driving scene into a *legal* pedestrian crossing scene or a *illegal* pedestrian crossing scene (Fig. 3). The semantic segmentation step is formulated using two scene-specific semantic segmentation frameworks. The first semantic segmentation framework is trained on the *legal* pedestrian crossing scene. The second semantic segmentation framework is trained on the *illegal* pedestrian crossing scenes. These semantic segmentation frameworks estimate the normal and jaywalking pedestrians in a given image. The proposed framework is validated on the FLIR public dataset, and is compared with baseline algorithms. The experimental results show that the hierarchical fusion framework is better than the baseline algorithms (Sect. 4), while reporting real-time computational complexity.

(a) Legal Pedestrian Crossing Scenes   (b) Illegal Pedestrian Crossing Scenes

Fig. 3. Scene partitions for the hierarchical framework.

To the best of our knowledge, the main contribution of our work are as follows:

- A hierarchical learning framework for jaywalking estimation
- Visible and thermal camera fusion for jaywalking estimation

The reminder of the paper is structured as follows. In Sect. 2 we review the literature in jaywalking estimation. The hierarchical learning framework is presented in Sect. 3, and the experimental results are presented in Sect. 4. Finally, we summarize our work in Sect. 5.

2   Related Work

Pedestrian detection is an important precursor for pedestrian behavior estimation, and has been well-researched [7–10]. Pedestrian detection methods are categorized into methods based on hand-crafted features [7–9] or methods based on deep learning [10,11]. Pedestrian spatial, contextual or temporal information obtained from pedestrian detection is used for pedestrian behavior estimation [12–14]. Pedestrian behavior estimation is based on probabilistic modeling [12,15–17], deep learning models [18–20], and traditional frameworks that incorporate spatial contextual cues [14]. The different pedestrian behavior estimation frameworks are surveyed in the work of Santosh et al. [5].

Probabilistic and traditional frameworks model pedestrian behaviour using extracted pedestrian features. The modeled pedestrian behavior are used to identify anomalous behavior [12,14–17]. Roshtkari et al. [14] model the pedestrian spatial-temporal information within a bag-of-words framework, which are then used to identify anomalous behavior. In the work of Bera et al. [17] where the pedestrian global and local features are extracted and used within a Bayesian framework to identify anomalous behavior. In recent years, deep learning models report state-of-the-art accuracy for different perception tasks [2,3,21]. Medel et al. [19] use an end-to-end composite Convolutional Long Short-Term Memory (LSTM) to estimate anomalous behavior. A similar approach is proposed by Xu et al. [22] using the Resnet and LSTM.

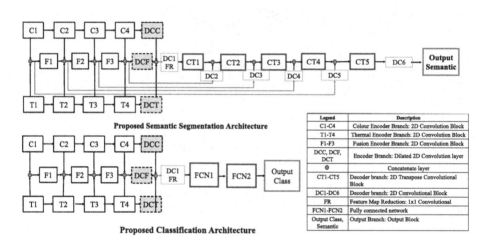

Fig. 4. Architecture of the classification and semantic segmentation network.

Compared to literature, in our work, we adopt a hierarchical deep learning framework using thermal and visible cameras to estimate jaywalking.

3   Algorithm

A two-step hierarchical framework using visible and thermal camera is proposed to identify jaywalking pedestrians. The initial step is formulated using a single deep learning-based classification network, while the second step is formulated using two semantic segmentation networks. The hierarchical framework

C1: C (64, 3, 1) P (2)	C2: C (128, 3,1) P (2)	C3: C (256, 3, 1) P (2)	C4: C (256, 3, 1) P (2)	DCC: C(256, 3) D(2)
T1: C (64, 3, 1) P (2)	T2: C (128, 3,1) P (2)	T3: C (256, 3, 1) P (2)	T4: C (256, 3, 1) P (2)	DCT: C(256, 3) D(2)
F1: C (256, 3, 1) P (2)	F2: C (256, 3, 1) P (2)	F3: C (256, 3, 1) P (2)	DCF: C(256, 3) D(2)	
DC1: C (256, 3, 1) Pad (S), FR: C(64,1,1)	DC2: C (256, 3, 1) Pad (S)	DC3: C (256, 3, 1) Pad (S)	DC4: C (256, 3, 1) Pad (S)	DC5: C (256, 3, 1) Pad (S)
CT1: TC (256, 5, 1)	CT2: TC (256, 4, 2)	CT3: TC (256, 4, 2)	CT4: TC (256, 5, 2)	CT5: TC (256, 4, 2)
DC6: C (64, 1, 1)	FN1: 512, FN2: 256	Output Semantic: Multiclass	Output Class: Binary	

Fig. 5. 2D Convolutional layer parameters: C (filters, kernel size, stride), D (dilation rate), Pad (S) "same" padding; Max pooling layer parameters: P (kernel size); 2D transpose convolutional layer parameters: TC (filters, kernel size, stride).

is formulated to reduce the following pedestrian behavior estimation errors: a) appearance similarities between jaywalking pedestrians and pedestrians in legal crossing scenes (Fig. 1); b) appearance variations across different *legal* pedestrians crossing scenes (Fig. 2).

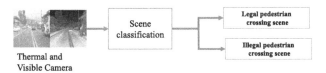

Fig. 6. Hierarchical framework step 1: classification.

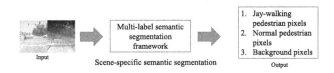

Fig. 7. Hierarchical framework step 2: semantic segmentation.

3.1 Classification Step

The first step in the hierarchical framework is a classification step, which categorises the driving scene into either a *legal* pedestrian crossing scene or a *illegal* pedestrian crossing scene (Fig. 3). An illustration of the classification step is shown in Fig. 6.

Architecture. A deep learning-based visible and thermal camera fusion architecture is used for the classification step. The architecture comprises of feature extraction, classification and output layers. The feature extraction layer contains three branches with two branches for visible camera and thermal camera feature extraction and one branch for fusion.

The two feature extraction branches contain 5 blocks. The first four blocks each contain a $2D$ convolutional layer with batch-normalization followed by a max-pooling layer. The fifth block contains a 2-dilated convolutional layer with batch-normalization.

The fusion branch also has 5 blocks. The first three blocks each contain a $2D$ convolutional layer with batch-normalization followed by a max-pooling layer. The fourth block contains a 2-dilated convolutional layer with batch-normalization. The final block contains a 1×1 convolutional layer functioning as a feature map reducing layer. The output of the feature map reducing layer is given as an input to the classification layer.

The classification layer contains two fully connected layers with 512 and 256 neurons and relu activation function. The final output layer contains 1 neuron and performs binary classification using the sigmoid activation.

3.2   Semantic Segmentation Step

This step contains two multi-class semantic segmentation networks. The first network is trained on the *legal* pedestrian crossing scenes, while the second network is trained on the *illegal* pedestrian crossing scenes. The trained semantic segmentation framework categorizes the image pixels as normal pedestrian, jaywalking pedestrian or background. An illustration of the semantic segmentation is shown in Fig. 7.

Architecture. A deep learning-based encoder-decoder architecture is utilized for the visible and thermal fusion and semantic segmentation. The encoder layers are the same as the feature extraction layers in the aforementioned classification network. This layer contains three feature extraction branches for visible camera feature extraction, thermal camera feature extraction and feature fusion.

The decoder layers contain 4 transpose convolutional layers and 5 convolutional layers. The transpose convolutional layers with batch-normalization upsample the encoder feature maps from the fusion branch. A skip connection is used to transfer the encoder feature maps to the decoder branches.

The output of the last decoder layer is fed into the output layer which performs the multiclass semantic segmentation using the softmax activation. The detailed architecture and the parameters are given in Fig. 4 and Fig. 5.

3.3   Hierarchical Framework: Training

The hierarchical framework is trained on the FLIR public dataset. Manually selected frames from the dataset are manually partitioned into *legal* pedestrian crossing and *illegal* pedestrian crossing scenes. The visible and thermal camera images for these frames are manually registered to ensure pixel-to-pixel correspondence.

During training, the single classification network is trained with all the frames (both legal and illegal pedestrian crossing scenes). On the other hand, the first semantic segmentation network is trained on the *legal* pedestrian crossing scenes, and the second semantic segmentation network is trained on the *illegal* pedestrian crossing scenes.

3.4   Hierarchical Framework: Testing

During testing, the registered thermal and visible camera images are first given as an input to the trained classification network. The classification network classifies the input images as either *legal* or *illegal* pedestrian crossing scene, assigning scene label c.

The estimated c-th scene label is used to retrieve the corresponding *trained* c-th scene-based semantic segmentation network (*illegal* or *legal*) for jaywalking estimation. Following the semantic segmentation network retrieval, the registered thermal and visible camera images are re-given as the network input and the jaywalking pedestrians are estimated. An overview of the testing is shown in Fig. 8.

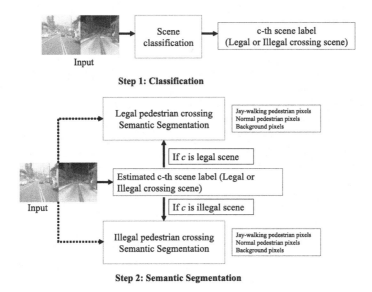

Fig. 8. Hierarchical framework.

4   Experimental Results

We validate the proposed framework on a manually selected subset from the FLIR public dataset. Our dataset contains 2799 training frames and 313 testing frames. Our algorithm was implemented using Tensorflow 2 on an Ubuntu 18.04 machine with two Nvidia 1080 GPUs. The algorithm was compared with six baseline algorithms and validated on the dataset. The proposed framework and the baseline algorithms were trained with batch size 4 for 30 epochs. The performance is measured using the pixel segmentation accuracy, the intersection-over-union (IOU) measure and classification accuracy. The IoU measure is the calculated from the overlap between the prediction and segmentation divided by the area of their union. We next briefly review the different baseline algorithms.

Hierarchical MFNet: The first baseline is a hierarchical framework based on the MFNet [23]. The MFNet is a visible-thermal camera based semantic segmentation framework with encoder-decoder architecture.

For comparative analysis, the MFNet encoder was used for feature extraction in the classification network. On the other hand, the entire MFNet was used for the two semantic segmentation networks.

Hierarchical Fusenet: The second baseline is a hierarchical framework based on the Fusenet [21]. The original Fusenet is a visible-depth based semantic segmentation framework with encoder-decoder architecture. For the comparative analysis, the original Fusenet input layers were modified for visible-thermal camera input.

The modified Fusenet's encoder was used for feature extraction in the classification network. The entire modified Fusenet was used for the two semantic segmentation networks in the second step.

Hierarchical with Single Encoder: The third baseline is a hierarchical framework where the classification network feature maps are reused for the semantic segmentation network.

The classification network is first trained on the dataset, and the feature maps for the dataset are obtained. The classification network feature maps are used for the semantic segmentation network training. The feature maps are the outputs of the $DC1 - FR$ block or the final fusion encoder block. Since the feature maps are re-used, there is no encoder layer in this baseline's semantic segmentation networks. The classification feature maps are directly given as input to the decoder branches and network is trained.

Hierarchical Visible: The fourth baseline is a hierarchical framework using the visible camera input as the sole input. The encoder branch of the proposed network for both the classification and segmentation networks contain a single branch for the visible camera.

Hierarchical Thermal: The fifth baseline is a hierarchical framework using the thermal camera as the sole input. The encoder branch of the proposed network for both the classification and segmentation networks contain a single branch for the thermal camera.

End-to-End Semantic Segmentation: The sixth baseline is a naive end-to-end semantic segmentation framework, formulated to evaluate the hierarchical framework. The performance of the hierarchical framework is compared with the end-to-end semantic segmentation framework.

In this baseline network, the jaywalking pedestrians are directly estimated using a "single" semantic segmentation framework. Unlike, the hierarchical semantic segmentation networks, this "single" semantic segmentation framework is trained with entire dataset, both legal and illegal pedestrian crossing scenes.

4.1   Comparative Analysis

The performance of the different algorithms are tabulated in Table 1, 2 and 3. The results are illustrated in Fig. 9 and Fig. 10.

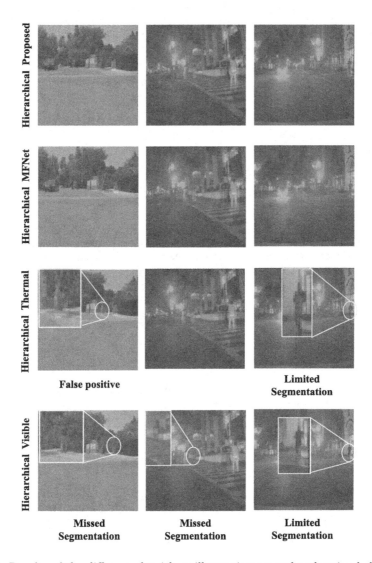

Fig. 9. Results of the different algorithms illustrating normal pedestrian behavior.

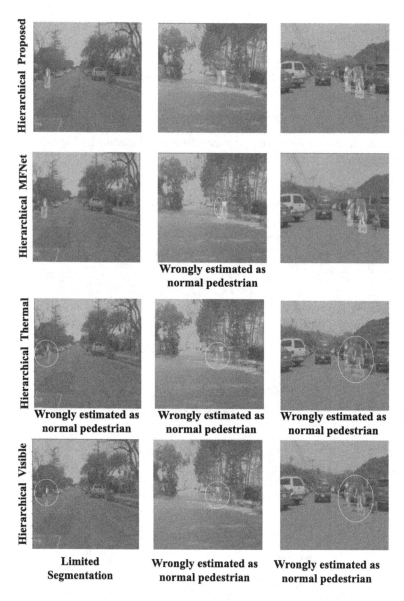

Fig. 10. Results of the different algorithms illustrating abnormal or jaywalking pedestrian behavior.

Hierarchical Framework with Varying Base Deep Learning Models: In Table 1, the results of the hierarchical framework with varying base deep learning models are tabulated. The results show that the hierarchical framework with the proposed deep learning architecture is better than the hierarchical framework with the MFNet and the Fusenet.

Table 1. Comparative analysis of the proposed hierarchical framework with different hierarchical frameworks.

Proposed Algo.	Pixel Acc. %		IOU (unit scale)		Class. Acc %	Time (ms)
	Normal Ped	Jaywalk Ped.	Normal Ped	Jaywalk Ped.		
Proposed Hier.	80.05	**82.75**	**0.71**	**0.73**	99	47
Hier. MFNet	**84.42**	68.10	0.69	0.59	96	38
Hier. Fusenet	51.40	59.08	0.46	0.52	96	35

Table 2. Comparative analysis of the sensor fusion of the proposed hierarchical framework.

Proposed Algo.	Pixel Acc. %		IOU (unit scale)		Class. Acc %	Time (ms)
	Normal Ped	Jaywalk Ped.	Normal Ped	Jaywalk Ped.		
Hier. fusion	**80.05**	**82.75**	**0.71**	**0.73**	99	47
Hier. visible	41.32	60.43	0.37	0.48	93	32
Hier. thermal	55.18	40.90	0.47	0.35	89	31

Table 3. Comparative analysis of the proposed hierarchical framework with different estimation approaches.

Proposed Algo.	Pixel Acc. %		IOU (unit scale)		Time (ms)
	Normal Ped	Jaywalk Ped.	Normal Ped	Jaywalk Ped.	
Proposed Hier.	**80.05**	**82.75**	**0.71**	**0.73**	47
End-to-End Seg.	78.99	71.58	0.70	0.64	36
Hier. single encoder	60.04	32.23	0.50	0.29	50

Hierarchical Framework with Varying Sensors: The results of the hierarchical framework with varying sensors are tabulated in Table 2. As expected, the advantages of the visible-thermal camera sensor fusion are clearly demonstrated.

Varying Estimation Approaches: Apart from the hierarchical formulation, we also investigate two different jaywalking estimation approaches namely end-to-end semantic segmentation and hierarchical with single encoder. The results of the different approaches are tabulated in Table 3. The results show that the proposed hierarchical approach is better than the other two approaches. The reuse of the classification feature maps (hierarchical with single encoder) or the use of a naive end-to-end segmentation network doesn't improve the accuracy.

5   Summary

A hierarchical deep learning framework is proposed for jaywalking estimation using thermal and visible cameras. The hierarchical framework is proposed to address the challenges in this perception task. The hierarchical framework contains two steps, an initial step with a single classification network and second step with two semantic segmentation networks. In the first step, the classification network classifies the scene into a legal or illegal pedestrian crossing scenes. In the second step, scene-specific semantic segmentation networks are used to estimate the jaywalking pedestrians. The proposed framework is validated on the FLIR public dataset, and a comparative analysis with baseline algorithms is performed. The results show that the proposed hierarchical approach reports better accuracy than baseline algorithm, while reporting computational complexity. In our future work, we will investigate the framework with a much larger dataset in varying countries.

References

1. John, V., Guo, C., Mita, S., Kidono, K., Guo, C., Ishimaru, K.: Fast road scene segmentation using deep learning and scene-based models. In: ICPR (2016)
2. John, V., Liu, Z., Guo, C., Mita, S., Kidono, K.: Real-time lane estimation using deep features and extra trees regression. In: Bräunl, T., McCane, B., Rivera, M., Yu, X. (eds.) PSIVT 2015. LNCS, vol. 9431, pp. 721–733. Springer, Cham (2016). https://doi.org/10.1007/978-3-319-29451-3_57
3. John, V., et al.: Sensor fusion of intensity and depth cues using the ChiNet for semantic segmentation of road scenes. In: IEEE Intelligent Vehicles Symposium, pp. 585–590 (2018)
4. John, V., Mita, S.: RVNet: deep sensor fusion of monocular camera and radar for image-based obstacle detection in challenging environments. In: Lee, C., Su, Z., Sugimoto, A. (eds.) PSIVT 2019. LNCS, vol. 11854, pp. 351–364. Springer, Cham (2019). https://doi.org/10.1007/978-3-030-34879-3_27
5. Chandola, V., Banerjee, A., Kumar, V.: Anomaly detection: a survey. ACM Comput. Surv. **41**, 1–58 (2009)
6. John, V., Tsuchizawa, S., Liu, Z., Mita, S.: Fusion of thermal and visible cameras for the application of pedestrian detection. Signal Image Video Process. **11**, 517–524 (2017)
7. Dollar, P., Appel, R., Belongie, S., Perona, P.: Fast feature pyramids for object detection. IEEE Trans. Pattern Anal. Mach. Intell. **36**, 1532–1545 (2014)
8. Zhang, S., Benenson, R., Schiele, B.: Filtered channel features for pedestrian detection. In: 2015 IEEE Conference on Computer Vision and Pattern Recognition (CVPR), pp. 1751–1760 (2015)
9. Ohn-Bar, E., Trivedi, M.M.: To boost or not to boost? On the limits of boosted trees for object detection. CoRR abs/1701.01692 (2017)
10. Brazil, G., Yin, X., Liu, X.: Illuminating pedestrians via simultaneous detection & segmentation. CoRR abs/1706.08564 (2017)
11. Du, X., El-Khamy, M., Lee, J., Davis, L.S.: Fused DNN: a deep neural network fusion approach to fast and robust pedestrian detection. CoRR abs/1610.03466 (2016)
12. Carvalho, J.F., Vejdemo-Johansson, M., Pokorny, F.T., Kragic, D.: Long-term prediction of motion trajectories using path homology clusters. In: 2019 IEEE/RSJ International Conference on Intelligent Robots and Systems, IROS 2019, Macau, SAR, China, November 3–8, 2019, pp. 765–772. IEEE (2019)
13. Yoo, Y., Yun, K., Yun, S., Hong, J., Jeong, H., Choi, J.: Visual path prediction in complex scenes with crowded moving objects. In: 2016 IEEE Conference on Computer Vision and Pattern Recognition (CVPR), pp. 2668–2677 (2016)

14. Javan Roshtkhari, M., Levine, M.D.: An on-line, real-time learning method for detecting anomalies in videos using spatio-temporal compositions. Comput. Vis. Image Underst. **117**, 1436–1452 (2013)
15. Rudenko, A., Palmieri, L., Arras, K.O.: Joint long-term prediction of human motion using a planning-based social force approach. In: 2018 IEEE International Conference on Robotics and Automation, ICRA 2018, Brisbane, Australia, May 21–25, 2018, pp. 1–7. IEEE (2018)
16. Solaimanpour, S., Doshi, P.: A layered HMM for predicting motion of a leader in multi-robot settings. In: ICRA, pp. 788–793. IEEE (2017)
17. Bera, A., Kim, S., Manocha, D.: Realtime anomaly detection using trajectory-level crowd behavior learning. In: 2016 IEEE Conference on Computer Vision and Pattern Recognition Workshops (CVPRW), pp. 1289–1296 (2016)
18. Chang, M.F., et al.: Argoverse: 3D tracking and forecasting with rich maps (2019)
19. Medel, J.R., Savakis, A.E.: Anomaly detection in video using predictive convolutional long short-term memory networks. CoRR abs/1612.00390 (2016)
20. Wu, X., Zhao, W., Yuan, S.: Skeleton-based pedestrian abnormal behavior detection with spatio-temporal model in public places. In: Journal of Physics Conference Series, vol. 1518, p. 012018 (2020)
21. Hazirbas, C., Ma, L., Domokos, C., Cremers, D.: FuseNet: incorporating depth into semantic segmentation via fusion-based CNN architecture. In: Lai, S.-H., Lepetit, V., Nishino, K., Sato, Y. (eds.) ACCV 2016. LNCS, vol. 10111, pp. 213–228. Springer, Cham (2017). https://doi.org/10.1007/978-3-319-54181-5_14
22. Xu, D., Ricci, E., Yan, Y., Song, J., Sebe, N.: Learning deep representations of appearance and motion for anomalous event detection. CoRR abs/1510.01553 (2015)
23. Ha, Q., Watanabe, K., Karasawa, T., Ushiku, Y., Harada, T.: MFNet: towards real-time semantic segmentation for autonomous vehicles with multi-spectral scenes. In: 2017 IEEE/RSJ International Conference on Intelligent Robots and Systems (IROS), pp. 5108–5115 (2017)

Towards Locality Similarity Preserving to 3D Human Pose Estimation

Shihao Zhou(iD), Mengxi Jiang, Qicong Wang, and Yunqi Lei(✉)

Department of Computer Science, Xiamen University, Xiamen 361005, China
{shzhou,jiangmengxi}@stu.xmu.edu.cn,
{qcwang,yqlei}@xmu.edu.cn

Abstract. Estimating 3D human pose from an annotated or detected 2D pose in a single RGB image is a challenging problem. A successful way to address this problem is the example-based approach. The existing example-based approaches often calculate a global pose error to search a single match 3D pose from the source library. This way fails to capture the local deformations of human pose and highly dependent on a large training set. To alleviate these issues, we propose a simple example-based approach with locality similarity preserving to estimate 3D human pose. Specifically, first of all, we split an annotated or detected 2D pose into 2D body parts with kinematic priors. Then, to recover the 3D pose from these 2D body parts, we recombine a 3D pose by using 3D body parts that are split from the 3D pose candidates. Note that joints in the combined 3D parts are refined by a weighted searching strategy during the inference. Moreover, to increase the search speed, we propose a candidate selecting mechanism to narrow the original source data. We evaluate our approach on three well-design benchmarks, including Human3.6M, HumanEva-I, and MPII. The extensive experimental results show the effectiveness of our approach. Specifically, our approach achieves better performance than compared approaches while using fewer training samples.

Keywords: 3D human pose estimation · Locality similarity

1 Introduction

3D human pose estimation from a single RGB image is quite an important task in the field of computer vision with a variety of practical applications, such as human-robot interaction, virtual reality, activity recognition, and abnormal behavior detection [1–6]. Estimating 3D human pose from a single image is a typical ill-posed problem since similar projections in low dimension may be derived from different 3D poses. To alleviate this problem, a wide range of approaches with different strategies have been introduced in recent years.

Most of the existing literature apply discriminative strategy, with its representative work (*i.e.*, neural networks model) [7–11]. Generally, these learning-based approaches intend to learn a mapping between images and 3D human

I. Sato and B. Han (Eds.): ACCV 2020 Workshops, LNCS 12628, pp. 136–153, 2021.
https://doi.org/10.1007/978-3-030-69756-3_10

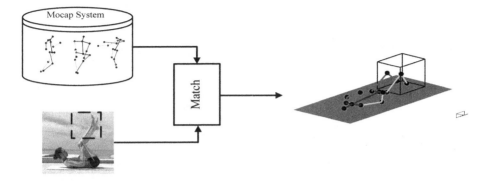

Fig. 1. Impact of global matching strategy to standard example-based approach.

poses with plenty of 2D-3D paired examples. As a result, a large number of training data are required to learn a satisfactory mapping function.

The other branch of discriminative strategy is example-based approaches [12–14]. These works usually search for a 3D human pose from the source data by calculating the global pose error rather than learning a mapping function. Such a global matching strategy may fail to capture the deformation of the local part in a human pose, as shown in Fig. 1. In this figure, the traditional example-based approach searches for the best match with minimum joints position error among the library. Moreover, this issue can be aggravated if there are insufficient source data. Intuitively, these approaches obtain a pose with a high global score, but fails in capturing the local deformations. Of course, this issue can be alleviated by augmenting more diverse samples (*e.g.*, different scenes, subjects, and actions) to the source library. However, since the deployment of capture equipment is constrained by the outdoor environment, it is difficult to obtain 3D annotations of real scenarios. Existing widely used datasets (*e.g.*, Human3.6M [15] and HumanEva-I [16]) collect 2D and 3D annotated poses performed by a few of subjects with specific actions indoors. Thus, available rich source samples are limited. Though some data augmentation strategies are proposed [17,18] for synthesizing the training examples, there is still a gap between the synthesized and complex real scenario data on the diversity [19]. As a result, in order to alleviate these issues, we propose a novel and simple example-based model to estimate the 3D pose.

Considering the fact that a 3D pose obtained by minimizing global pose error may mismatch in local parts (*i.e.*, small global pose error and relatively large error in pose local parts, as shown in Fig. 1), while two poses with huge global pose error may perfect match in a few of local parts. Inspired by these observations, we argue that combine similar local parts from different poses could obtain pose with similar parts preserving and further boost the performance. However, the traditional example-based approach usually search a single pose match using the global error, which often fails to capture similar local part. Therefore, in this paper, instead of searching for a single best match as traditional

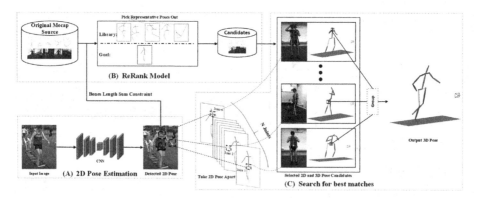

Fig. 2. Overview. Our approach can be mainly divided into three parts. The first part is about 2D pose estimation. We train a 2D detector Hourglass Network for 2D poses estimation. After that, we take both the detected 2D pose and the original mocap source into the reRank model. With a bone length sum constraint, we filter a lot of poses out, and narrow the training source into a quite small candidate set. Finally, we take the estimated 2D pose into different parts and search the best match for every single point with a weight mechanism. Then, we group different key points from all searched best matches into a whole 3D pose. Since we get a final pose from different candidates, we can nearly avoid generating predictions in Fig. 1.

example-based ways, we proposed to search for multiple candidates with similar local parts. More specifically, we split a pose into different parts and search the matched poses for each part. Then, we use key points extracted from different parts (*e.g.*, a limb or a trunk) to group a pose, as illustrated in Fig. 2.

We evaluate our approach on several datasets, including indoor 3D datasets Human3.6M [15] and HumanEva-I [16] for quantitative evaluation and outdoor 2D dataset MPII [20] for qualitative evaluation. On all the evaluation datasets, we achieve competitive results to example-based approaches and our approach even outperforms some learning-based ways.

The main contributions of our work include:

(1) In this study, to alleviate the pose local structure match issue, we propose a simple example-based approach with locality similarity preserving. This work, for the first time, introduces a novel body parts match of splitting a 2D and 3D human pose into the body parts with kinematic priors.

(2) In our approach, a source library narrowing strategy is designed to increase the searching speed, while remaining the most representative candidates.

(3) Extensive evaluated experiments are conducted on three public benchmarks. Our approach achieves superior estimation performance than considered comparison approaches. Especially, comparing with several approaches, our approach uses fewer training samples while obtaining better estimation accuracy.

2   Related Work

3D human pose estimation has been a well-studied problem these years. Traditionally, approaches proposed to solve this problem can be simply divided into two classes, generative ways [21–26] and discriminative ones [13,14,27,28]. The greatest strength for generative approaches is that they need quite a small size of the training set. While discriminative approaches generally take as input plenty of 2D-3D training samples. Moreover, discriminative ways can be classified into two subtypes, learning-based approachess [29–33] and example-based ones [34–36]. Prior to these traditional approaches, recent works raise interest in weak or unsupervised learning for wild human pose estimation [37–40]. Some other approaches combine tasks for both shape and pose estimation together [41–43].Considering the graph nature of human body, [28,44] make a great breakthrough by introducing graph operation. Although numerous methods have boosted the interest for 3D human pose estimation, we will focus our review on example-based pose estimation.

2.1   Example-based Approaches

Exampled-based approaches, also called pose retrieval methods, intended to search for the best match from the library with the goal one. Such methods benefit in fitness on anthropology from searching in training source, composed completely of the realistic human 3D pose. While other kinds of approaches (*i.e.* learning-based approaches and generative ways) are more likely to predict human poses as an outlier with less mean per joint position errors (MPJPE) [45,46]. Noted the performance of the example-based ways may not as good as learning-based approaches, but the obtained poses based on sample retrieval are usually more in line with the physical constraints. Moreover, example-based approaches never generate unreasonable pose, which is the main flaw of learning-based ways. So this topic is still worth exploring.

Recently, exampled-based works have attempted to acquire better results via introducing networks or other priors. Yasin et al. [14] utilized a dual-source approach to do 3D pose estimation from a single image and became the-state-of-art at that time. Chen and Ramanan [13] proposed to split the task 3D poses estimation apart into 2D pose estimation and matching to the 3D poses in Library. Li et al. [34] introduced a deep-network to do pose prediction auxiliary task and transferred the prediction problem into maximum-margin structured learning. However, these traditional retrieval approaches usually deal with the whole human pose, which hardly captures local deformations. Therefore, we propose to solve this by introducing a local similarity preserving strategy.

2.2   Locality Similarity Preserving for Human Pose Estimation

Many works have made efforts to keep local part preserving. For preserving local structure in the original space, Tian et al. [47] introduced Latent Variable Models to learn latent spaces for both image features and 3D poses. Fan et al. [48]

developed a block-structural pose dictionary to explicitly encourage pose local-ity in human-body modeling. Rogez and Schmid [12] selected different images patches for a 3D pose in the library via keeping their 2D pose similar. Yasin [35] learned a 3D local pose model in low Principle Component Analysis space via retrieving nearest neighbors. Zhou et al. [7] embedded kinematic function as part of the network for fully exploited geometric validity. Varolet al. [17] addressed segmentation by training a pixel-wise classifier. Tang and Wu [30] trained a part-based branching network for leaning specific feature. ke et al. [49] proposed a local refinement part for more compact limbs.

However, they are either greedy for plenty of training data, which without considering unaffordable computational cost, or aiming for local compact struc-ture in the 2D dimension [50]. Hence, our approach designs a new model for simple and fast pose estimation with keeping local similarity. Instead of sim-ply implementing constraints or synthesizing data for learning-based ways, we redesign the search rule from the whole body into local parts.

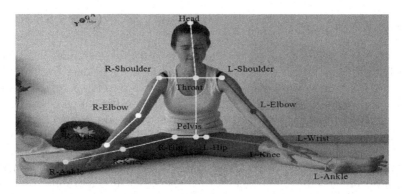

Fig. 3. Skeleton. As shown in the figure, a human pose can be presented with 15 joints and divided into various five groups. Note that, joints belong to the same group are painted with the same color. (Color figure online)

3   Background

In this section, we introduce the background knowledge of this paper, including the problem definition and the standard example-based approaches [13,14].

In this paper, we represent a human body as a skeleton with N joints. The 2D and 3D pose corresponding to the human body are denoted as $\boldsymbol{X} = \{x_i\}_{i=1}^{N} \in \mathbb{R}^{2 \times N}$ and $\boldsymbol{Y} = \{y_i\}_{i=1}^{N} \in \mathbb{R}^{3 \times N}$ respectively.

To estimate a 3D human pose from an annotated or detected 2D pose $\boldsymbol{X}$, traditional example-based ways firstly search for the best match through mini-mizing the distance between the annotated or detected 2D pose and the retrieved 2D pose $\hat{\boldsymbol{X}} = \{\hat{x}_i\}_{i=1}^{N} \in \mathbb{R}^{2 \times N}$. Normally, the distance function in 2D space can be formulated as:

$$\arg\min_{\hat{X}} \|x_i - \hat{x}_i\|_2 \tag{1}$$

where x_i and $\hat{x}_i$ denote the i-th joint position of the annotated or detected 2D pose and the retrieved pose, respectively. Then, by minimizing $Eq.\,(1)$, the traditional example-based approach obtains a best global match 2D pose whose corresponding 3D pose is the final 3D prediction. However, two poses with the global minimum error may have large local differences in some body parts as Fig. 1 shown, and the estimation performance of the traditional examples-based approach is affected since they fail to capture the local deformation.

4   Proposed Model

To alleviate the issue discussed above, we propose our solution in this paper. Specifically, firstly, we propose to represent a whole 2D human pose as different parts that satisfy human body kinematic constraints. Then, instead of searching a single match 3D pose from the source library as most of the example-based approaches, we retrieve body parts that come from different source poses. In this work, our aim is to enable our model to preserve the locality similarity of the local parts within human bodies for pose estimation.

4.1   Human Pose Split Using Kinematic Priors

Kinematic priors [7,51] interpret the interrelationship between the body components, which capture the inherent connectivity of human pose. In this paper, in order to split the 2D human pose while preserving correlation within the local structure, we provide local structural descriptions of an annotated or detected 2D human pose in terms of the kinematic priors. Specifically, considering that the arms and feet of the human body belong to different local parts, a human pose can be divided into various groups. For example, a pose with 15 joints can be divided into five sub-groups in total, including: (1) right elbow and right wrist, (2) left elbow and left wrist, (3) right knee and right ankle, (4) left knee and left ankle, and (5) head, throat, right shoulder, left shoulder, pelvis, right hip and left rip, as shown in Fig. 3. As a result, to formulate such local structure, a 2D human posture with N joint nodes can be rewritten as $X = \{P_k\}_{k=1}^{K}$, where K indicates the number of the subgroups, P_k is the specific part. Such a split strategy allows us to search for the best match through part by part.

4.2   The Locality Similarity Preserving for Human Pose

In our retrieval strategy, instead of searching the whole pose as traditional example-based approaches, we retrieve parts $\hat{P}_k$ for locality similarity preserving.

$$\arg\min_{\hat{P}_k} \|P_k - \hat{P}_k\|_2 \tag{2}$$

By minimizing $Eq.\,(2)$, we obtain the best match part $\hat{\boldsymbol{P}}_k$ for each part $\boldsymbol{P}_k$. In practice, $Eq.\,(2)$ is too strict to be satisfied due to the annotated or detected 2D pose is usually wild (*i.e.* the annotated or detected 2D pose is not included in the indoor source library). Thus, it may leads to a inferior retrieval part.

To further improve the parts retrieval performance, we aim to search each joint in the part carefully rather than a whole part. To obtain each joint in the part, we future reformulate $Eq.\,(2)$ as:

$$\underset{\hat{x}_a}{\arg\min}\ \boldsymbol{W}_k^a * \|\boldsymbol{P}_k - \hat{\boldsymbol{P}}_k\|_2,\ \forall a \in \{1, 2, ..., M_k\} \tag{3}$$

where $\hat{x}_a \in \hat{\boldsymbol{P}}_k$ denotes the query joint in the k-th part. $\boldsymbol{W}_k^a = \{\omega_k^{an}\}_{n=1}^{M_k}$ is used to increase the impact of adjacent joints of $\hat{x}_a$, which helps to find a better match [12]. M_k is the number of joints in the k-th part. Moreover, the weight ω_k^{an} is calculated by

$$\omega_k^{an} = \begin{cases} \dfrac{1}{\|x_a - x_n\|_2} + \dfrac{1}{\|\hat{x}_a - \hat{x}_n\|_2}, & a \neq n \\ 0, & a = n \end{cases} \tag{4}$$

where $\hat{x}_n$ is the n-th joint in k-th part, $n \in \{1, 2, ..., M_k\}$. x_a, x_n are the corresponding joints of $\hat{x}_a, \hat{x}_n$ in the given 2D parts. ω_k^{an} is the sum of inversely proportional to the distance between joint n-th and the a-th joint. $Eq.\,(4)$ implies that the joint closer to the a-th joint is given a higher weight.

By minimizing the $Eq.\,(3)$ M_k times, we obtain a list of M_k match joints $\{\hat{x}_a\}_{a=1}^{M_k}$. Since parts are paired (2D-3D) samples in source libary, we can acquire another list of M_k match joints in 3D space at the same time and denote as $\{\hat{y}_a\}_{a=1}^{M_k}$, which is illustrated in (B) of Fig. 2. By combining these joints $\{\hat{x}_a\}_{a=1}^{M_k}$, we obtain the final k-th part as

$$\hat{\boldsymbol{P}}_k = \{\hat{x}_a\}_{a=1}^{M_k} \tag{5}$$

Similarly, we can obtain the final k-th part in according 3D space as:

$$\hat{\boldsymbol{Q}}_k = \{\hat{y}_a\}_{a=1}^{M_k} \tag{6}$$

where $\hat{\boldsymbol{Q}}_k$ is the k-th part in 3D space, and $\hat{y}_a \in \hat{\boldsymbol{Q}}_k$ denotes the 3D coordinate of query joint in the k-th part. After retrieving the all K parts $\hat{\boldsymbol{Q}}_k$, we assemble them into one pose as the final prediction Y.

Given a source pose library $\boldsymbol{S}$, we can search the joints in $\hat{\boldsymbol{P}}_k$ and $\hat{\boldsymbol{Q}}_k$. Therefore, the speed of the workflow is largely influenced by the size of the source pose library $\boldsymbol{S}$. In order to increase the search speed, we propose a candidate mechanism to narrow the source library $\boldsymbol{S}$. By introducing a weak physical constraint, we improve the retrieval speed by selecting the representative source poses from the library $\boldsymbol{S}$. Especially, our strategy can be formulated as:

Algorithm 1. The locality similarity preserving algorithm

Input: $\boldsymbol{X}$, $\boldsymbol{\mathcal{S}}$ //2D human pose,source pose libary
Output: $\boldsymbol{Y}$ //Predicted 3D human pose
Parameter: N, K, M_k //joints of a human pose, parts of the split strategy, joints in each part

1: Calculate C by $Eq.$ (7).
2: Split $\boldsymbol{X}$ into K parts with kinematic priors.
3: **for** $k = 1$ to K **do**
4:    **for** $a = 1$ to M_k **do**
5:       Calculate $\hat{x}_a$ by $Eq.$ (3).
6:    **end for**
7:    Calculate $\hat{\boldsymbol{P}}_k$ by $Eq.$ (5).
8:    Calculate $\hat{\boldsymbol{Q}}_k$ by $Eq.$ (6).
9: **end for**
10: Calculate $\boldsymbol{Y} = \{\hat{\boldsymbol{Q}}_k\}_{k=1}^{K}$.

$$C = \arg\min_{S}(L(\boldsymbol{X}), L(\boldsymbol{S})), \ \boldsymbol{S} \in \boldsymbol{\mathcal{S}} \tag{7}$$

where $C = \{\boldsymbol{S}_1^c, \boldsymbol{S}_2^c, ..., \boldsymbol{S}_{N_c}^c\}$ represents the candidate set including a set of representative source poses, $\boldsymbol{S}_1^c$ is one of the poses, N_c is the number of candidate pose in the C. $L(\boldsymbol{X})$, $L(\boldsymbol{S})$ are the sum of bones length to the annotated or detected 2D pose and the retrieval 2D pose, and $L(\boldsymbol{X}) = \sum_{i=1}^{N-1}\|x_i - parent(x_i)\|_2$, $x_i \in \boldsymbol{X}$. $\|x_i - parent(x_i)\|_2$ is the length of the joint x_i to its parent in 2D pose $\boldsymbol{X}$. By minimizing $Eq.$ (7), we pick up poses with similar bones length sum from $\boldsymbol{\mathcal{S}}$, and these poses are combined as candidate set C. As a result, we narrow source pose library $\boldsymbol{\mathcal{S}}$ into a limited set, which accelerates the searching speed.

The complete workflow of the proposed approach is described in Algorithm 1.

5   Experiment

Since various datasets provide different human pose representation, we unify all these original poses into a single one, with N = 15 points. We quantitatively evaluate our approach on two different datasets: **Human3.6M** dataset [15], one of the largest indoor human pose datasets, and **HumanEva-I** dataset [16]. We qualitatively verify our approach on **MPII** dataset [20]. In this paper, to verity the effectiveness of the proposed approach, we conduct the experiments using annotated and detected 2D pose as input, respectively. Following the same setting of previous works [10,37,39], we apply the stacked hourglass network (SH) [52] to obtain the detected 2D pose for the fair comparison. Note that SH is pre-trained on the MPII dataset at first and then fine-tuned on the Human3.6M dataset to be in line with the literature [10,37,39].

Table 1. Mean reconstruction errors (mm) under Protocol #1 and mean per joint errors (mm) under Protocol #2 of Human3.6M. − indicates that the result for the specific action is not reported. 'GT' means ground truth (annotated) 2D input. 'DT' means detected 2D input. 'IM' means image input. † indicates learning-based approach. Best result in bold.

Protocol #1	Dir.	Disc.	Eat	Greet	Phone	Pose	Purch.	Sit	SitD.	Smoke	Photo	Wait	Walk	WalkD.	WalkT.	AVG
Rogez (IM) (NIPS'16) [12]	-	-	-	-	-	-	-	-	-	-	-	-	-	-	-	88.1
†Nie et al. (DT) (ICCV'17) [8]	62.8	69.2	79.6	78.8	80.8	72.5	73.9	96.1	106.9	88.0	86.9	70.7	71.9	76.5	73.2	79.5
Chen (DT) (CVPR'17) [13]	71.6	66.6	**74.7**	79.1	70.1	67.6	89.3	90.7	195.6	83.5	93.3	71.2	**55.8**	85.8	62.5	82.7
†Moreno-Noguer (DT) (CVPR'17) [9]	66.1	**61.7**	84.5	73.7	**65.2**	**67.2**	60.9	67.3	103.5	**74.8**	92.6	**69.6**	71.5	78.0	73.2	**74.0**
ADSA (DT) (CVPR'16) [14]	88.4	72.5	108.5	110.2	97.1	81.6	107.2	119.0	170.8	108.2	142.5	86.9	92.1	165.7	102.0	108.3
Ours (DT)	67.9	65.4	77.7	**69.3**	68.9	75.9	86.5	105.3	**81.5**	86.3	**73.6**	102.3	59.1	**69.8**	52.6	76.1
ADSA (GT)(CVPR'16) [14]	60.0	**54.7**	71.6	67.5	63.8	**61.9**	**55.7**	**73.9**	110.8	**78.9**	96.9	**67.9**	**47.5**	89.3	53.4	70.5
Ours (GT)	59.1	63.3	**70.6**	**65.1**	**61.2**	73.2	83.7	84.9	**72.7**	84.3	**68.4**	81.9	57.5	**75.1**	49.6	**70.0**
Protocol #2	Dir.	Disc.	Eat	Greet	Phone	Pose	Purch.	Sit	SitD.	Smoke	Photo	Wait	Walk	WalkD.	WalkT.	AVG
Li et al. (IM) (ICCV'15) [34]	-	149.1	109.9	136.9	-	-	-	-	-	-	179.9	-	83.6	147.2	-	135.6
†Du et al. (IM) (ECCV'16) [32]	85.1	112.7	104.9	122.1	139.1	105.9	166.2	117.5	226.9	120.0	135.9	117.7	99.3	137.4	106.5	126.5
Rogez et al. (IM) (NIPS'16) [12]	-	-	-	-	-	-	-	-	-	-	-	-	-	-	-	121.2
†Zhou et al. (IM) (ECCVW'16) [7]	91.8	102.4	97.0	98.8	113.4	90.0	**93.9**	132.2	159.0	106.9	125.2	94.4	79.0	126.0	99.0	107.3
Chen (DT) (CVPR'17) [13]	89.9	97.6	90.0	107.9	107.3	93.6	136.1	133.1	240.1	106.7	139.2	106.2	87.0	114.1	90.6	114.2
†Kudo et al. (DT) (arXiv'18) [37]	161.3	174.3	143.1	169.2	161.7	180.7	178.0	170.6	191.4	157.4	174.1	182.3	180.3	180.7	193.4	173.2
†Novotný et al. (DT) (ICCV'19) [10]	-	-	-	-	-	-	-	-	-	-	-	-	-	-	-	153.0
†Wandt et al. (DT) (CVPR'18) [39]	77.5	85.2	82.7	93.8	93.9	82.9	102.6	**100.5**	125.8	88.0	**101.0**	84.8	72.6	**78.8**	79.0	89.9
†Li et al. (IM) (ICCV'19) [11]	**70.4**	83.6	76.6	77.9	85.4	**72.3**	102.9	115.8	165.0	82.4	106.1	**74.3**	**60.2**	94.6	**70.7**	88.8
ADSA (DT) (CVPR'16) [14]	97.3	103.2	97.2	110.4	115.1	127.3	90.7	104.6	160.2	173.8	103.0	117.2	99.7	93.1	94.9	112.5
Ours (DT)	75.5	**80.0**	**75.3**	71.8	**77.0**	84.3	97.2	105.4	**101.0**	**78.1**	132.3	96.5	92.8	88.8	79.2	89.5
†Kudo et al. (GT) (arXiv'18) [37]	125.0	**44.4**	107.2	65.1	115.1	147.7	128.7	134.7	139.8	114.5	127.3	147.1	125.6	130.8	151.1	130.9
†Novotný et al. (GT) (ICCV'19) [10]	-	-	-	-	-	-	-	-	-	-	-	-	-	-	-	101.8
ADSA (GT)(CVPR'16) [14]	80.5	77.0	**72.1**	90.4	92.1	103.1	84.7	**72.0**	103.9	107.1	**87.5**	83.1	84.6	79.8	67.6	85.7
Ours (GT)	88.1	64.3	73.0	**62.1**	**84.4**	**77.1**	70.8	96.3	**89.9**	**68.8**	128.5	**62.7**	**65.9**	64.8	67.5	**79.8**

5.1 Datasets

Human3.6M. It is a large-scale indoor dataset with 3D annotations. For there are many protocols proposed these years and it is quite difficult to perform a comprehensive comparison to all the existing experiments. We followed the standard protocol according to [14] noted as Protocol #1, and Protocol #2 from [33]. Under Protocol #1, training is performed on subjects (1,5,6,7,8,9), and the valid set consists of subject (11). While the train set is made up of subjects (1,5,6,7,8) and test on the subjects (9,11) is Protocol #2.

HumanEva-I. It is a common used benchmark with annotated 3D pose. Following the same setting of pervious works [14,23,53], we take all the training sequences as input while validate on the "walking" and "jogging" actions.

MPII. It is an in-the-wild dataset with 2D annotations. For only 2D annotation is provided, we perform qualitatively validation on it.

5.2 Comparison Approaches

A dual-source approach (**ADSA**) proposed by Yasin et al. [14], which used images with annotated 2D poses and accurate 3D motion capture data to do 3D pose estimation from a single image. ADSA is a standard example-based approach, in which a single 3D pose in the source library is selected as the final best match by minimizing the global pose error. In our approach, in order to preserve the local part similarity, we combine a 3D pose by using multiple candidates that are searched via a weighted similarity mechanism. Moreover, recent three other example-based approaches [12,13,34] and several representative works [7–11,23,24,32,37,39,53,54], including generative and discriminative ways, are also considered in the comparison.

Table 2. Mean reconstruction errors (mm) under Protocol #1 of Human3.6M. Comparison to example-based approaches with different size of training data. Best result in bold.

Method	2D source	3D source	AVG
Rogez (NIPS'16) [12]	207k	190k	88.1
Chen (CVPR'17) [13]	180k	180k	82.4
ADSA (CVPR'16) [14]	64,000k	380k	108.3
Ours	375k	375k	**76.1**

5.3 Evaluation Protocols

There are two popular criterions to evaluate the pose estimation accuracy, the **per joint error** and the **reconstruction error** [21]. The **per joint error** calculates the average Euclidean distance of the estimated joints to ground truth. While the **reconstruction error** makes the same calculation but with a rigid transformation. Following the same evaluation protocols in most literature [8–14, 24,54], we take per joint error as the evaluation metric for Human3.6M Protocol #1 while reconstruction error for HumanEva-I and Human3.6M Protocol #2.

5.4 Quantitative Evaluation on Human3.6M

We first report the results of our approach and the representative works both under Protocol #1 and #2 in Table 1. It is easy to find out that there is a huge promotion between our approach and the baseline (ADSA). More specifically, under Protocol #1, we demonstrate that our pipeline on the standard benchmark with a relative error reduction greater than **30%** to the baseline (ADSA) and 13% on average to other compared approaches. Under Protocol #2, our approach also outperforms the baseline (ADSA) by 20%. Moreover, as expected our proposed approach outperforms all example-based approaches [12–14,34]. It should be noted that our approach can even beyond many learning-based approaches [7,8,32,37], and comparative to some recent representative works [10,39]. Even though our proposed approach performs slightly worse than learning-based approaches [9,39] on average, we outperform both of the two approaches on more than half categories. While [39] trains subject-wise models relying on multiple priors and [9] use more training data (400k), comparing to ours. Moreover, both [9,39] report their results after a fine-tuning process while our approach needs no hyperparameter and training stage. Noted that, all compared results are taken from original papers except for [14] under Protocol #2, which we implement with their publicly available code.

Table 3. Mean reconstruction errors (mm) on the HumanEva-I. 'GT' means ground truth (annotated) 2D input. 'DT' means detected 2D input. † indicates learning-based approach. Best result in bold.

Approaches	Walking			Jogging			AVG
	S1	S2	S3	S1	S2	S3	
Radwan et al. (DT) (ICCV'13) [24]	75.1	99.8	93.8	79.2	89.8	99.4	89.5
Wang et al. (DT) (CVPR'14) [54]	71.9	75.7	85.3	62.6	77.7	54.4	71.3
ADSA (DT)(CVPR'16) [14]	59.5	43.9	**63.4**	61.0	51.2	**55.7**	55.8
Ours (DT)	**39.1**	**21.2**	87.5	**39.1**	**48.2**	64.5	**53.2**
†Simo-Serra et al. (GT) (CVPR'13) [53]	65.1	48.6	73.5	74.2	46.6	**32.2**	56.7
Kostrikov et al. (GT) (BMVC'14) [23]	44.0	30.9	41.7	57.2	35.0	33.0	39.6
ADSA (GT)(CVPR'16) [14]	41.1	39.9	48.4	53.4	36.0	43.1	43.6
Ours (GT)	**27.3**	**13.2**	**37.6**	**44.0**	**34.1**	50.2	**34.4**

As mentioned above, we achieve quite competitive results on both two protocols. Under Protocol #1, our approach can achieve the best results for only several actions, while the average results show that our approach can be competitive with the learning-based ways [8, 9]. We attribute this to effective of our split strategy, which is easier to handle challenges of intricate actions comparing to the previous approaches, as shown in Fig. 2. In general, intricate actions, such as "SitDown", can be harder to make predictions for heavy self-occlusion than the simple ones like "Direction" or "Discuss". However, our proposed pipeline works for such challenging actions, which is difficult to traditional example-based ways [13, 14]. Under Protocol #2, beyond greater scores in most categories, we also found out that our approach meets slight degradation in some specific actions, such as "Sit" and "Photo". We argue that this may be attributed to the unrepresentative candidates. In our pipeline, we simply generate candidates with similarity bones sum, which is work for most cases. While we do not take other poses with similar shape but different scale into consideration. We believe the proposed approach could boost the performance by a margin through considering translate poses into a similar scale. Moreover, we found that actions like "Purchase" and "WalkDog" can not achieve the best results. This may due to strong occlusions of these specific categories.

Moreover, we can notice that there is no great gap after replacing the estimated 2D pose with ground truth. We argue that estimated 2D ground truth rather than reprojected one can explain this phenomenon, and also this can show that our approach still works with a slightly worse 2D estimated pose. Noted that, some recent works [28, 31] tend to take as input 2D pose reprojected via 3D pose with responding camera parameter, while this is impractical in the real world. Therefore we regard as input 2D pose the dataset provided, which is estimated and leads to less accuracy at first as ground truth and harder for making an accurate prediction. However, this input can be more close to a practical case.

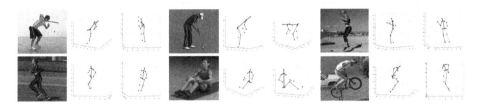

Fig. 4. Examples successes on MPII. For each example, the first column is the input image with its 2D pose, the second and the third columns are estimated 3D poses from different views.

Fig. 5. Qualitative comparison. For each example, the images from left-to-right correspond to input the image with its 2D pose, estimated 3D poses from ADSA [14] and ours, respectively. Note that the reconstruction results of the body local parts are highlighted by red cubes. (Color figure online)

We compare the results with different approaches take as input various size of the training set in Table 2. For our approach can be roughly classified into example-based ways, we are supposed to do the comparison with the same group, *e.g.*, [12–14,34]. We can observe that our approach achieves the best scores with quite a small size of data as the training source. For this, we argue the strategy to take pose into pieces does help enlarge the search space. We believe this module improves performance, but in the same way, could increase the time to do the search process. Therefore, we conduct a relevant experiment to verify our thoughts in Sect. 5.7.

5.5   Quantitative Evaluation on HumanEva-I

In this section, the results of HumanEva-I are presented. Since this dataset is quite small, few recent learning-based approaches treat it as significant as Human3.6M and conduct experiments on it [31]. Therefore, we compare representative learning-based ways (*e.g.*, [53]) with lightweight architecture to avoid overfitting. As shown in Table 3, we can outperform most works and achieve best for several sequences, except for the "Walking" and "Jogging" sequence of S3 subject. It is easy to find out many works degrade on the "Walking" sequence of subject S3, and this may due to inaccurate annotations that exist in the testing data [55]. Similar to human3.6M, due to the heavy self-occlusion, the performance of the proposed approach has also been affected ("Jogging" sequence of subject S3). Visual inspection of these results suggests that the extremely rare 3D poses are beyond the representational capacity of the model. Noted that all compared results are taken from original papers except for [14], which we implement with their publicly available code. For a fair comparison, we report the result with the same "CMU" skeleton [14].

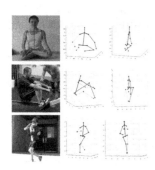

Fig. 6. Example fails on MPII. For this example, the first column is the input image with its 2D pose, the second and the third column are estimated 3D poses from different views.

Table 4. Per joint errors (mm) under Protocol #1 of Human3.6M. Comparison with various strategies for local similarity preserving. 'SH' means detected 2D input with Stacked Hourglass Networks. 'GT' means ground truth (annotated) 2D input. Best result in bold.

Strategy	MPJPE (SH)	MPJPE (GT)
Pose-Pose	110.0	101.4
Part-Part	92.5	75.2
Part-Joint	**76.1**	**70.0**

Table 5. Per joint errors (mm) under Protocol #1 of Human3.6M. Comparison with various strategies for adjacent joints weight calculation. 'SH' means detected 2D input with Stacked Hourglass Networks. 'GT' means ground truth (annotated) 2D input. Best result in bold.

Strategy	MPJPE (SH)	MPJPE (GT)
Pose	93.7	86.4
Part	**76.1**	**70.0**

5.6   Qualitative Evaluation on MPII

We also implement qualitative validation on MPII dataset. The successful results can be viewed in Fig. 4. In Fig. 5, the qualitative results from ADSA [14] and our approach are provided. It is clear observer that our approach achieve the better local part reconstruction than ADSA. Moreover, there are some failure cases are presented in Fig. 6. This may due to great depth ambiguity and severe occlusions.

5.7   Ablation Study

Different Size of Candidate Set. Our approach introduces a module called reRank to narrow the searching space S into a relatively small one C, as shown in (B) of Fig. 2. Various settings of the size of the candidate N_c for C will generate different results and take diverse seconds to complete the search process. Therefore, we do a series of experiments to find out the best parameter for the whole process. As shown in Fig. 7, the MPJPE decreases with the growth of N_c, while the time cost surge at the same time. Thus, we are not simply increasing N_c, but choose a proper value for good performance with sustainable time cost, and in this experiment, we set N_c as 35,000 for comparison in Table 1.

Different Local Similarity Preserving Strategies. We compare different strategies to estimate 3D human pose, including: **(i)** searching the whole pose via $Eq.$ (1) as the prediction (denoted as Pose-Pose); **(ii)** searching pre-defined body parts via $Eq.$ (2) and assemble the 3D pose (denoted as Part-Part); and **(iii)** searching joints via $Eq.$ (5) from different parts to reconstruct the 3D pose (denoted as Part-Joint). Our proposed strategy searching joints **(iii)** achieves **31%** improvement than searching the whole pose **(i)**, and **7%** improvement than searching parts **(ii)**, which is shown in Table 4.

Table 6. Cross-dataset validation. Mean reconstruction error (mm) on HumanEva-I given training source from Human3.6M (under Protocol #1). Best result in bold.

Size	Strategy	Walking			Jogging			AVG
		S1	S2	S3	S1	S2	S3	
30k	Pose-Pose	104.1	108.1	138.9	125.3	129.2	135.7	123.6
	Part-Joint	65.6	74.4	94.8	85.3	87.5	**88.6**	82.7
375k	Pose-Pose	77.5	76.4	107.3	91.7	96.4	105.7	92.5
	Part-Joint	**65.4**	**69.7**	**91.9**	**80.5**	**84.0**	89.2	**80.1**

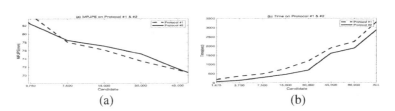

(a)   (b)

Fig. 7. Different size of Candidate Set. Figure 7 (a) and (b) show the different parameter C can impact the whole workflow on accuracy and time cost.

Different Adjacent Joints Weights W_k^a. We take different ways to calculate the weight of adjacent joints, including: **(i)** treating joints in the whole pose as neighbors in $Eq.$ (4) to calculate the similarity (denoted as Pose); **(ii)** treating joints in the pre-defined body part as neighbors to do the calculation in $Eq.$ (4)

(denoted as Part). As shown in Table 5, the results demonstrate proposed adjacent joints weights calculation can pick up the similar local parts effectively.

Cross-Dataset Validation. To further verify the generalization of the proposed approach, we quantitatively evaluate the cross-dataset ability, in which we perform accuracy evaluation on HumanEva-I given training source from Human3.6M (under Protocol #1). We take the ground-truth (annotated) 2D pose as input. Various sizes of training sources (30k and 375k) and different local similarity preserving strategies (Pose-Pose and Part-Joint) are taken into consideration. As shown in Table 6, increasing the number of training sources would boost the accuracy generally. However, different from the Pose-Pose strategy, our strategy (Part-Joint) is insensitive to the training source. More specifically, though both two strategies obtain promotion with more training sources, there is a huger gap for the Pose-Pose strategy. Moreover, with fewer training sources, our pipeline still performs superior. Noted that our strategy performs better with 30k training size on "Jogging" of S3, and this may due to the representative candidates.

6   Conclusion

In our work, we propose a simple yet effective approach to estimate 3D human pose by taking the 2D pose apart and searching a group of 3D poses to assemble a new one. Noted, our approach has dramatically reduced reliance on massive samples and improve the performance. Extensive experiments demonstrate the effectiveness of our approach. For example, under Protocol #1 of Human3.6M, we achieve a relative error reduction greater than **30%** to ADSA and **13%** on average to other compared approaches. More interesting, our approach yields competitive results with only 1% training data of ADSA.

Acknowledgement. This research was supported by the National Natural Science Foundation of China (Grant no. 61671397).

References

1. Wang, Y., et al.: 3dv: 3D dynamic voxel for action recognition in depth video. In: Proceedings of the IEEE Conference on Computer Vision and Pattern Recognition (CVPR), pp. 508–517 (2020)
2. Wang, Z., et al.: Learning diverse stochastic human-action generators by learning smooth latent transitions. In: Proceedings of the AAAI Conference on Artificial Intelligence, vol. 34, pp. 12281–12288 (2020)
3. Weng, J., Liu, M., Jiang, X., Yuan, J.: Deformable pose traversal convolution for 3D action and gesture recognition. In: European Conference on Computer Vision (ECCV), pp. 142–157 (2018)
4. Tu, Z., Li, H., Zhang, D., Dauwels, J., Li, B., Yuan, J.: Action-stage emphasized spatiotemporal VLAD for video action recognition. IEEE Trans. Image Process. **28**, 2799–2812 (2019)

5. Tu, Z., et al.: Multi-stream CNN: learning representations based on human-related regions for action recognition. Pattern Recognit. **79**, 32–43 (2018)
6. Tu, Z., Xie, W., Dauwels, J., Li, B., Yuan, J.: Semantic cues enhanced multi-modality multistream CNN for action recognition. IEEE Trans. Circ. Syst. Video Technol. **29**, 1423–1437 (2019)
7. Zhou, X., Sun, X., Zhang, W., Liang, S., Wei, Y.: Deep kinematic pose regression. In: European Conference on Computer Vision Workshops (ECCVW), pp. 186–201 (2016)
8. Nie, B.X., Wei, P., Zhu, S.: Monocular 3D human pose estimation by predicting depth on joints. In: Proceedings of IEEE International Conference on Computer Vision (ICCV), pp. 3447–3455 (2017)
9. Moreno-Noguer, F.: 3D human pose estimation from a single image via distance matrix regression. In: Proceedings of the IEEE Conference on Computer Vision and Pattern Recognition (CVPR), 1561–1570 (2017)
10. Novotny, D., Ravi, N., Graham, B., Neverova, N., Vedaldi, A.: C3dpo: canonical 3D pose networks for non-rigid structure from motion. In: Proceedings of IEEE International Conference on Computer Vision (ICCV), pp. 7688–7697 (2019)
11. Li, Z., Wang, X., Wang, F., Jiang, P.: On boosting single-frame 3D human pose estimation via monocular videos. In: Proceedings of IEEE International Conference on Computer Vision (ICCV), pp. 2192–2201 (2019)
12. Rogez, G., Schmid, C.: MoCap-guided data augmentation for 3D pose estimation in the wild. In: Advances in Neural Information Processing Systems (NIPS), pp. 3108–3116 (2016)
13. Chen, C., Ramanan, D.: 3D human pose estimation = 2D pose estimation + matching. In: Proceedings of the IEEE Conference on Computer Vision and Pattern Recognition (CVPR), 5759–5767 (2017)
14. Hashim, Y., Umar, I., Björn, K., Andreas, W., Juergen, G.: A dual-source approach for 3D pose estimation from a single image. In: Proceeding of the IEEE Conference on Computer Vision and Pattern Recognition (CVPR), pp. 4948–4956 (2016)
15. Ionescu, C., Papava, D., Olaru, V., Sminchisescu, C.: Human3.6m: large scale datasets and predictive methods for 3D human sensing in natural environments. IEEE Trans. Pattern Anal. Mach. Intell. **36**, 1325–1339 (2014)
16. Sigal, L., Balan, A., Black, M.J.: HumanEva: synchronized video and motion capture dataset and baseline algorithm for evaluation of articulated human motion. Int. J. Comput. Vision **87**, 4–27 (2010)
17. Varol, G., et al.: Learning from synthetic humans. In: Proceedings of the IEEE Conference on Computer Vision and Pattern Recognition (CVPR), pp. 109–117 (2017)
18. Chen, W., et al.: Synthesizing training images for boosting human 3D pose estimation. In: Proceedings of International Conference on 3D Vision (3DV), pp. 479–488 (2016)
19. Wu, J., et al.: Single image 3D interpreter network. In: European Conference on Computer Vision (ECCV), pp. 365–382 (2016)
20. Andriluka, M., Pishchulin, L., Gehler, P., Schiele, B.: 2D human pose estimation: New benchmark and state of the art analysis. In: Proceeding of the IEEE Conference on Computer Vision and Pattern Recognition (CVPR), pp. 3686–3693 (2014)
21. Zhou, X., Zhu, M., Pavlakos, G., Leonardos, S., Derpanis, K.G., Daniilidis, K.: Monocap: monocular human motion capture using a CNN coupled with a geometric prior. IEEE Trans. Pattern Anal. Mach. Intell. **41**, 901–914 (2019)

22. Jiang, M., Yu, Z.L., Zhang, Y., Wang, Q., Li, C., Lei, Y.: Reweighted sparse representation with residual compensation for 3D human pose estimation from a single RGB image. Neurocomputing **358**, 332–343 (2019)
23. Kostrikov, I., Gall, J.: Depth sweep regression forests for estimating 3D human pose from images. In: Proceedings of the British Machine Vision Conference (BMVC), vol. 1, page 5 (2014)
24. Radwan, I., Dhall, A., Goecke, R.: Monocular image 3D human pose estimation under self-occlusion. In: Proceedings of IEEE International Conference on Computer Vision (ICCV), pp. 1888–1895 (2013)
25. Zhou, X., Zhu, M., Leonardos, S., Daniilidis, K.: Sparse representation for 3D shape estimation: a convex relaxation approach. IEEE Trans. Pattern Anal. Mach. Intell. **39**, 1648–1661 (2017)
26. Jiang, M., Yu, Z., Li, C., Lei, Y.: SDM3d: shape decomposition of multiple geometric priors for 3D pose estimation. Neural Comput. Appl. (2020). https://doi.org/10.1007/s00521-020-05086-0
27. Sarafianos, N., Boteanu, B., Ionescu, B., Kakadiaris, I.A.: 3D human pose estimation. Comput. Vision Image Understand. **152**, 1–20 (2016)
28. Zhao, L., Peng, X., Tian, Y., Kapadia, M., Metaxas, D.N.: Semantic graph convolutional networks for 3D human pose regression. In: Proceedings of the IEEE Conference on Computer Vision and Pattern Recognition (CVPR), pp. 3425–3435 (2019)
29. Li, S., Chan, A.B.: 3D human pose estimation from monocular images with deep convolutional neural network. In: Proceedings of Asian Conference on Computer Vision (ACCV), pp. 332–347 (2014)
30. Tang, W., Wu, Y.: Does learning specific features for related parts help human pose estimation? In: Proceedings of the IEEE Conference on Computer Vision and Pattern Recognition (CVPR), pp. 1107–1116 (2019)
31. Martinez, J., Hossain, R., Romero, J., Little, J.J.: A simple yet effective baseline for 3D human pose estimation. In: Proceedings of IEEE International Conference on Computer Vision (ICCV), pp. 2659–2668(2017)
32. Du, Y., et al.: Marker-less 3D human motion capture with monocular image sequence and height-maps. In: European Conference on Computer Vision (ECCV), pp. 20–36 (2016)
33. Luo, C., Chu, X., Yuille, A.L.: Orinet: a fully convolutional network for 3D human pose estimation. arXiv:1811.04989 (2018)
34. Li, S., Zhang, W., Chan, A.B.: Maximum-margin structured learning with deep networks for 3D human pose estimation. In: Proceedings of IEEE International Conference on Computer Vision (ICCV), pp. 2848–2856 (2015)
35. Yasin, H.: Towards efficient 3D pose retrieval and reconstruction from 2D landmarks. In: Proceedings of International Symposium on Multimedia (ISM), pp. 169–176 (2017)
36. Yu, J., Hong, C.: Exemplar-based 3d human pose estimation with sparse spectral embedding. Neurocomputing **269**, 82–89 (2017)
37. Kudo, Y., Ogaki, K., Matsui, Y., Odagiri, Y.: Unsupervised adversarial learning of 3D human pose from 2D joint locations. arXiv: 1803.08244 (2018)
38. Tung, H.F., Harley, A.W., Seto, W., Fragkiadaki, K.: Adversarial inverse graphics networks: learning 2D-to-3D lifting and image-to-image translation from unpaired supervision. In: Proceedings of IEEE International Conference on Computer Vision (ICCV), pp. 4364–4372 (2017)

39. Wandt, B., Rosenhahn, B.: Repnet: weakly supervised training of an adversarial reprojection network for 3D human pose estimation. In: Proceedings of the Computer Vision and Pattern Recognition (CVPR), pp. 7782–7791 (2019)
40. Dong, J., Jiang, W., Huang, Q., Bao, H., Zhou, X.: Fast and robust multi-person 3D pose estimation from multiple views. In: Proceedings of the IEEE Conference on Computer Vision and Pattern Recognition (CVPR), pp. 7792–7801 (2019)
41. Kanazawa, A., Black, M.J., Jacobs, D.W., Malik, J.: End-to-end recovery of human shape and pose. In: Proceedings of the IEEE Conference on Computer Vision and Pattern Recognition (CVPR), pp. 7122–7131 (2018)
42. Pavlakos, G., Zhu, L., Zhou, X., Daniilidis, K.: Learning to estimate 3D human pose and shape from a single color image. In: Proceedings of the IEEE Conference on Computer Vision and Pattern Recognition (CVPR), pp. 459–468 (2018)
43. Xu, Y., Zhu, S., Tung, T.: Denserac: joint 3D pose and shape estimation by dense render-and-compare. In: Proceedings of IEEE International Conference on Computer Vision (ICCV), pp. 7760–7770 (2019)
44. Cai, Y., et al.: Exploiting spatial-temporal relationships for 3D pose estimation via graph convolutional networks. In: Proceedings of IEEE International Conference on Computer Vision (ICCV), pp. 2272–2281 (2019)
45. Kocabas, M., Karagoz, S., Akbas, E.: Self-supervised learning of 3D human pose using multi-view geometry. In: Proceedings of the IEEE Conference on Computer Vision and Pattern Recognition (CVPR), pp. 1077–1086 (2019)
46. Bogo, F., Kanazawa, A., Lassner, C., Gehler, P., Romero, J., Black, M.J.: Keep it SMPL: automatic estimation of 3D human pose and shape from a single image. In: European Conference on Computer Vision (ECCV), pp. 561–578 (2016)
47. Tian, Y., Sigal, L., La Torre, F.D., Jia, Y.: Canonical locality preserving latent variable model for discriminative pose inference. Image Vision Comput. **31**, 223–230 (2013)
48. Fan, X., Zheng, K., Zhou, Y., Wang, S.: Pose locality constrained representation for 3D human pose reconstruction. In: European Conference on Computer Vision (ECCV), pp. 174–188 (2014)
49. Sun, K., Lan, C., Xing, J., Zeng, W., Liu, D., Wang, J.: Human pose estimation using global and local normalization. In: Proceedings of IEEE International Conference on Computer Vision (ICCV), pp. 5600–5608 (2017)
50. Luo, Y., Xu, Z., Liu, P., Du, Y., Guo, J.: Combining fractal hourglass network and skeleton joints pairwise affinity for multi-person pose estimation. Multimed. Tools Appl. **78**, 7341–7363 (2019)
51. Isack, H., et al.: Repose: learning deep kinematic priors for fast human pose estimation. arXiv:2002.03933 (2020)
52. Newell, A., Yang, K., Deng, J.: Stacked hourglass networks for human pose estimation. In: European Conference on Computer Vision (ECCV), pp. 483–499 (2016)
53. Simo-Serra, E., Quattoni, A., Torras, C., Moreno-Noguer, F.: A joint model for 2D and 3D pose estimation from a single image. In: Proceeding of the IEEE Conference on Computer Vision and Pattern Recognition (CVPR), pp. 3634–3641 (2013)
54. Wang, C., Wang, Y., Lin, Z., Yuille, A.L., Gao, W.: Robust estimation of 3D human poses from a single image. In: Proceedings of the IEEE Conference on Computer Vision and Pattern Recognition (CVPR), pp. 2369–2376 (2014)
55. Pavllo, D., Feichtenhofer, C., Grangier, D., Auli, M.: 3D human pose estimation in video with temporal convolutions and semi-supervised training. In: Proceedings of the IEEE Conference on Computer Vision and Pattern Recognition (CVPR), pp. 7745–7754 (2019)

Iterative Self-distillation for Precise Facial Landmark Localization

Shigenori Nagae$^{(\boxtimes)}$ and Yamato Takeuchi

OMRON Corporation, 9-1 Kizugawadai, Kizugawa-City, Kyoto 619-0283, Japan
{shigenori.nagae,yamato.takeuchi}@omron.com

Abstract. In this paper, we propose a novel training method to improve
the precision of facial landmark localization. When a facial landmark
localization method is applied to a facial video, the detected landmarks occasionally jitter, whereas the face apparently does not move. We
hypothesize that there are two causes that induce the unstable detection:
(1) small changes in input images and (2) inconsistent annotations. Corresponding to the causes, we propose (1) two loss terms to make a model
robust to changes in the input images and (2) self-distillation training
to reduce the effect of the annotation noise. We show that our method
can improve the precision of facial landmark localization by reducing the
variance using public facial landmark datasets, 300-W and 300-VW. We
also show that our method can reduce jitter of predicted landmarks when
applied to a video.

1 Introduction

Facial landmark localization is widely used as a pre-process of many computer
vision tasks, such as face recognition [1], face reconstruction [2], and measurement of biometrics from face, such as gaze estimation [3] and heart rate estimation [4]. High precision of the facial landmark localization is required for the
reproducible results of these methods.

Although recent studies on facial landmark localization have significantly
improved its accuracy, less attention has been paid to its precision. In fact,
many landmark detectors output jittering landmarks when applied to a video
(Fig. 4). Our assumption is that the imprecise detection is caused by two factors:
(1) small changes in the input images and (2) inconsistent annotations of facial
landmark datasets.

Consider when landmark localization is carried out on a face in a video.
Generally facial images in consecutive frames are similar but slightly different.
If a landmark detector is not trained to be robust to such a small change, the
exact position of the predicted landmarks will be different among the frames
and the difference appears as jitter of the landmarks. We found that a loss term

Electronic supplementary material The online version of this chapter (https://
doi.org/10.1007/978-3-030-69756-3_11) contains supplementary material, which is
available to authorized users.

© Springer Nature Switzerland AG 2021
I. Sato and B. Han (Eds.): ACCV 2020 Workshops, LNCS 12628, pp. 154–167, 2021.
https://doi.org/10.1007/978-3-030-69756-3_11

called Equivalent Landmark Transform (ELT), which is used in semi-supervised training, can make the model robust to the changes in the input images in supervised training.

Inconsistent annotations are another cause of the unstable localization. We found that in the 300-W dataset, some faces are annotated twice and the a clear difference can be observed between the two annotations (Fig. 1). Such noisy annotations will confuse a trained model and lead to unstable landmark localization. To reduce the effect of the noise contained in the annotated landmarks, we propose training a model in an unsupervised fashion using its output as a supervision instead of the annotated landmarks after the model is trained in a supervised way.

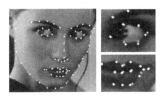

Fig. 1. In the 300-W dataset, some faces have two different annotations. An example of the two annotations are shown in the figure as the white and green circles. There are large differences between the two annotations at some landmarks (e.g., facial contours). Even at discriminative landmarks such as the tail of the eye, small differences are observed. (Color figure online)

Our contributions are: (1) present a novel training method on the basis of iterative self-distillation and two loss terms to improve the precision of the facial landmark localization, (2) show that our method can reduce the variance of the detection result in a facial dataset 300-W and actually suppress jitter of predicted landmarks on a facial video dataset 300-VW.

2   Related Works

2.1   Facial Landmark Localization

Facial landmark localization has been intensively studied for over two decades. Active Appearance Models (AAM) is an early successful method [5]. The method solves the facial landmark localization problem by modeling a whole facial shape consistent with the appearance. More recently, Cao et al. used cascaded regressors that map facial appearances to the landmark coordinates [6]. Ren et al. used local binary features to improve the performance up to 3000 FPS [7].

Since convolutional neural networks (CNNs) were introduced in this field, significant progress has been achieved [8–10]. Sun et al. used three cascaded networks to gradually improve landmark prediction [8]. Zhang et al. improved localization robustness with a multi-task learning framework, in which landmark coordinates, facial attributes and head poses are predicted simultaneously [9]. Merget et al. proposed a global context network to complement local features extracted by fully CNN [10].

Most of these studies focused on localizing facial landmarks on static images. When these detectors are applied to a video in a tracking-by-detection fashion, the detected landmarks occasionally jitter. Although some studies used video datasets to train their models [11–14], they focused on difficulties specific to faces on video, such as the change of the illumination and large changes in facial pose. The jittering problem is often ignored.

To overcome the unstable detection, Dong et al. uses a temporal constraint among successive frames in an unsupervised way to track landmarks [15]. Although this method effectively reduces the jitter of the detected landmarks, it requires a video dataset to train a network. Our training framework requires only static images, showing that the temporal information is not required for precise landmark localization.

2.2 Self-distillation

Knowledge distillation (KD) is commonly used to train a smaller student network effectively by using information acquired by a larger teacher network. Hinton et al. uses the final output of a teacher network as a soft target to train a student network [16]. Recently, Gao et al. applied the technique to facial landmark localization by transferring intermediate features of a teacher network to a smaller student network [17].

Whereas KD is used to train a small network by transferring knowledge from a larger network, student and teacher networks have the same architecture in self-distillation (SD). Furlanello et al. trained a series of students iteratively [18]. The output of a trained network in the previous iteration is used as a supervision to a student model in the next iteration. Finally, an ensemble of the students is used to obtain additional gains [18]. Interestingly, SD has been used to refine erroneous ground-truth labels [19,20]. Bagherinezhad et al. iteratively trained a student model one-by-one and observed the knowledge from the previous iteration can help to refine the noisy labels [19]. Kato et al. used the output of the trained model to recover erroneous labels or missing labels in multi-person pose estimation [20]. Similar to these studies, we used the output of a trained model to remove the annotation noise.

3   Method

We assume that the unstable landmark localization is caused by two factors: small changes in input images and the annotation noise. Corresponding to the factors, our method consists of two components: (1) two loss terms and (2) iterative self-distillation. The loss terms are introduced to make a model robust to small changes of the input images. The self-distillation technique is used to reduce the effect of the annotation noise contained in ground-truth labels.

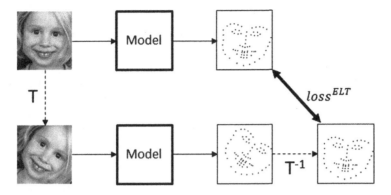

Fig. 2. An input image is transformed by an affine transformation T. The output to the transformed image is then transformed by the inverse transformation T^{-1}. The ELT loss is defined as a distance between the inversely transformed output and the output of the original image.

3.1   Loss Terms

Equivariant Landmark Transformation (ELT) Loss. When a landmark localization method is applied to a video, most successive frames are very similar but not the same. The small difference in the input images is caused by some reasons and one of them is small facial movements. If a landmark detector cannot perfectly follow the movement, a slight difference occurs between the predicted and actual landmarks. The difference will appear as jittering landmarks. We believe that this is one of the main causes of unstable landmark localization.

To address the problem, we directly force the model to follow the movement of input images by adding a loss term. Let T be an arbitrary affine transformation, and the loss is expressed as below:

$$loss^{ELT} = \frac{1}{N} \sum_n g(f(I_n), T^{-1} \otimes f(T \otimes I_n)) \tag{1}$$

where f is a trained model, $I_n \in \mathbb{R}^{h \times w \times 3}$ is the n th input image, N is the number of training images in a batch, and g is a loss function.

The loss means that if an input image is transformed by an affine transformation, the output should be equally transformed (Fig. 2). This loss is proposed by Honari et al. as Equivariant Landmark Transformation (ELT) [21]. The ELT loss is first introduced for images without annotations in semi-supervised training because the loss does not require any annotation. In this paper we found that the loss effectively reduces the variance of the detected landmarks as described in Sect. 4.

Scale Compensation Term (SCT). The ELT loss works well for making a model robust to small changes of input images. However, we found that the model's output slightly moves towards the center of images when the ELT loss is used. This may be because points near to the center of the image move less than points far from the center by affine transformation induced in calculation of the ELT loss, especially by rotation and resize transformation. Therefore, it may be easier for the model to track points near to the center. To overcome the shrinking effect of the ELT loss, we introduce a second loss term, scale compensation term (SCT). The SCT loss penalizes the change of the scale of the output landmarks through training. The SCT loss is defined as

$$loss^{SCT} = \frac{1}{N} \sum_n |\sigma(f(I_n)) - \sigma(l_n)| \qquad (2)$$

where $l_n \in \mathbb{R}^{2L}$ is the ground-truth landmarks of the n th sample and σ is a scale function that measures a scale of predicted landmarks defined as

$$\sigma_x(l_n) = \sum_i \|l_{n,i} - \overline{l_n}\|_1 \qquad (3)$$

where $l_{n,i} \in \mathbb{R}^2$ is a i th landmark in l_n and $\overline{l_n}$ is the average of $l_{n,i}$ (i.e. the centroid of the landmarks).

Overall Loss. In addition to the two loss terms, we also use a standard loss term:

$$loss^{GT} = \frac{1}{N} \sum_n g(f(I_n), l_n) \qquad (4)$$

The overall loss is the weighted sum of the loss terms:

$$loss = loss^{GT} + w^{ELT} loss^{ELT} + w^{SCT} loss^{SCT} \qquad (5)$$

where w^{ELT} and w^{SCT} are fixed coefficients. In this paper, we use $w^{ELT} = 1$ and $w^{SCT} = 1$.

3.2   Self-distillation (SD)

We found that the ground-truth labels may contain noise (Fig. 1). One source of the noise is a variance among annotators. It is common to hire multiple annotators to make a large dataset. The definition of landmarks is usually shared among the annotators, but it is difficult for the annotators to point the exactly same position in a facial image [15]. In fact, we found two different annotations to the same image in the 300-W dataset and the difference between the annotations can be observed (Fig. 1). The inconsistency of the annotation may confuse a trained model and lead to unstable detection.

We observed that a trained model with the above loss terms output landmarks more consistently than the ground-truth (Supplementary Fig. 1) and we hypothesize that the outputs of the model can be used as a ground-truth with less noise. Thus, we use a self-distillation (SD) method iteratively to reduce the effect of the annotation noise. In SD, a student model in an iteration is trained to fit the output of a teacher model trained in the previous iteration, where the student and the teacher have the same architecture. Specifically, the student model in the i th iteration is trained to minimize $loss_i^{ST}$ defined as

$$loss_i^{SD} = \frac{1}{N} \sum_n g(f_i(I_n),\ f_{i-1}(I_n)) \tag{6}$$

where f_i is a trained model in i th iteration and f_{i-1} is a model trained in the previous iteration. The parameters of f_{i-1} are fixed in the i th iteration.

The ELT loss and the SCT loss are also used in the SD part. The ELT loss in the SD is the same as the one in the supervised training part except for using f_i instead of f in Eq. 1. The SCT loss has more important role in the SD because the shrinking effect of the ELT loss becomes more significant with longer epochs by iterative training. To keep the scale of output landmarks through the iteration, we used the output of the model trained in the supervised training as a reference and is fixed throughout the SD training (Fig. 3):

$$loss_i^{SCT} = \frac{1}{N} \sum_n |\sigma(f(I_n)) - \sigma(f_0(I_n))| \tag{7}$$

where f_0 is the model trained in the supervised training part. The parameters of the model f_0 are fixed during the SD training.

The training process in the i th iteration is shown in Fig. 3. The overall loss in the i th iteration is

$$loss_i = loss_i^{SD} + w_i^{ELT} loss_i^{ELT} + w_i^{SCT} loss_i^{SCT} \tag{8}$$

where w_i^{ELT} and w_i^{SCT} are coefficients and fixed during each iteration. We use $w_i^{ELT} = w_i^{SCT} = i + 1$ for i th iteration ($i = 1$ at the first iteration).

4   Result

4.1   Dataset

We used 300-W facial landmark datasets [22–24] to train our models. The 300-W dataset re-annotated various datasets, including LFPW [25], AFW [26], HELEN [27], and XM2VTS [28] with 68 landmarks. We split the dataset into four subsets following [29]: training, common testing, challenging testing, and full testing. For facial landmark localization in video, we used the 300-VW dataset [30–32], which contains video clips of training subjects and testing subjects. We used the dataset only to evaluate our trained models. Therefore, we used only the testing clips in this paper. The test dataset contains 64 clips with 123,405 frames in total.

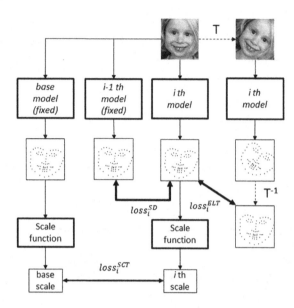

Fig. 3. Overview of our training method in the i th iteration. First, the base model is trained to minimize $loss$ in Eq. 5. The $i-1$ th model is a model trained in the previous iteration. Both models are fixed and only the i th model is trained in the i th iteration. Outputs from the $i-1$ th model are used instead of a ground truth and are compared with outputs from the i th model ($loss_i^{SD}$). Outputs from the base model are used to keep the scale of the outputs among iterations unchanged ($loss_i^{SCT}$). The input image is transformed with an affine transformation and fed into the i th model. The output is inversely transformed and compared with the output of the original image ($loss_i^{ELT}$).

4.2   Model

We tested our method with two kinds of neural networks. One is based on residual networks [33]. We removed an average pooling layer and a softmax layer at the end of the network because the average pooling removes positional information and the softmax operation is not appropriate with our regression tasks. We also change the output dimension of the last fully connected layer from 1,000 to $2L$. We denote the model as "ResNet18". The other is based on the Face Alignment Network (FAN) [34]. Although the FAN has four Hour-Glass (HG) modules, we used two HG modules to reduce the computational burden and we observed little effect on the accuracy by reducing the HG modules. We denote the models with two HG as "FAN2HG".

We used different loss function g for the two kinds of models because the outputs from the models are different. Whereas ResNet18 outputs landmark coordinates $l_o \in \mathbb{R}^{L \times 2}$, FAN2HG outputs a heatmap of the same size with the input image for each landmark. Therefore, the total output dimension of FAN2HG is $h \times w \times L$ where h and w is the height and the width of input images. We calculated the landmark coordinates as the centroids of the heatmaps as below:

$$l_{o,i} = \sum_p \frac{pH_i(p)}{\sum_{p'} H_i(p')} \tag{9}$$

where H_i is the output heatmap for the i th landmark, $l_{o,i} \in \mathbb{R}^2$ is the coordinate of the landmark and $p, p' \in \mathbb{R}^2$ is iterated over all the pixels in H_i.

We used a L2 loss function as the loss function for ResNet18. For FAN2HG, we have two kinds of output: landmark coordinates and heatmaps. We applied the L2 loss function to the both outputs. The overall loss is the sum of the values. The ground-truth heatmaps are not provided by the datasets, so we generated them from the ground-truth landmarks as below:

$$H_i^{GT}(p) = A exp(-\frac{\|p - l_i\|_2^2}{\sigma^2}) \tag{10}$$

where A and σ are constants and l_i is the i th landmark position of ground-truth. We used A = 4096 and $\sigma = 1$ in this paper.

The ResNet18 and FAN2HG models were trained with the 300-W training set for experiments using 300-W and 300-VW. First, the models were trained using ground-truth landmarks. Then six and three iterations of self-distillation were carried out for ResNet18 and FAN2HG, respectively. Note that at the beginning of each SD iteration, parameters of the student network were initialized with the parameters of the teacher network (i.e. the same parameters at the end of the previous iteration were used), because we found that initializing the student network with random values leads to worse result.

4.3   Implementation Detail

We used Chainer as a deep learning framework [35–37]. We cropped faces and resized to 256 × 256. The crop size is determined by 1.4 × the size of a bounding box of the landmarks. They were then normalized by the mean and the variance of 300-W and augmented by random flips and scaling (0.5–1.1). For the affine transformation of the ELT loss, we used a combination of random translation (±8 pixels), scaling (0.8–1.0) and rotation (±30°). The Adam optimizer was used for training with a weight decay of 5.0×10^{-4}, β_1 of 0.9, and β_2 of 0.999 with a mini-batch size of 12. The initial learning rate was 10^{-2} and decreased by one tenth at 150 and 230 epochs. The training ended at 250 epochs. In subsequent SD iterations, the learning rate was reset to 10^{-2} and decreased by one tenth at 100 and 130 epochs. The training in each SD iteration ended at 150 epochs.

4.4   Experimental Result

Evaluation Metric. To analyze the variance of detected landmarks, we calculated normalized root mean square error (NRMSE) and decomposed it into bias and standard deviation (std). Bias, std, and NRMSE are calculated as below:

$$d_{im} = \frac{l_{o,im} - l_{im}}{D_m} \tag{11}$$

$$bias = \frac{1}{LM} \| \sum_{i,m} d_{im} \|_2 \tag{12}$$

$$std = \sqrt{\frac{1}{LM} \sum_{i,m} \| d_{im} - \overline{d_{im}} \|_2^2} \tag{13}$$

$$NRMSE = \sqrt{\frac{1}{LM} \sum_{i,m} \| d_{im} \|_2^2} \tag{14}$$

where L is the number of landmarks, M is the number of test samples, $l_{o,im} \in \mathbb{R}^2$ is the i th predicted landmark of the m th sample, $l_{im} \in \mathbb{R}^2$ is the ground-truth landmark, D_m is a normalized factor (i.e., distance between outer corners of the eye) of the m th sample, and d_{im} is the normalized displacement between the predicted and the ground-truth landmarks.

Mislocalized landmarks generally have large errors and dominant effects on the NRMSE. We are interested in measuring the small vibrations of correctly localized landmarks, so we removed such incorrect detections by rejecting landmarks with a large error. Specifically, if an error of a predicted landmark $\| d_{im} \|_2 > \alpha$, the landmark is not used in calculating bias, std and NRMSE. We used $\alpha = 0.05$ in this paper but qualitatively the same results were obtained with other values of α.

Result on 300-W. We trained ResNet18 and FAN2HG models with the 300-W training set and calculated bias, std and NRMSE on the full test set. The results are shown in Table 1. In both models, our loss terms reduced the std. The iterative SD further improves the std and achieved the lowest value compared with the recent models, indicating that the FAN2HG with our method was most precise among the compared models. Although we did not observe a consistent effect of the loss terms on the bias, SD iterations decreased the bias in both cases. The loss terms and the SD decreased NRMSE in both models, indicating that our method also improves the accuracy in addition to the precision.

Result on 300-VW. To evaluate whether our method can actually reduce the jitter of landmarks, we used a video dataset, 300-VW. The FAN2HG trained with 300-W with or without our method was used as landmark detectors. An example of the detected landmarks is shown in Fig. 4. In the figure, detected landmarks during one second (25 frames) are plotted to show how the detected landmarks move during the period. Figure 4(a) and (b) shows the movement of detected landmarks was actually smaller with our method than without it. Figure 4(c) and (d) shows that the movement of the landmark is not directional, indicating that the movement is not driven by a movement of the face.

The bias, standard deviation, and NRMSE on 300-VW with FAN2HG are shown in Table 2. The proposed loss terms reduces the std but increases the

Table 1. Bias, standard deviation (std) and NRMSE of landmark localization by ResNet18 and FAN2HG on 300-W. '+ loss' means that the model was trained with the ELT and the SCT losses. '+ SD' means that SD iterations were carried out. All the values in the table are scaled by 10^3.

Method	Bias	Std	NRMSE
SAN [38]	0.87	20.8	22.6
SBR [15]	**0.50**	19.1	**19.1**
HRNet [39]	5.14	23.7	24.3
ResNet18	5.92	25.4	26.1
ResNet18 + loss	7.28	20.3	21.6
ResNet18 + loss + SD	7.07	20.1	21.3
FAN2HG	6.41	20.0	21.0
FAN2HG + loss	5.64	19.2	20.0
FAN2HG + loss + SD	4.00	**18.7**	**19.1**

Table 2. Bias, standard deviation (std) and NRMSE of landmark localization on 300-VW by FAN2HG trained with 300-W. '+ loss' means that the model was trained with the ELT and the SCT losses. '+ SD' means that SD iterations were carried out. All the values in the table are scaled by 10^3.

Method	Bias	Std	NRMSE
SAN [38]	9.20	28.0	29.5
SBR [15]	5.51	26.9	27.4
HRNet [39]	17.9	26.5	32.0
FAN2HG	4.86	26.9	27.3
FAN2HG + loss	7.62	25.6	26.7
FAN2HG + loss + SD	**4.49**	**25.3**	**25.7**

bias. Iterative SD cancelled the decrease of the bias and further improved the std, indicating that our method can improve the precision of the model. As in the case of 300-W, the FAN2HG with our method achieved the lowest std.

Ablation Study. We showed that our method decreased the variance of the localization result and reduced the jitter of predicted landmarks. Our method has three key components: iterative self-distillation, ELT loss and SCT loss. To clarify the effect of each component, we trained the FAN2HG model with the 300-W dataset with four conditions of loss terms:

- only $loss^{GT}$
- $loss^{GT}$ and $loss^{ELT}$
- $loss^{GT}$ and $loss^{SCT}$
- all losses

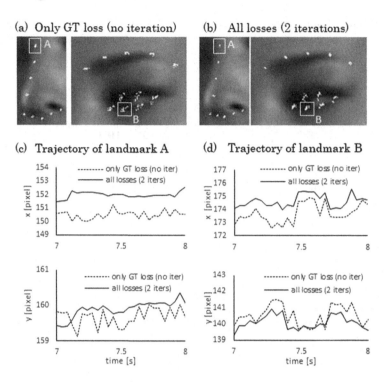

Fig. 4. An example of localization result in 300-VW. (a, b) Detected landmarks around the nose and the left eye during one second (25 frames) are plotted. The detector was FAN2HG trained with 300-W without (a) or with (b) SD iterations, ELT loss and SCT loss. (c) Trajectories of a representative landmark (specified as A in (a) and (b)). (d) Trajectories of other representative landmark (specified as B in (a) and (b)).

The result is shown in Fig. 5. When $loss^{ELT}$ was used ('GT + ELT loss' and 'all losses' in Fig. 5), the bias was initially high but rapidly decreased to values comparable to other conditions when SD is applied. In contrast, the standard deviation (std) consistently decreased by using $loss^{ELT}$. $loss^{SCT}$ slightly improves the std but we did not observe a consistent effect on the bias. SD improved the std and also the bias, but more than two iterations was harmful in the case of FAN2HG.

In conclusion:

- $loss^{ELT}$ can decrease the variance but may increases the bias.
- $loss^{SCT}$ slightly improves the variance.
- SD improves the variance. It also improves the bias with small iterations.

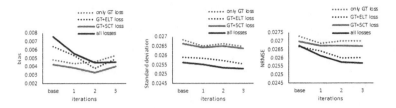

Fig. 5. Bias, standard deviation and NRMSE on 300-VW was measured. The detector was FAN2HG trained on 300-W with some combination of loss functions.

4.5   Conclusion

In this paper, we propose a novel training method to improve the stability of landmark localization. We assume that there are two causes of the instability: (1) the small changes in input images and (2) annotation noise. Corresponding to the causes, we proposed a training method using (1) ELT and SCT losses and (2) self-distillation to stabilize the localization result. We showed our method successfully reduces the variance of the localization result and suppresses the jitter of the predicted landmarks in videos.

We introduced the ELT loss to make a model robust to the small changes in input images. In calculation of the ELT loss, The affine transformation is used to mimic the small changes in input images. However, the changes in input images are caused by various reasons, such as camera noises and local facial movements, which are not considered in this paper. Incorporating these reasons to our framework might lead to a better training method and it is an interesting future direction.

References

1. Koestinger, M., Wohlhart, P., Roth, P.M., Bischof, H.:Annotated facial landmarks in the wild: a large-scale, real-world database for facial landmark localization. In: 2011 IEEE International Conference on Computer Vision Workshops (ICCV Workshops), pp. 2144–2151. IEEE (2011)
2. Gilani, S.Z., Mian, A., Eastwood, P.: Deep, dense and accurate 3D face correspondence for generating population specific deformable models. Pattern Recogn. **69**, 238–250 (2017)
3. Wang, K., Zhao, R., Ji, Q.: A hierarchical generative model for eye image synthesis and eye gaze estimation. In: Proceedings of the IEEE Conference on Computer Vision and Pattern Recognition, pp. 440–448 (2018)
4. Wang, Z., Yang, X., Cheng, K.T.: Accurate face alignment and adaptive patch selection for heart rate estimation from videos under realistic scenarios. PLoS ONE **13**, e0197275 (2018)
5. Cootes, T.F., Edwards, G.J., Taylor, C.J.: Active appearance models. IEEE Trans. Pattern Anal. Mach. Intell. **23**, 681–685 (2001)
6. Cao, X., Wei, Y., Wen, F., Sun, J.: Face alignment by explicit shape regression. Int. J. Comput. Vision **107**, 177–190 (2014). https://doi.org/10.1007/s11263-013-0667-3

7. Ren, S., Cao, X., Wei, Y., Sun, J.: Face alignment at 3000 FPS via regressing local binary features. In: Proceedings of the IEEE Conference on Computer Vision and Pattern Recognition, pp. 1685–1692 (2014)
8. Sun, Y., Wang, X., Tang, X.: Deep convolutional network cascade for facial point detection. In: Proceedings of the IEEE Conference on Computer Vision and Pattern Recognition, pp. 3476–3483 (2013)
9. Zhang, Z., Luo, P., Loy, C.C., Tang, X.: Facial landmark detection by deep multi-task learning. In: Fleet, D., Pajdla, T., Schiele, B., Tuytelaars, T. (eds.) ECCV 2014. LNCS, vol. 8694, pp. 94–108. Springer, Cham (2014). https://doi.org/10.1007/978-3-319-10599-4_7
10. Merget, D., Rock, M., Rigoll, G.: Robust facial landmark detection via a fully-convolutional local-global context network. In: Proceedings of the IEEE Conference on Computer Vision and Pattern Recognition, pp. 781–790 (2018)
11. Liu, H., Lu, J., Feng, J., Zhou, J.: Two-stream transformer networks for video-based face alignment. IEEE Trans. Pattern Anal. Mach. Intell. **40**, 2546–2554 (2017)
12. Sánchez-Lozano, E., Tzimiropoulos, G., Martinez, B., De la Torre, F., Valstar, M.: A functional regression approach to facial landmark tracking. IEEE Trans. Pattern Anal. Mach. Intell. **40**, 2037–2050 (2017)
13. Belmonte, R., Ihaddadene, N., Tirilly, P., Bilasco, I.M., Djeraba, C.: Video-based face alignment with local motion modeling. In: 2019 IEEE Winter Conference on Applications of Computer Vision (WACV), pp. 2106–2115. IEEE (2019)
14. Guo, M., Lu, J., Zhou, J.: Dual-agent deep reinforcement learning for deformable face tracking. In: Ferrari, V., Hebert, M., Sminchisescu, C., Weiss, Y. (eds.) ECCV 2018. LNCS, vol. 11214, pp. 783–799. Springer, Cham (2018). https://doi.org/10.1007/978-3-030-01249-6_47
15. Dong, X., Yu, S.I., Weng, X., Wei, S.E., Yang, Y., Sheikh, Y.: Supervision-by-registration: An unsupervised approach to improve the precision of facial landmark detectors. In: Proceedings of the IEEE Conference on Computer Vision and Pattern Recognition, pp. 360–368 (2018)
16. Hinton, G., Vinyals, O., Dean, J.: Distilling the knowledge in a neural network. arXiv preprint arXiv:1503.02531 (2015)
17. Gao, P., Lu, K., Xue, J.: EfficientFAN: deep knowledge transfer for face alignment. In: Proceedings of the 2020 International Conference on Multimedia Retrieval, pp. 215–223 (2020)
18. Furlanello, T., Lipton, Z., Tschannen, M., Itti, L., Anandkumar, A.: Born-again neural networks. In: International Conference on Machine Learning, pp. 1602–1611 (2018)
19. Bagherinezhad, H., Horton, M., Rastegari, M., Farhadi, A.: Label refinery: improving imagenet classification through label progression. arXiv preprint arXiv:1805.02641 (2018)
20. Kato, N., Li, T., Nishino, K., Uchida, Y.: Improving multi-person pose estimation using label correction. arXiv preprint arXiv:1811.03331 (2018)
21. Honari, S., Molchanov, P., Tyree, S., Vincent, P., Pal, C., Kautz, J.: Improving landmark localization with semi-supervised learning. In: Proceedings of the IEEE Conference on Computer Vision and Pattern Recognition, pp. 1546–1555 (2018)
22. Sagonas, C., Antonakos, E., Tzimiropoulos, G., Zafeiriou, S., Pantic, M.: 300 faces in-the-wild challenge: database and results. Image Vis. Comput. **47**, 3–18 (2016)
23. Sagonas, C., Tzimiropoulos, G., Zafeiriou, S., Pantic, M.: 300 faces in-the-wild challenge: the first facial landmark localization challenge. In: Proceedings of the IEEE International Conference on Computer Vision Workshops, pp. 397–403 (2013)

24. Sagonas, C., Tzimiropoulos, G., Zafeiriou, S., Pantic, M.: A semi-automatic methodology for facial landmark annotation. In: Proceedings of the IEEE Conference on Computer Vision and Pattern Recognition Workshops, pp. 896–903 (2013)
25. Belhumeur, P.N., Jacobs, D.W., Kriegman, D.J., Kumar, N.: Localizing parts of faces using a consensus of exemplars. In: CVPR 2011, pp. 545–552. IEEE (2011)
26. Ramanan, D., Zhu, X.:Face detection, pose estimation, and landmark localization in the wild. In: 2012 IEEE Conference on Computer Vision and Pattern Recognition, pp. 2879–2886. IEEE (2012)
27. Le, V., Brandt, J., Lin, Z., Bourdev, L., Huang, T.S.: Interactive facial feature localization. In: Fitzgibbon, A., Lazebnik, S., Perona, P., Sato, Y., Schmid, C. (eds.) ECCV 2012. LNCS, vol. 7574, pp. 679–692. Springer, Heidelberg.(2012). https://doi.org/10.1007/978-3-642-33712-3_49
28. Messer, K., Matas, J., Kittler, J., Luettin, J., Maitre, G.: XM2VTSDB: the extended m2vts database. In: Second International Conference on Audio and Video-Based Biometric Person Authentication, vol. 964, pp. 965–966 (1999)
29. Zhu, S., Li, C., Change Loy, C., Tang, X.: Face alignment by coarse-to-fine shape searching. In: Proceedings of the IEEE Conference on Computer Vision and Pattern Recognition, pp. 4998–5006 (2015)
30. Chrysos, G.G., Antonakos, E., Zafeiriou, S., Snape, P.: Offline deformable face tracking in arbitrary videos. In: Proceedings of the IEEE International Conference on Computer Vision Workshops, pp. 1–9 (2015)
31. Shen, J., Zafeiriou, S., Chrysos, G.G., Kossaifi, J., Tzimiropoulos, G., Pantic, M.: The first facial landmark tracking in-the-wild challenge: benchmark and results. In: Proceedings of the IEEE International Conference on Computer Vision Workshops, pp. 50–58 (2015)
32. Tzimiropoulos, G.: Project-out cascaded regression with an application to face alignment. In: Proceedings of the IEEE Conference on Computer Vision and Pattern Recognition, pp. 3659–3667 (2015)
33. He, K., Zhang, X., Ren, S., Sun, J.: Deep residual learning for image recognition. In: Proceedings of the IEEE Conference on Computer Vision and Pattern Recognition, pp. 770–778 (2016)
34. Bulat, A., Tzimiropoulos, G.: How far are we from solving the 2D & 3D face alignment problem? (and a dataset of 230,000 3d facial landmarks). In: Proceedings of the IEEE International Conference on Computer Vision, pp. 1021–1030 (2017)
35. Tokui, S., et al.: Chainer: a deep learning framework for accelerating the research cycle. In: Proceedings of the 25th ACM SIGKDD International Conference on Knowledge Discovery & Data Mining, pp. 2002–2011. ACM (2019)
36. Tokui, S., Oono, K., Hido, S., Clayton, J.: Chainer: a next-generation open source framework for deep learning. In: Proceedings of Workshop on Machine Learning Systems (LearningSys) in The Twenty-ninth Annual Conference on Neural Information Processing Systems (NIPS) (2015)
37. Akiba, T., Fukuda, K., Suzuki, S.: ChainerMN: scalable distributed deep learning framework. In: Proceedings of Workshop on ML Systems in The Thirty-first Annual Conference on Neural Information Processing Systems (NIPS) (2017)
38. Dong, X., Yan, Y., Ouyang, W., Yang, Y.: Style aggregated network for facial landmark detection. In: Proceedings of the IEEE Conference on Computer Vision and Pattern Recognition, pp. 379–388 (2018)
39. Wang, J., et al.: Deep high-resolution representation learning for visual recognition. IEEE Trans. Pattern Anal. Mach. Intell. (2020)

Multiview Similarity Learning for Robust Visual Clustering

Ao Li$^{(\boxtimes)}$ ⓘ, Jiajia Chen ⓘ, Deyun Chen ⓘ, and Guanglu Sun ⓘ

School of Computer Science and Technology, Harbin University of Science
and Technology, Harbin, China
`dargonboy@126.com, 544953065@qq.com,`
`{chendeyun,sunguanglu}@hrbust.edu.cn`

Abstract. Multiview similarity learning aims to measure the neighbor
relationship between each pair of samples, which has been widely used
in data mining and presents encouraging performance on lots of applications. Nevertheless, the recent existing multiview similarity learning
methods have two main drawbacks. On one hand, the comprehensive
consensus similarity is learned based on previous fixed graphs learned
from all views separately, which ignores the latent cues hidden in graphs
from different views. On the other hand, when the data are contaminated with noise or outlier, the performance of existing methods will
decline greatly because the original true data distribution is destroyed.
To address the two problems, a Robust Multiview Similarity Learning
(RMvSL) method is proposed in this paper. The contributions of RMvSL
includes three aspects. Firstly, the recent low-rank representation shows
some advantage in removing noise and outliers, which motivates us to
introduce the data representation via low-rank constraint in order to generate clean reconstructed data for robust graph learning in each view.
Secondly, a multiview scheme is established to learn the consensus similarity by dynamically learned graphs from all views. Meanwhile, the consensus similarity can be used to propagate the latent relationship information from other views to learn each view graph in turn. Finally, the
above two processes are put into a unified objective function to optimize
the data reconstruction, view graphs learning and consensus similarity
graph learning alternatively, which can help to obtain overall optimal
solutions. Experimental results on several visual data clustering demonstrates that RMvSL outperforms the most existing methods on similarity
learning and presents great robustness on noisy data.

1 Introduction

Similarity learning is a key and fundamental issue in data mining and machine
learning, which not only is used to measure the data neighbor relationship, but
also plays an important role in constructing the graph from data. Graph is
a significant structure for presenting the relationships among large amount of
objects, which is consist of nodes and their edges. Each node of graph corre-
sponds to a object, and the edges represent the linkage among objects. By the

© Springer Nature Switzerland AG 2021
I. Sato and B. Han (Eds.): ACCV 2020 Workshops, LNCS 12628, pp. 168–183, 2021.
https://doi.org/10.1007/978-3-030-69756-3_12

graph, the global and local data structure can be obtained simultaneously, which is widely used in many data analysis based applications. Thanks for the distinguished ability in relationship measurement, a good partition will be produced by the learned graph, which shows encouraging performance on clustering task. Therefore, graph-based clustering approaches attract increased attention and are widely studied in recent years. It is worth noting that similarity structure is at the core of graph-based clustering, so the quality of graph learning is crucial to final performance. In a direct way, the gaussian kernel can be used to construct a graph by computing exponential Euclidean distance between instances, such as k nearest neighbor graph. Nevertheless, the direct way would be failed because the data within similar distribution may suffer large gap in Euclidean space due to external outlier. To considered structural similarity on distribution, a l_1-graph learning method is proposed in [1] with the help of data representation model, where each weight edge of graph is learned by the l_1-norm based reconstruction from instances. Motivated by l_1-graph, Fang et al. [2] seek the non-negative low-rank representation from data for subspace clustering, which can be used to explore the more meaningful similarity relationship by exploiting subspace structure. From the viewpoint of probability, Nie et al. [3] propose a probabilistic graph learning approach based on adaptive neighbors. In their method, all the instances are connected to each other as a neighbor with a probability s_{ij}, which should be large if the distance between instance x_i and x_j is small while verse vice. So, the obtained s_{ij} can be utilized as a well similarity measurement. To earn extra robustness, Kang et al. [4] introduces the robust principle component analysis (RPCA) to probabilistic graph, where the similarity probability is assigned based on latent data component.

Nevertheless, the above graph learning methods are designed in a single view. More recently, multiview learning breeds a new paradigm in machine learning, which aims to establish the learning model from different views. In essence, multiview data often presents in our life. For example, an image can be characterized by different types of features, a piece of news can be described by different languages, et al. Hence, thanks for the ability in utilizing the redundant and complementary information across views, multiview learning has been widely studied in many literatures [5–11]. Specially, many multiview graph learning approaches are proposed and applied to clustering problem. Multiview graph learning aims to seek a more accurate fusion similarity graph from the cues in all views. And then, the corresponding clustering algorithm can be implemented on the learned fusion graph to obtain low-dimensional data representation for final cluster results. In [12], a multiple graph learning method is presented to share a same cluster indicator matrix. Also, a auto-weighted scheme is adopt to assign the optimal parameter-free weight for each view graph. Nie et al. [13] supposes that graphs from all views are closed to each other, and they would like to seek the centroid of graphs by exploring the Laplacian rank constraint as the fusion graph. Meanwhile, the self-weighted scenario with hyperparameter is designed to compute the confidences for different graphs. Inspired by it, to further make full use of data correlation among views, Zhan et al. [14] proposes a concept

Factorization-based multivew clustering. In this approach, affinity weights from different views are correlated to jointly learn the unified graph matrix. Assuming that the underlying cluster structure is shared across multiple views, a common graph is learned by minimizing the disagreement between each pair of views in [15]. Moreover, the rank constraints are also imposed on each Laplacian matrix for further improving the graph consensus. Similarly, a multi-graph fusion scheme is proposed in [16] for multiview clustering, which enforces the fusion graph to be approximated to original graph from each view but with an explicit cluster structure. Although these multiview graph learning methods have shown promising results and proved to be effective in clustering, they are still limited in two aspects. Firstly, the noise and outlier influence are ignored when individual graph is learned from each view, by which the true similarity structure in graph might be damaged. Secondly, the graphs from each view are isolated pre-learned and fixed when multiview learning is implemented, which leads that the complementary information cross views is not considered sufficiently. Finally, the robust modeling, individual view graph learning and common graph learning are not be well unified to improve each other. Hence, the correlations among these three aspects are not utilized efficiently.

Towards the mentioned problems, in this paper, we proposes a robust multi-view similarity learning method for visual data clustering, which can be used in many practical applications, such as image annotation, visual pattern analysis and so on. Thanks for the help of robust representation and multiview learning, RMvSL can learn an effective graph with reliable similarity relationship from robust multiple graphs. The contributions of RMvSL are summaried as follows.

1) Data representation model is introduced to seek a robust space via low-rank constraint, by which the corrupted data can be recovered with linear combination of instances. That is, what we want is to learn the view graphs from the robust compensated counterpart of corrupted data.
2) A consensus similarity graph learning scheme will be designed in a multivew way to cover multiple cues from all views, in which the latent true similarity can be well explored in the learned consensus graph. Meanwhile, the complementary information can be propagated among views by common graph when the individual view graph is constructed.
3) We put the data compensation model, view graphs and consensus graph learning into a unified framework where variables can be jointly optimized to benefit each other and obtain the overall optimal solutions with a developed numerical algorithm.

The comprehensive idea of our proposed approach is shown in Fig. 1. The joint learning framework is presented, in which the iterations are conducted among the data reconstruction, view graph and consensus graph learning. And then, the spectral clustering will be implemented on the learned consensus graph to get the final cluster structures.

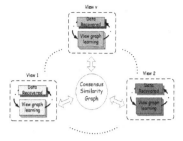

Fig. 1. The joint learning framework of RMvSL.

2   Related Works

2.1   Graph Learning Revisited

As illustrated in [3], learning similarity with adaptive neighbors is a kind of easy and elegant graph constructed method. In this branch, it emphasizes that the connectivity of neighbor is a useful strategy for similarity learning. Inspired by it, the neighbors of instance can be connected to each other with a probability. Assuming s_{ij} denotes the probabilistic similarity between two instance x_i and x_j respectively, the similarity with adaptive neighbors can be formulated as follows.

$$\min_{s_i^T \mathbf{1}=1, 0 \leq s_{ij} \leq 1} \sum_{j=1}^{n} \|x_i - x_j\|_2^2 s_{ij} \tag{1}$$

where $\|\cdot\|_2$ denotes the l_2-norm. The Eq. (1) is established with an intuitive assumptions that samples closed to each other should have a large connected probability s_{ij}. In other words, the s_{ij} has a negative correlation to the distance of each pair of instances. In addition, to avoid the trivial solution, an additional l_2-norm based constraint is imposed on the similarity matrix in Eq. (1) as follows.

$$\min_{s_i \in \mathbb{R}^{n \times 1}} \sum_{i,j}^{n} Tr(XLX^T) + \lambda \|S\|_F^2 \tag{2}$$

$$s.t. \forall i, s_i^T \mathbf{1} = 1, 0 \leq s_{ij} \leq 1$$

where $L = D - S$ denotes the graph Laplacian matrix, and D is a diagonal matrix with $D_{ii} = 0.5 \left(\sum S_{i*} + \sum S_{*i} \right)$.

By Eq. (2), the larger probability will be assigned to the closed instances pair, and the obtained S can be used as the similarity matrix to present the neighbor relationship among data. Next, the spectral clustering can be implemented on S to obtain the final cluster result. Moreover, many other applications based on the above graph learning model are further studied in literatures [17–19].

Nevertheless, from Eq. (2), we can see that the similarity probability is learned from raw data directly. It means that the true similarity relationship may be damaged when the data are contaminated with noise or outlier, which will destroy the latent distribution property belongs to clean data. Meanwhile, in practice, it is easy to collect more noisy data while few clean data in the open visual environment. So, a more robust learning method is urgently expected to obtain high quality graph with noisy data recently.

2.2 Self-representation via Low-Rank Constraint

Low-rank representation (LRR) is a typical representation model to learn subspace structure hidden among data, which attracts much attention and has shown promising performance in data recovery problem [20]. In general, the LRR can be formulated as

$$\min_Z \|Z\|_* + \tau \|E\|_l$$
$$s.t. X = DZ + E \tag{3}$$

where $X \in R^{d \times n}$ denotes the data matrix including n instances with d dimensions, D is the dictionary used to span the space for X, and Z is the representation coefficient matrix. E denotes the residual matrix for modeling kinds of typical noise with different norm, such as Frobenius norm for Gaussian noise, l_1 norm for random corruptions, et al. $\|\cdot\|_*$ and $\|\cdot\|_l$ indicate the nuclear norm and l norm respectively.

Specially, if the dictionary is replaced by data matrix X itself, the above formulation are changed into a self-representation based LRR problem as follows.

$$\min_Z \|Z\|_* + \tau \|E\|_l$$
$$s.t. X = XZ + E \tag{4}$$

With the Eq. (4), the intrinsic subspace structure of data is uncovered, and the robust recovered data may be reconstructed from two aspects. On one hand, thank for Z, a nearly clean counterpart of raw data are recovered by the linear combination of all the data as XZ, and much useful detail can be reconstructed by the instances mainly drawn from the same subspace due to the block diagonal character of Z. Meanwhile, the damaged latent distribution hidden in data would be complementary with the help of combination of other instances. On the other hand, the error matrix E can also remove extra noise influence existed in the noisy raw data. So, if the LRR is introduced into the neighbor graph learning model to form a unified framework that learns the recovered data and similarity probability alternately, a more robustness similarity graph will be constructed to improve the subsequent clustering results.

3   The Proposed Framework of RMvSL

Multiview graph learning aims to learn a fusion graph from the different views, which can cover all the useful cues from all views and obtain further performance improvement. For the most existing multiview graph learning approaches, they generally focus on the elegant graphs construction model and their corresponding multiview learning mechanism but ignore the data themselves, especially for uncertain noisy data. In the open environment, the data are easily contaminated with kinds of noise, which will damage the original data distribution greatly and lead to awful similarity measurement obviously. However, the data quality restoration are not sufficiently and especially considered in the most existing multiview graph learning approaches.

Motivated by the above considerations, the details of our proposed RMvSL will be discussed in this section. Firstly, we will talk about how to learn the similarity probability with the cleaning recovered data to earn a reliable graph matrix from the noisy raw data in each view. And then, a multiview scheme is designed to not only learn the consensus fusion graph but also propagate the cues from other views for each single view graph learning.

For each view v, the robust graph learning method is formulated as

$$\min_{Z^v, E^v, S^v} \|Z^v\|_* + \alpha \|E^v\|_l + \beta \sum_{i,j} \|X^v Z_i^v - X^v Z_j^v\|_2^2 S_{ij}^v + \gamma \|S^v\|_F^2 \tag{5}$$

$$s.t. X^v = X^v Z^v + E^v, S^v \mathbf{1} = \mathbf{1}, 0 \leq S_{ij}^v \leq 1$$

where $X^v \in R^{d \times n}$ denotes the data in v-th view, $Z^v \in R^{n \times n}$ and Z_i^v present the low-rank representation matrix and its i-th column. α, β and γ are the positive parameters to balance the constrained terms. By our proposed framework in Eq. (5), the view graph $S^v \in R^{n \times n}$ is learned from the compensated data $X^v Z_i^v$ with LRR model instead of the noisy raw data X_i^v, which can further preserve true data distribution when the similarity probability S_{ij}^v is assigned. In turn, the learned similarity graph S_{ij}^v can also be used to guide representation matrix (Z^v) learning, which helps to obtain more rational recovered data. The two mutual parts will benefit each other during the iterations. Furthermore, different from the direct two-stage operation that separates the data recovery and graph learning, we put them into a unified framework. It should be noted that graph presents the neighbor relationship between pair of instances, which is believed to be capable of providing useful correlation information when the subspace representation is learned. Hence, the unified framework will improve the two variables each other effectively. That is, in this framework, the more accurate subspace structure will be learned for better data recovering, and it helps to obtain a higher quality view graph with nearly clean compensated data in turn.

As mentioned above, to fuse cues from other views, a consensus graph learning scheme is designed in a multiview manner, which makes the view graphs and their consensus fusion version to be mutually optimized by jointly learning. Assuming G is the consensus fusion graph, which can be solved with the following weighted learning model as

$$\min_G \sum_{v=1}^m w_v \|G - S^v\|_F^2 \tag{6}$$

$$s.t. \forall_i, g_{ij} \geq 0, \mathbf{1}^T \mathbf{g}_i = 1$$

where m denotes the total number of views, and g_i presents the i-th row of G. Similarly, to keep the probability property, the nonnegative and normalization constraints are enforced on G in Eq. (6). w_v is the weighted constraint coefficient for the v-th view, which is computed automatically in our designed multiview graph learning scheme. Naturally, a compact form is set to be the reciprocal of distance between pair of graphs as $w_v = \frac{1}{2\sqrt{\|G-S^v\|_F^2}}$. In practice, the weighted coefficient for each view is determined during the iteration dynamically to present stronger adaption than the fixed situation.

Incorporating Eq. (6) into Eq. (5), our proposed RMvSL model is turned into

$$\min_{Z,E,S,G} \sum_{v=1}^{m} \left(\|Z^v\|_* + \alpha\|E^v\|_l + \beta \sum_{i,j} \|X^v Z_i^v - X^v Z_j^v\|_2^2 S_{ij}^v \right.$$

$$\left. + \gamma\|S^v\|_F^2 + w_v\|G - S^v\|_F^2 \right) \tag{7}$$

$$s.t. X^v = X^v Z^v + E^v, S^v \mathbf{1} = \mathbf{1}, 0 \le S_{ij}^v \le 1, v = 1, ..., m,$$

$$\forall i, g_{ij} \ge 0, \mathbf{1}^T \mathbf{g}_i = 1$$

Based on the comprehensive formulation in RMvSL, the view subspace structure Z^v, view graph S^v and consensus graph G are jointly learned in a unified framework, resulting in the alternating optimizing among the recovered data and graph learning to improve each variable. That is to say, by Eq. (7), we establish a multiview graph learning framework with dynamic data compensation mechanism, which could mutually learn the recovered data, view graphs and fusion graph and show some advantage on similarity learning for uncertain noisy data. Furthermore, with the proposed unified framework, each variable is not optimized in isolation during iteration. For example, when the subspace structure Z^v is updated, the view graph S^v is involved to provide relationships between data, which is benefit to intrinsic structure exploration and data reconstruction. Similarly, for each view graph leaning, the cues from all other views are propagated by the fusion graph G. So, the overall optimal solutions can be obtained by our proposed framework, which is believed to learn a more robust and high quality graph finally. In the next section, a numerical algorithm is developed to solve the objective function in RMvSL efficiently.

3.1 Numerical Algorithm

Solving all the variables at once is a challenging problem because they are coupled in objective function. So, we adopt an alternating scheme to optimize variables iteratively. That is, we updates only one variable once while fixing others.

Equation (7) can be solved by using the inexact augmented Lagrange multiplier method (IALM). Introducing the auxiliary variable J, it can be changed into:

$$\min_{Z,E,S,G} \sum_{v=1}^{m} \left(\|Z^v\|_* + \alpha\|E^v\|_l + \beta Tr(X^v Z^v L^v (X^v Z^v)^T) \right.$$

$$\left. + \gamma\|S^v\|_F^2 + w_v\|G - S^v\|_F^2 \right) \tag{8}$$

$$s.t. X^v = X^v Z^v + E^v, S^v \mathbf{1} = \mathbf{1}, 0 \le S_{ij}^v \le 1, v = 1, ..., m,$$

$$\forall i, g_{ij} \ge 0, \mathbf{1}^T \mathbf{g}_i = 1, Z^v = J^v.$$

Removing the equality constraints on X^v and Z^v, we can get the following Lagrangian functions:

$$\min_{Z,E,S,J,G} \sum_{v=1}^{m} \left(\|J^v\|_* + \alpha\|E^v\|_l + \beta Tr(X^v Z^v L^v (X^v Z^v)^T) + \gamma\|S^v\|_F^2 \right.$$
$$\left. + w_v\|G - S^v\|_F^2 + \|X^v - X^v Z^v - E^v - \frac{R_1^v}{\mu}\|_F^2 + \|Z^v - J^v - \frac{R_2^v}{\mu}\|_F^2 \right) \tag{9}$$

where μ is penalty parameter. R_1 and R_2 are Lagrange multipliers. Next, the variables in (9) will be solved one by one.

Updating E^v for Each View:

$$\min_{E^v} \alpha\|E^v\|_l + \|X^v - X^v Z^v - E^v - \frac{R_1^v}{\mu}\|_F^2 \tag{10}$$

For different types of noise, the error matrix can be solved with the corresponding l-norm based optimization. For example, if l_1 norm is enforced, then $E_{ij} = (|t_{ij}| - \alpha/\mu)^+ \cdot sign(t_{ij})$, where $T = X^v - X^v Z^v - \frac{R_1^v}{\mu}$.

Updating Z^v for Each View:

$$\min_{Z} \|Z^v - J^v - \frac{R_2}{\mu}\|_F^2 + \beta Tr(X^v Z^v L^v (X^v Z^v)^T) + \|X^v - X^v Z^v - E^v - \frac{R_1^v}{\mu}\|_F^2 \tag{11}$$

Setting its derivative to be zero, we have

$$2\beta Z^v L^v + ((X^v)^T X^v)^{-1}(2I + 2(X^v)^T X^v)Z^v = ((X^v)^T X^v)^{-1}D \tag{12}$$

where $D = 2J^v + 2\frac{R_1}{\mu} + 2(X^v)^T X^v - 2(X^v)^T E^v - 2(X^v)^T \frac{R_2}{\mu}$, and I denotes the identity matrix. Equation (12) is a standard Sylvester equation, which can be solved by existing method [21].

Updating J^v for Each View:

$$\min_{J} \|J^v\|_* + \|Z^v - J^v - \frac{R_2^v}{\mu}\|_F^2 \tag{13}$$

Equation (13) is a nuclear norm based minimization problem, which can be easily solved by using the singular value shrinkage operator proposed in [22].

Updating Graph S^v for Each View: To make it more clear, the S^v is solved in a row-wise way by

$$\min_{s_i} \sum_{j=1}^{n} \frac{\beta}{2}\|o_i - o_j\|^2 s_{ij} + \gamma s_{ij}^2 + (g_{ij} - s_{ij})^2 \tag{14}$$

where $O = X^v Z^v$ is the recovered data by linear combination of raw data, and o_i denotes its i-th column. Assuming $f_{ij} = \|o_i - o_j\|^2 - \frac{4}{\beta} g_{ij}$, Eq. (14) can be converted to

$$\min_{s_i^T \mathbf{1}=1, 0 \le s_{ij} \le 1} \left\| s_i + \frac{\beta}{4\gamma} f_i \right\|^2 \tag{15}$$

Equation (15) have a natural sparse solution due to the neighborhood connections. Therefore, we only need to update its first k neighborhoods. In other words, s_i has k positive entries. The Lagrangian function of Eq. (15) can be expressed as follows:

$$\Gamma(s_i, \eta, \zeta) = \left\| s_i + \frac{\beta}{4\gamma_i} f_i \right\|^2 - \eta(s_i^T \mathbf{1} - 1) - \zeta_i^T s_i \tag{16}$$

where η and $\zeta \in R^{n \times 1}$ are Lagrangian multipliers. By the Karush-Kuhn-Tucker condition, it produces $s_i = ((\eta/2) - (\beta f_i / 4\eta))_+$.

Ranking f_i in ascending order, we have

$$\begin{cases} s_{ik} = \frac{\eta}{2} - \frac{\beta f_{ik}}{4\gamma_i} > 0 \\ s_{i,k+1} = \frac{\eta}{2} - \frac{\beta f_{i,k+1}}{4\gamma_i} \in 0 \\ s_i^T \mathbf{1} = \sum_{j=1}^{k} (\frac{\eta}{2} - \frac{\beta f_{ij}}{4\gamma_i}) = 1 \end{cases} \tag{17}$$

After inferring, we can get

$$\begin{cases} s_{ij} = \frac{f_{i,k+1} - f_{ij}}{k f_{i,k+1} - \sum_{r=1}^{k} f_{ir}}, j \le k \\ \gamma_i = \frac{\beta}{4}(k f_{i,k+1} - \sum_{j=1}^{k} f_{ij}) \\ \eta = \frac{2}{k} + \frac{\beta}{2k\gamma_i} \sum_{j=1}^{k} f_{ij} \end{cases} \tag{18}$$

Updating Consensus Similarity Graph G: When the above variables of all views are solved, the consensus fusion graph G can be optimized by

$$\min_{G} \sum_{v=1}^{m} w_v \|G - S^v\|_F^2 \tag{19}$$
$$s.t. g_i^T \mathbf{1} = 1, g_{ij} > 0$$

The solution can be obtained by solving its each row separately as

$$\min_{g_i^T \mathbf{1}=1, g_{ij}>0} \sum_{v=1}^{m} \|w_v(g_i - s_i^v)\|_F^2 \tag{20}$$

Equation (20) can be solved by an effective iterative scheme proposed in [23].

In summary, the developed scheme for solving our proposed objective function of **RMvSL** in Eq. (7) is listed in **Algorithm 1** as follows.

Algorithm 1

Input: Multiview Data $\{X^v\}_{v=1}^m$, Parameters α, β, γ, μ;

Initialize: $E^v = 0$, $Z^v = \left(X^{vT}X^v + 10^{-3}I\right)^{-1}X^{vT}X^v$, $R_1^v = R_2^v = 0$;

S^v is initialized with normalized Euclidean distance;

while not converged do

for each view do

1. Update J^v using Eq.(14);
2. Update Z^v according to Eq.(13);
3. Update S^v using Eq.(18);
4. Update E^v by Eq.(11);
5. $R_1^v = R_1^v + \mu(X^vZ^v + E^v - X^v)$
6. $R_2^v = R_2^v + \mu(J^v - Z^v)$

end for

7. Update G according to Eq.(20), and $w_v = \dfrac{1}{2\sqrt{\|G - S^v\|_F^2}}$

until convergence

Output: Similarity graph G

---

4   Experiments

In this part, we will verify the performance of our RMvSL model via visual clustering experiments on four datasets, including two facial datasets, a digital handwritten dataset and a object dataset. The detailed description and setting for each dataset will be elaborated later. Our proposed RMvSL is compared with six recent similarity graph learning approaches, including two single-view based approaches and four multiview based approaches: classical k-nearest neighbor Graph Construction with Gaussian distance (GCG), Robust Graph Clustering (RGC) [4], Graph-based Multi-view Clustering (GMC) [24], Multi-Graph Fusion for Multi-view Spectral Clustering (GFSC) [16], parameter-free Auto-weighted Multiple Graph Learning (AMGL) [12], Self-weighted Multiview Clustering with Multiple Graphs (SwMC) [13], Multiview concept factorization (MVCF) [14] and Multiview consensus graph clustering (MCGC) [15]. Among them, RGC and GCG are single-view based methods that are implemented on each view and the average indicator of all views are taken as the final clustering performance. To be balanced, the same spectral clustering are implemented on the learned graphs from comparison methods, and the obtained clustering indicators are used to evaluate their performance. Three classical clustering evaluation indicators (accuracy (ACC), normalized mutual information (NMI) and purity (PUR)) are used in our experiments.

4.1   Datasets

ORL/YALE Dataset: The **ORL** contains 400 facial images from 40 different people. **YALE** contains total 165 facial images from 15 people, each of whom has 11 photos under different lighting, posture and expression. We extract three kinds of features for these datasets that are gray intensity, Local Binary Pattern (LBP) [25] and Gabor feature [26] as three views for each subject.

COIL20 Dataset: COIL-20 is a collection of gray-scale images, including 20 objects taken from different angles. The image is taken every 5° and size of 32 × 32, and each object has 72 images, a total of 1440 images. We directly divide them into four different views according to the taken degree: V1[0°, 85°], V2[90°, 175°], V3[180°, 265°], V4[270°, 360°]. In essence, by this setting, each object has 18 individuals, meanwhile each individual has 4 views from different taken degree interval.

UCI-Handwritten (UCI-H) Dataset: UCI-H contains ten kinds of hand-written images, which are 0, 1, 2, ..., 9. Each subject has 200 samples, so the entire dataset has 2000 samples and 10 clusters. We select 500 samples and use three views for each instance. The first view is the profile-correlation feature with 216 dimensions, the second is the Fourier-coefficient with 76 dimensions, and the third is morphological feature with 6 dimensions.

4.2   Experimental Results and Analysis

In our experiments, there are two types of representative noise will be introduced to valid the robust performance of comparison methods under noisy visual data, which are Gaussian noise and feature missing respectively. The test on each dataset are repeated five times and the average indicator performance are reported. We add the Gaussian noise to normalized view feature with different variances with interval 0.01, and take l_2 norm as the constraint on error matrix E. The average clustering results and their variances in parenthesis are shown in Table 1, 2, 3 and 4. The best results are highlighted in boldface. Specially, only the variance larger than 10^{-3} is presented while others are shown as $\rightarrow 0$. For feature missing, we randomly select part of the features of data in each view to be zero. Meanwhile, the l_1 norm is taken to be enforced on E. The average clustering results under different missing rates are plotted in Fig. 2, 3, 4 and 5.

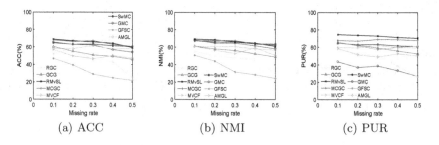

(a) ACC   (b) NMI   (c) PUR

Fig. 2. Clustering results on **YALE** with missing rate.

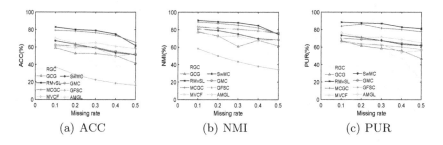

Fig. 3. Clustering results on **ORL** with missing rates.

From the results in tables, we can see that, when the data are contaminated with Gaussian noise, our proposed method outperforms other compared methods on visual clustering task in almost all experiments, which demonstrates the robust performance of RMvSL. In particular, thank for the introduced low-rank representation model, the view graph can be learned from the clean reconstructed data, which will help to obtain a better similarity metric with nearly true data distribution.

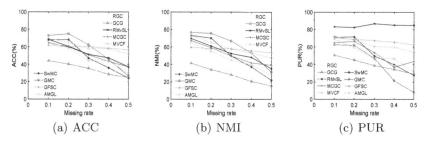

Fig. 4. Clustering results on **UCI-H** with missing rates.

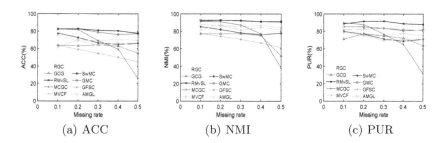

Fig. 5. Clustering results on **COIL20** with missing rates.

Table 1. Clustering results on **UCI-H** (%).

	Metric	SwMC	GMC	GFSC	AMGL	RGC	GCG	MCGC	MVCF	RMvSL
σ = 0.02	ACC	70.56(→0)	**74.24**(→0)	39.16(→0)	72.88(0.008)	35.66(→0)	40.27(→0)	72.36(0.005)	16.64(→0)	73.12(0.004)
	NMI	75.24(→0)	**76.10**(→0)	42.98(→0)	75.63(0.003)	33.78(→0)	36.31(→0)	70.02(0.003)	3.65(→0)	75.85(0.003)
	PUR	75.08(→0)	60.48(→0)	73.22(→0)	75.64(0.006)	36.33(→0)	51.20(→0)	72.52(0.004)	16.52(→0)	**88.68**(→0)
σ=0.03	ACC	69.96(0.005)	**73.80**(0.002)	38.75(0.0004)	69.56(0.005)	34.49(→0)	44.60(0.0008)	73.12(→0)	15.88(→0)	72.84(0.001)
	NMI	72.83(0.001)	**76.19**(0.001)	40.21(0.0004)	73.27(0.003)	34.40(→0)	38.66(0.0007)	70.48(→0)	3.49(→0)	72.95(0.002)
	PUR	74.16(0.002)	58.94(0.006)	75.16(→0)	73.16(0.003)	40.13(→0)	50.07(→0)	73.6(→0)	16.52(→0)	**86.80**(→0)
σ=0.04	ACC	69.36(0.003)	72.51(→0)	32.80(0.002)	**74.92**(0.002)	36.67(→0)	37.34(0.003)	67.48(0.002)	17.0(→0)	73.24(0.001)
	NMI	70.69(0.001)	**74.35**(→0)	33.32(0.002)	72.09(0.002)	32.85(→0)	30.89(→0)	63.07(0.001)	4.66(→0)	73.92(0.005)
	PUR	71.96(0.001)	57.61(0.002)	81.20(0.001)	74.92(0.004)	51.34(→0)	43.87(→0)	67.76(0.001)	18.2(→0)	**87.28**(→0)
σ=0.05	ACC	67.88(→0)	**69.20**(0.006)	31.66(0.001)	66.28(0.004)	32.66(→0)	39.87(→0)	66.16(0.007)	17.8(→0)	68.16(0.003)
	NMI	67.96(→0)	70.35(0.004)	30.72(0.001)	65.76(0.002)	30.10(→0)	30.13(→0)	62.67(0.003)	5.22(→0)	67.27(0.004)
	PUR	71.44(→0)	45.36(0.012)	80.55(0.002)	67.84(0.003)	38.26(→0)	47.40(→0)	67.52(0.003)	19.0(→0)	**88.88**(→0)
σ=0.06	ACC	60.56(0.003)	58.72(0.005)	29.33(0.001)	**61.25**(0.003)	32.34(→0)	33.60(→0)	62.72(0.003)	15.4(→0)	60.94(0.002)
	NMI	61.16(0.002)	60.06(0.001)	27.60(0.001)	58.69(0.001)	27.37(→0)	25.17(→0)	56.27(0.002)	3.58(→0)	58.81(0.002)
	PUR	65.08(0.003)	30.42(0.007)	82.51(0.002)	64.92(0.002)	41.00(→0)	40.93(→0)	63.04(0.003)	15.8(→0)	**89.80**(0.001)

For experiments on feature missing, RMvSL achieves almost best performance among comparison methods on all evaluation indicators in Yale, ORL and COIL20. Only for UCI-H dataset, the GMC and AMGL are a little better than our proposed method on ACC and NMI under a few of missing rates. Nevertheless, the competitive results can still show advantage of RMvSL on robustness under feature missing situation.

4.3   Parameters Sensitivity and Convergence

There are total five parameters α, β, γ, and μ in our proposed method. We set $\alpha = 1/\sqrt{(max\,(d,n))}$ for all the experiments according to [22]. As for γ, it can be computed with Eq. (18) during the iteration. So, the unknown parameters are just β and μ. To evaluate their influence on the clustering performance, we take the ORL as testing dataset. The experimental results under missing rate 0.3 are drawn with varying parameters. As shown in Fig. 6, the two unknown parameters are not quite sensitive to three evaluation indicators. Moreover, the experimental results in Sect. 4.2 on each dataset are obtained with the empirical parameters setting in this way. In addition, $max\,\{\|X^v Z^v + E^v - X^v\|_\infty, \|J^v - Z^v\|_\infty\}$ is taken as the criteria to evaluate the convergence in each iteration. The convergence curves with increasing iterative step on two selected datasets are shown in Fig. 7, from which it is confirmed that our proposed method converges fast within a few of iterations.

Table 2. Clustering results on **YALE** (%).

	Metric	SwMC	GMC	GFSC	AMGL	RGC	GCG	MCGC	MVCF	RMvSL
σ = 0.02	ACC	52.97(0.001)	54.30(0.001)	47.96(→0)	55.03(0.001)	48.28(→0)	41.82(→0)	**60.36**(→0)	41.82(0.006)	58.30(0.003)
	NMI	56.94(0.002)	58.88(→0)	52.10(→0)	55.87(0.001)	50.66(→0)	49.96(→0)	**59.85**(→0)	45.96(0.007)	59.52(0.001)
	PUR	54.67(0.001)	29.21(0.003)	64.62(→0)	56.85(0.002)	51.92(→0)	48.69(→0)	64.48(→0)	44.85(0.005)	**70.55**(→0)
σ=0.03	ACC	43.15(0.002)	32.85(0.006)	43.67(→0)	44.91(→0)	33.73(→0)	29.29(→0)	**46.12**(0.002)	33.94(→0)	44.91(0.001)
	NMI	45.13(0.002)	42.43(0.001)	44.75(→0)	**47.78**(0.003)	33.73(→0)	32.60(→0)	47.26(0.003)	41.25(0.001)	43.47(0.001)
	PUR	44.00(0.002)	7.67(→0)	63.90(→0)	49.21(0.003)	37.57(→0)	31.92(→0)	49.33(0.002)	35.15(→0)	**67.52**(→0)
σ=0.04	ACC	25.58(→0)	25.82(0.001)	27.07(→0)	28.79(→0)	23.23(→0)	24.24(→0)	31.87(0.001)	27.27(0.001)	**28.94**(→0)
	NMI	28.59(0.001)	30.75(0.001)	28.26(→0)	**30.34**(→0)	27.59(0.009)	26.57(0.009)	31.61(0.002)	31.31(0.001)	29.33(0.02)
	PUR	27.88(→0)	3.52(→0)	64.05(→0)	32.97(→0)	26.46(→0)	25.66(→0)	62.90(0.002)	29.70(0.001)	**75.39**(0.002)
σ=0.05	ACC	21.24(→0)	19.06(→0)	16.10(→0)	21.15(→0)	21.41(→0)	18.61(→0)	20.96(0.001)	22.42(→0)	**21.32**(→0)
	NMI	23.28(→0)	23.11(→0)	21.60(→0)	**25.89**(→0)	25.83(→0)	25.59(→0)	20.16(→0)	26.71(→0)	23.46(→0)
	PUR	24.48(→0)	0.72(→0)	64.40(→0)	28.85(→0)	23.03(→0)	25.86(→0)	22.66(0.001)	24.45(→0)	**77.33**(→0)
σ=0.06	ACC	17.82(→0)	18.42(→0)	15.89(→0)	**21.30**(→0)	19.62(→0)	20.61(→0)	17.33(→0)	18.18(→0)	20.84(→0)
	NMI	18.1(→0)	**24.71**(→0)	21.37(→0)	22.57(→0)	21.20(→0)	20.43(→0)	17.45(→0)	18.72(→0)	22.86(→0)
	PUR	18.91(→0)	0.36(→0)	63.76(→0)	23.76(→0)	23.84(→0)	22.42(→0)	18.66(→0)	20.00(→0)	**79.52**(→0)

Table 3. Clustering results on **ORL** (%).

	Metric	SwMC	GMC	GFSC	AMGL	RGC	GCG	MCGC	MVCF	RMvSL
$\sigma = 0.02$	ACC	51.55(→0)	49.10(→0)	41.17(→0)	59.50(→0)	43.58(→0)	37.50(→0)	70.00(→0)	20.00(0.03)	**72.65**(0.002)
	NMI	65.76(→0)	73.88(→0)	61.58(→0)	76.96(→0)	61.64(→0)	43.33(→0)	80.50(→0)	37.56(0.03)	**83.37**(0.007)
	PUR	60.60(→0)	59.30(→0)	68.47(→0)	65.95(→0)	46.67(→0)	44.08(→0)	75.85(→0)	21.5(0.04)	**82.05**(0.001)
$\sigma=0.03$	ACC	33.40(→0)	36.25(→0)	38.54(→0)	49.15(0.002)	31.25(→0)	26.25(→0)	46.70(0.001)	47.00(→0)	**50.80**(→0)
	NMI	41.91(0.001)	60.89(→0)	59.68(→0)	**64.69**(0.001)	51.59(→0)	47.29(→0)	56.78(0.002)	64.67(→0)	62.16(→0)
	PUR	40.15(→0)	45.70(→0)	68.34(→0)	54.85(0.001)	34.08(→0)	30.83(→0)	52.60(0.002)	52.50(→0)	**75.05**(→0)
$\sigma=0.04$	ACC	19.05(→0)	18.70(→0)	18.51(→0)	**28.50**(→0)	17.92(→0)	20.00(→0)	22.00(→0)	32.00(0.01)	28.15(→0)
	NMI	23.71(→0)	37.42(→0)	33.16(→0)	**42.92**(→0)	36.47(→0)	37.98(→0)	29.84(→0)	48.54(→0)	40.79(→0)
	PUR	21.25(→0)	23.60(→0)	67.04(→0)	31.20(→0)	23.08(→0)	22.83(→0)	24.55(→0)	95.75(0.001)	76.40(→0)
$\sigma=0.05$	ACC	13.75(0.008)	14.00(→0)	13.82(→0)	18.40(→0)	16.66(→0)	16.42(→0)	14.80(→0)	**19.5**(→0)	18.45(→0)
	NMI	19.32(→0)	30.29(→0)	38.23(→0)	35.87(→0)	**39.87**(→0)	37.50(→0)	22.90(→0)	37.46(→0)	38.68(→0)
	PUR	15.20(→0)	16.35(→0)	65.59(→0)	20.80(→0)	19.34(→0)	22.00(→0)	16.10(→0)	24.50(→0)	**77.00**(→0)
$\sigma=0.06$	ACC	12.50(→0)	13.20(→0)	12.87(→0)	17.05(→0)	16.34(→0)	15.92(→0)	13.25(→0)	**17.00**(→0)	16.94(→0)
	NMI	18.61(0.001)	31.03(→0)	33.42(→0)	34.60(→0)	39.69(→0)	32.02(→0)	21.38(→0)	32.06(→0)	**36.30**(→0)
	PUR	13.90(→0)	14.80(→0)	64.73(→0)	17.90(→0)	44.84(→0)	19.58(→0)	14.30(→0)	18.50(→0)	**77.45**(→0)

Table 4. Clustering results on **COIL20** (%).

	Metric	SwMC	GMC	GFSC	AMGL	RGC	GCG	MCGC	MVCF	RMvSL
$\sigma = 0.02$	ACC	77.15(→0)	82.22(→0)	64.22(→0)	66.56(0.002)	76.80(→0)	65.07(→0)	**84.61**(→0)	59.28(0.001)	83.50(0.001)
	NMI	85.56(→0)	92.71(→0)	77.52(→0)	83.37(→0)	84.51(→0)	77.68(→0)	**93.50**(→0)	76.45(→0)	91.09(→0)
	PUR	80.55(→0)	85.17(→0)	82.22(→0)	74.50(0.001)	80.07(→0)	73.75(→0)	90.11(→0)	66.67(0.001)	**90.72**(→0)
$\sigma=0.03$	ACC	66.60(0.002)	77.94(→0)	62.31(→0)	64.00(→0)	77.08(→0)	59.16(→0)	**79.66**(→0)	63.06(→0)	79.06(0.002)
	NMI	78.36(→0)	90.86(→0)	76.13(→0)	83.20(→0)	84.66(→0)	70.81(→0)	90.50(→0)	75.81(→0)	**91.13**(→0)
	PUR	71.55(→0)	81.17(→0)	82.77(→0)	72.06(0.001)	80.83(→0)	63.68(→0)	**90.11**(→0)	66.67(→0)	89.78(→0)
$\sigma=0.04$	ACC	62.25(0.003)	72.00(0.002)	57.95(→0)	64.56(0.003)	71.88(→0)	46.88(→0)	72.27(→0)	61.44(→0)	**72.33**(→0)
	NMI	73.20(0.002)	89.07(→0)	73.31(→0)	80.72(→0)	80.37(→0)	58.14(→0)	**89.38**(→0)	70.44(→0)	86.92(→0)
	PUR	66.65(0.002)	78.17(0.001)	83.06(→0)	70.89(→0)	77.03(→0)	53.33(→0)	85.50(→0)	63.72(→0)	**85.83**(→0)
$\sigma=0.05$	ACC	57.25(0.001)	56.78(→0)	51.68(→0)	57.89(0.001)	52.56(→0)	35.76(→0)	58.72(0.002)	50.61(→0)	**59.17**(→0)
	NMI	67.92(→0)	**76.45**(→0)	72.04(→0)	74.73(→0)	64.94(→0)	45.18(→0)	75.21(→0)	61.75(→0)	73.78(0.001)
	PUR	61.65(0.002)	63.11(→0)	70.5(→0)	64.22(0.001)	58.68(→0)	40.91(→0)	73.66(0.001)	54.44(→0)	**76.44**(→0)
$\sigma=0.06$	ACC	50.35(→0)	46.33(0.002)	46.68(→0)	**48.61**(0.004)	42.15(→0)	28.68(→0)	48.00(0.001)	42.0(0.005)	47.22(→0)
	NMI	63.73(→0)	67.98(→0)	69.22(→0)	64.98(0.002)	54.98(→0)	35.58(→0)	**70.35**(0.001)	52.56(0.003)	61.77(→0)
	PUR	57.10(→0)	50.39(0.001)	66.61(→0)	56.33(0.002)	46.87(→0)	32.15(→0)	60.22(0.001)	44.78(0.004)	**75.50**(→0)

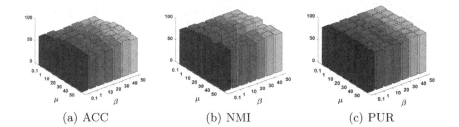

(a) ACC   (b) NMI   (c) PUR

Fig. 6. The influence of β and μ on clustering performance of **ORL**

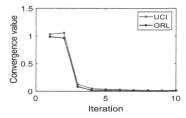

Fig. 7. Convergence curves on two selected datasets.

5   Conclusions

This paper presents a novel multiview similarity graph learning method named RMvSL for visual clustering task. With a unified objective function, RMvSL can optimize the view graphs, consensus fusion graph and constructed data alternately, which can greatly improve each other during the iteration. By introducing the low-rank self-representation model, the recovered data with distribution compensation can be obtained to learn the true similarity between pairs of instances, which shows more advantage than raw data and help to construct meaningful graphs. With the learned fusion graph, spectral clustering can be implemented to obtain the final cluster results. Extensive experiments on four visual datasets demonstrate the superior and robustness of RMvSL compared with various existing excellent similarity graph learning approaches.

Acknowledgments. This work was supported in part by the National Natural Science Foundation of China under Grant 62071157, University Nursing Program for Young Scholars with Creative Talents in Heilongjiang Province under Grant UNPYSCT-2018203, Natural Science Foundation of Heilongjiang Province under Grant YQ2019F011, Fundamental Research Foundation for University of Heilongjiang Province under Grant LGYC2018JQ013, and Postdoctoral Foundation of Heilongjiang Province under Grant LBH-Q19112.

References

1. Cheng, B., Yang, J., Yan, S., Fu, Y., Huang, T.S.: Learning with l1-graph for image analysis. IEEE Trans. Image Process. **19**, 858–66 (2010)
2. Fang, X., Xu, Y., Li, X., Lai, Z., Wong, W.K.: Robust semi-supervised subspace clustering via non-negative low-rank representation. IEEE Trans. Syst. **46**, 1828–1838 (2016)
3. Nie, F., Wang, X., Huang, H.: Clustering and projected clustering with adaptive neighbors. In: ACM SIGKDD International Conference on Knowledge Discovery and Data Mining, pp. 977–986 (2014)
4. Kang, Z., Pan, H., Hoi, S.C.H., Xu, Z.: Robust graph learning from noisy data. IEEE Trans. Cybern. **50**, 1833–1843 (2019)
5. Liu, M., Luo, Y., Tao, D., Xu, C., Wen, Y.: Low-rank multi-view learning in matrix completion for multi-label image classification. In: National Conference on Artificial Intelligence, pp. 2778–2784 (2015)
6. Wang, Q., Dou, Y., Liu, X., Lv, Q., Li, S.: Multi-view clustering with extreme learning machine. Neurocomputing **214**, 483–494 (2016)
7. Zhang, C., Hu, Q., Fu, H., Zhu, P., Cao, X.: Latent multi-view subspace clustering. In: Computer Vision and Pattern Recognition, pp. 4333–4341 (2017)
8. Li, B., et al.: Multi-view multi-instance learning based on joint sparse representation and multi-view dictionary learning. IEEE Trans. Pattern Anal. Mach. Intell. **39**, 2554–2560 (2017)
9. Jing, X., Wu, F., Dong, X., Shan, S., Chen, S.: Semi-supervised multi-view correlation feature learning with application to webpage classification. In: Proceedings of the Thirty-First AAAI Conference on Artificial Intelligence, pp. 1374–1381 (2017)

10. Wu, J., Lin, Z., Zha, H.: Essential tensor learning for multi-view spectral clustering. IEEE Trans. Image Process. **28**, 5910–5922 (2019)
11. Xing, J., Niu, Z., Huang, J., Hu, W., Zhou, X., Yan, S.: Towards robust and accurate multi-view and partially-occluded face alignment. IEEE Trans. Pattern Anal. Mach. Intell. **40**, 987–1001 (2018)
12. Nie, F., Li, J., Li, X.: Parameter-free auto-weighted multiple graph learning: a framework for multiview clustering and semi-supervised classification. In: International Joint Conference on Artificial Intelligence, pp. 1881–1887 (2016)
13. Nie, F., Li, J., Li, X.: Self-weighted multiview clustering with multiple graphs. In: International Joint Conference on Artificial Intelligence, pp. 2564–2570 (2017)
14. Zhan, K., Shi, J., Wang, J., Wang, H., Xie, Y.: Adaptive structure concept factorization for multiview clustering. Neural Comput. **30**, 1080–1103 (2018)
15. Zhan, K., Nie, F., Wang, J., Yang, Y.: Multiview consensus graph clustering. IEEE Trans. Image Process. **28**, 1261–1270 (2019)
16. Kang, Z., et al.: Multi-graph fusion for multi-view spectral clustering. Knowl. Based Syst. **189**, 102–105 (2020)
17. Zhang, L., Zhang, Q., Du, B., You, J., Tao, D.: Adaptive manifold regularized matrix factorization for data clustering. In: International Joint Conference on Artificial Intelligence, pp. 3399–3405 (2017)
18. Du, L., Shen, Y.: Unsupervised feature selection with adaptive structure learning. In: ACM SIGKDD International Conference on Knowledge Discovery and Data Mining, pp. 209–218 (2015)
19. Cai, S., Kang, Z., Yang, M., Xiong, X., Peng, C., Xiao, M.: Image denoising via improved dictionary learning with global structure and local similarity preservations. Symmetry **10**, 167 (2018)
20. Liu, G., Lin, Z., Yan, S., Sun, J., Yu, Y., Ma, Y.: Robust recovery of subspace structures by low-rank representation. IEEE Trans. Pattern Anal. Mach. Intell. **35**, 171–184 (2013)
21. Bartels, R.H., Stewart, G.W.: Solution of the matrix equation ax + xb = c [f4]. Commun. ACM **15**, 820–826 (1972)
22. Candes, E.J., Li, X., Ma, Y., Wright, J.: Robust principal component analysis. J. ACM **58**, 11 (2011)
23. Duchi, J.C., Shalevshwartz, S., Singer, Y., Chandra, T.D.: Efficient projections onto the l1-ball for learning in high dimensions. In: International Conference on Machine Learning, pp. 272–279 (2008)
24. Wang, H., Yang, Y., Liu, B.: GMC: graph-based multi-view clustering. IEEE Trans. Knowl. Data Eng. **32**, 1116–1129 (2019)
25. Ojala, T., Pietikainen, M., Maenpaa, T.: Multiresolution gray-scale and rotation invariant texture classification with local binary patterns. IEEE Trans. Pattern Anal. Mach. Intell. **24**, 971–987 (2002)
26. Lades, M., et al.: Distortion invariant object recognition in the dynamic link architecture. IEEE Trans. Comput. **42**, 300–311 (1993)

Real-Time Spatio-Temporal Action Localization via Learning Motion Representation

Yuanzhong Liu, Zhigang Tu$^{(\boxtimes)}$, Liyu Lin, Xing Xie, and Qianqing Qin

Wuhan University, Wuhan 430079, China
{yzliu.me,tuzhigang,linliyu,Qqqin}@whu.edu.cn, rd_xiex@163.com

Abstract. Most state-of-the-art spatio-temporal (S-T) action localization methods explicitly use optical flow as auxiliary motion information. Although the combination of optical flow and RGB significantly improves the performance, optical flow estimation brings a large amount of computational cost and the whole network is not end-to-end trainable. These shortcomings hinder the interactive fusion between motion information and RGB information, and greatly limit its real-world applications. In this paper, we exploit better ways to use motion information in a unified end-to-end trainable network architecture. First, we use knowledge distillation to enable the 3D-Convolutional branch to learn motion information from RGB inputs. Second, we propose a novel motion cue called short-range-motion (SRM) module to enhance the 2D-Convolutional branch to learn RGB information and dynamic motion information. In this strategy, flow computation at test time is avoided. Finally, we apply our methods to learn powerful RGB-motion representations for action classification and localization. Experimental results show that our method significantly outperforms the state-of-the-arts on dataset benchmarks J-HMDB-21 and UCF101-24 with an impressive improvement of ~8% and ~3%.

1 Introduction

Many breakthroughs have been witnessed in spatio-temporal action localization [1–6] mainly due to the progress of deep learning, and the emergence of large datasets [7–9]. Spatio-temporal action localization aims to not only identify the action category, but also localize it in both time and space. Inspired by the success of object detection, most current spatio-temporal action localization methods utilize the popular object detection frameworks [10–17], action bounding boxes are predicted in frame-level, then a dynamic linking strategy is used to generate human action tubes.

The key to accurately recognize human actions in videos is to effectively use both RGB information and motion information [6,18–20], however, the 2D CNNs can not well model motion information. Many approaches have been proposed to extract motion. Using additional inputs, e.g. RGB difference and optical flow,

© Springer Nature Switzerland AG 2021
I. Sato and B. Han (Eds.): ACCV 2020 Workshops, LNCS 12628, pp. 184–198, 2021.
https://doi.org/10.1007/978-3-030-69756-3_13

are the common practices to learn motion information. Although using optical flow has indeed achieved good results, its disadvantages are obvious. Optical flow needs to be calculated and stored in advance, where the computation of optical flow is very time-consuming. Since both the training and testing phases require optical flow, the previous optical flow based methods cannot be applied in real-time scenarios. The dual-stream network architecture [21,22] also makes the network unable to be trained in an end-to-end way. Moreover, the motion information cannot be interactively integrated with the RGB information spatio-temporally.

To enable the network to learn motion features from RGB input and avoid the above shortcomings, we use the knowledge distillation method to train the network, which is effective to improve the performance of the network by learning motion features. To better fuse the long distance temporal information in the video, we also added the non-local module at the last layer of the 3D-Convolutional branch. For the 2D-Convolutional branch, which aims to predict the bounding box of the key frame, we use the short-range motion information extraction sub-network to further enhance the motion information near the key frame, so that the final generated action tube is smoother. In summary, we only use optical flow in the training stage of 3D-Convolutional branch, and the pre-trained model which is obtained through knowledge transfer is used in the spatio-temporal positioning task, and in this task optical flow is not required in both the training and the testing stage.

Our method is superior to the existing methods in the frame-mAP and the video-mAP with different thresholds. On the J-HMDB-21 dataset, the frame-mAP and video-mAP under the threshold 0.5 outperforms the second place by 5.8% and 3.9% respectively. On the UCF101-24 data set, compared to the baseline method [4], the accuracy of our method is improved by 2.8% in Frame-mAP (0.5), which is the current best result, and the video-mAP (0.5) is increased by 2%, which is close to the best result. To sum up, our contributions are as follows:

1. We use knowledge distillation to learn motion information from the optical flow stream. Non-local block is also used to help capture accurate long range temporal information.
2. We propose a novel motion cue called short-range-motion (SRM) module to learn short range temporal information, which makes the 2D-Convolutional branch to learn dynamic motion information.
3. The proposed method achieves the state-of-the-art performance by fusing the long and short-term motion information with RGB input.

This paper is organized as follows. In Sect. 2, we review the related work on S-T action localization. We introduce our method in Sect. 3. Section 4 presents the experimental results. We conclude our method in Sect. 5.

2   Related Work

Action Recognition. Currently, the most successful action recognition methods [21–25] involve the use of optical flow in a two-stream way, which typically consists of two branches to learn the appearance and motion information using RGB image and optical flow respectively. Although optical flow has been proven to be an effective motion information, but its estimation is very time-consuming and storage takes up a lot of space. Meanwhile, the contained information between optical flow and RGB images are redundant. How to accurately and efficiently model the motion information in the video to improve the extraction of spatiotemporal features is still far from being solved.

Spatio-Temporal Action Localization. Most spatio-temporal action localization methods are expanded under the popular 2D target detection framework. The extensions mainly include: (1) optical flow is used to capture motion cues; (2) linking algorithms are applied to connect frame-level detections to form action tubes [5]. Although these methods achieved promising results, the temporal property of videos is not fully exploited. The use of pre-calculated optical flow not only hinders the interaction between the motion information and RGB information, but also makes the network unable to be trained end-to-end. Zhang [6] used PWC-Net [26] as a subnet integrated into the action localization network, so flow pre-computation is avoided. But this integration is simply placing the optical flow network before the action positioning network, and its results on the J-HMDB-21 and AVA datasets are not ideal. Köpüklü et al. [4] utilized a single-stage architecture with two branches to extract temporal and spatial information concurrently, and predict bounding boxes and action probabilities directly from video clips in one evaluation. The unified CNN architecture they proposed is novel, but it is unable to make full use of motion information. To fully use temporal information, a long-term feature bank (LFB) [27] is applied to utilize longer clip at inference time. Although the performance is significantly improved, it also brings a lot of extra computation burden and performs poorly on the J-HMDB-21 dataset.

Knowledge Distillation. Integrating many models together and then averaging all the results is a simple way to improve model performance. However, the method of model integration causes multiple models to take up a lot of memory and also leads to huge calculations. Hinton et al. [28] put forward the concept of knowledge distillation. First, train a teacher network, and then use the output of the teacher network and the real labels of the data to train the student network. In this way, the small network can learn the knowledge of the large network. When the knowledge of a network is transferred to a network, the similar effect of model integration can be achieved. Nieves et al. [25] used the means of knowledge distillation to pre-train the action recognition stream with optical flow as input, then fix the network parameters, use the optical flow branch and the video action label to jointly train the RGB input branch, so that the network can learn from RGB. The motion information is learned from the input, which effectively improves the accuracy of action classification.

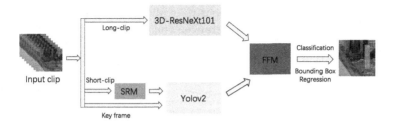

Fig. 1. MENet's architecture.

3   Learning Motion Representation

Modeling the motion information in the video is the key to realize the analysis and understanding of the video information. Two-stream method is the most popular S-T action localization methods. In the two-stream architecture, RGB images are usually used as an stream to extract RGB appearance information, and optical flow is used as another stream to extract motion information. The two branchs are independent, and the results are averaged at the end. Although the two-stream methods have achieved great success, its shortcomings are also obvious: First, Optical flow estimation is very time-consuming, and pre-saved on the hard disk will also take up a lot of storage space, which limits its real-world application. Second, there is a lot of redundant information between streams, which leads to a lot of unnecessary computing overhead. Third, the two separate branches make it impossible to train the network end-to-end, thus the motion information and RGB information cannot be interactively fused to obtain more robust spatio-temporal features, this leads to the video features obtained may be sub-optimal.

For frame-level video action localization, most algorithms extract key frame RGB information, and then use nearby consecutive n-frames of RGB input to extract temporal information. For the prediction of action categories, motion information at different times may be equally important, but for action positioning tasks, intuitively speaking, the importance of motion at different time distances is obviously different, the closer the time distance is, the more important for generating accurate key frame's action bounding box. Two-stream method ignores this fact, thus performance maybe harmed.

So, how to avoid the use of optical flow while achieving efficient extraction of motion information? How to strengthen motion representation at closer temporal distances?

Now, we propose our long short-term motion enhance method to solve the two problems. By using knowledge distillation and migration, while maintaining the performance of the two-stream method, we avoid using optical flow on the task of S-T action localization. At the same time, in order to enhance the motion information near the video key frames, we use a short-range-motion module (SRM) to extract short-range motion information. Since the motion information near the key frame is additionally extracted and input into the network together with the RGB information, this is equivalent to explicitly increasing the importance of the motion with a shorter time distance. The experimental results show that our enhancement of long short-term motion effectively improves the accuracy of S-T action localization. We call the network enhanced by long short-term motion as motion-enhanced network (MENet).

3.1   MENet

MENet is based on the recently popular unified network YOWO [4]. YOWO has two branches, a 3D-CNN branch and a 2D-CNN branch, the key frame and the previous n (n = 8/16) frames are input into the 3D backbone to extract spatio-temporal video features, key frame is input into 2D backbone to extract RGB features. The features of the two branches are merged together through a channel fusion and attention mechanism (CFAM) module. And then use a convolution layer to predict the action class and bounding box in Yolov2 style. The Yolov2 trained for 2D image target detection is applied to the 2D branch, thus only RGB appearance information can be obtained. Although the 3D-ResNeXt-101 network used in the 3D branch uses 3D convolution to extract video spatio-temporal information and is pre-trained in Kinetics, it does not make good use of motion information, and it has defects in its ability to extract long-range dependencies in videos. YOWO does not use optical flow. Good results are achieved on the J-HMDB-21 and UCF101-24 datasets by YOWO, but there are two obvious shortcomings: one is insufficient extraction of spatio-temporal information in the video, and the other is not using motion information.

The architecture of our MENet is as Fig. 1, which enhance long range temporal information in 3D-Convolutional branch and short range motion information is strengthened in 2D-Convolutional branch. A feature fusion module (FFM) is used to fusion 3D and 2D features to generate frame-level action detections. FMM is the collective name of CFAM and Yolov2 head. Frame-level outputs are then linked to generate action tubes using the same link strategy as YOWO [4].

3.2   Long Range Motion Information

The typical application of knowledge distillation is to allow small models to learn from large models and obtain knowledge of large models, which is one of the ways of knowledge transfer. To enable the CNNs to learn the motion features provided by optical flow from continuous RGB frames, we use the knowledge distillation method to train the 3D CNN so that the network learns long range optical-flow-like motion features. 3D-ResNeXt-101 are selected as 3D backbone to make full use of long range motion information. As many frames as possible are used to extract long-range motion information, here we put 16 frames of images, which is the limit of YOWO. In video action recognition, Crasto [25] proposed a training method that uses motion to enhance RGB flow, so that the network can avoid calculating optical flow in the test phase. We used the same strategy for the human action localization task. First, separately use RGB images and optical flow to train 3D-ResNext101 to classify videos. While the

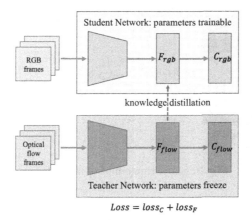

Fig. 2. Use knowledge distillation to train 3D-ResNeXt-101.

two CNNs are fully trained, the optical flow network parameters are fixed, and then the cross-entropy loss and the mean square error of the output of the global average pooling layer of the RGB branch network and the output of the global average pooling layer of the optical flow branch network are used as the joint loss to train the RGB network, the loss function is (Fig. 2):

$$Loss_{K.D.} = CrossEntropy(C_{rgb}, \hat{y}) + \alpha \|F_{flow} - F_{rgb}\|^2 \tag{1}$$

where F_{flow} is the flow feature, F_{rgb} is the RGB feature, $\hat{y}$ is the video ground truth label, C_{rgb} is the predict label, α is a scalar weight modulating the influence of motion features.

In CNNs, the size of the receptive field of convolution and pooling operations is limited, so they are processing local block information, and can't well capture the long-range dependence in the video. Non-local module [29] is proven to be a way to effectively enhance long-range motion information in video. We adopted this practice and added a layer of non-local module at the last layer of the network to enhance the network's ability to extract long-range motion information.

3.3 Short Range Motion Information

An optical flow frame is generally calculated from two adjacent frames, it represents the movement of pixels in the time interval of two images. Assuming that the time interval between the two frames is Δt, n optical flow frames represents the movement within $n\Delta t$. The smaller the value of n, the closer the time distance to the key frame. In the two-stream methods, n generally takes the value 16, 32, 64, which does not highlight the importance of a shorter time distance for positioning the motion in the key frame. Considering that the motion of shorter time distance can help better locate the motion in the key frame, while

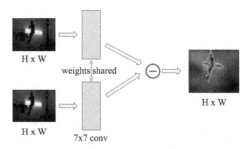

Fig. 3. Short-range-motion module.

extracting the long-range spatiotemporal information, we explicitly extract the motion information in the n neighboring video frames.

In order to verify that short-range motion information as input can indeed enhance the performance of S-T action localization tasks. We first use today's best-performing optical flow estimation method [30] to extract a frame of optical flow near the key frame and input it into the 2D backbone network together with the RGB key frame. The experimental results show that using optical flow as input can indeed greatly enhance the performance of the CNNs. But is optical flow the most appropriate way to express motion characteristics?

Many optical flow estimation algorithms [26, 30–32] today use parameter-sharing twin networks to extract the features of adjacent RGB video frames, and then use the correlation operation to construct a minimum cost volume to match the pixels in the two frames of images. With many methods such as crose-to-fine, downsampling, warp, and parameter sharing, the speed and accuracy of the optical flow have been greatly improved. But for video tasks that frequently input dozens of consecutive frames, embedding the optical flow estimation network as a sub-network in the video task will cause a large amount of graphics card memory consumption. And the training process will be more difficult and slow. In our practice, it will increase the training time by 2 to 3 times. Research [33] shows that RGB difference can also effectively represent motion information, which can be regarded as a rough representation of motion information. Although RGB difference as one of the motion information representation methods does not improve the performance of video tasks as well as optical flow, it can be obtained simpliy by only performing one subtraction. Based on the above observations, we propose our short-range motion information modeling module (SRM). In our SRM, feature encoding network of parameter sharing is used to extract features from RGB video frames, and then the features are subtracted to obtain motion features.

During our review of the literature, we found that Zhang et al. [34] have made relevant attempts. We implemented our SRM (as Fig. 3) based on the suggestions given in their experiments, and tested our ideas in the 2D backbone. Experimental results show that with only a small increase in calculations, SRM can quickly and accurately extract motion information and effectively enhance the network's spatiotemporal feature extraction capabilities.

4   Experiments

To evaluate the performance of the algorithm, UCF101-24 and J-HMDB-21 datasets are selected. We strictly follow the official evaluation metrics to measure the performance of the algorithm and compare our results with other state-of-the-art methods.

4.1   Datasets and Metrics

JHMDB-21. In order to promote an in-depth understanding of action recognition algorithms, Jhuang et al. [8] used part of the HMDB-51 [35] dataset to annotate human joint points to create the JHMDB-21 dataset. Since the 928 videos they extracted from HMDB-51 belong to 21 action categories, this dataset is also called the JHMDB-21 dataset. The labeled data in the JHMDB-21 dataset includes motion segmentation, dense optical flow, and human joint points. 928 video clips all contain 15 or more video frames.

UCF101-24. UCF101-24 [18] has more data than the JHMDB-21 dataset. Based on the UCF-101 data set, 3194 video action frames are labeled. Since they belong to 24 action categories, they are called UCF101-24 datasets. Although the UCF101-24 dataset has not been officially released, it has been revised by many scholars and its labels is relatively reliable.

Metrics. We use general indicators for target detection tasks to measure the performance of the algorithm on the task of action positioning. This paper will report the Frame-mAP (F-mAP) index when the IOU threshold is 0.5 and the Video-mAP (V-mAP) index under various IOU thresholds.

4.2   Training Settings

We choose 3D-ResNeXt101 as the 3D backbone and Yolov2 as the 2D backbone. The consecutive 16 frames (including key frames) before the key frame are input into the 3D backbone, the consecutive 4 frames (including key frames) before the key frame are input into the SRM, the key frame will be concated with the output of SRM into the 2D backbone. For the 3D backbone network, a non-local module is added in the last layer, then we use the same training settings as crasto et al. [25] for knowledge distillation training, the pre-trained weights are used to initialize the 3D branch of MENet. For the 2D backbone network, we initialize the network with Yolov2s pretrained weights, the number of input channels of the first layer of convolution is modified to 6 to accommodate the input. We use momentum stochastic gradient descent optimization algorithm for training, the momentum value is set to 0.9, and the weight decay rate is set to 0.0005.

For the JHMDB-21 dataset, set the initial learning rate to 0.0001 and the batch size to 16, and the weight is decayed by half every 10000 batch iterations. For the UCF101-24 dataset, set the initial learning rate to 0.001 and the batch size to 32. When the number of iterations reaches 20000, 30000, 40000, and 50000 nodes, the learning rate will be reduced by half.

4.3   Ablation Study

Long-Range-Motion-Enhancement. In common practice, usually 16, 32, 64 frames of continuous images are used as input for video tasks. Limited by the requirements of the network architecture, only 16 frames can be input at most in MENet. We first use knowledge distillation to enhance the motion information, and then add a non-local layer to the last layer of the backbone network to enhance the long-range motion information in the network. In order to verify the validity of the results, we separately use the 3D branch to conduct experiments in the UCF101-24 data set, results are shown in the Table 1.

We compared various metrics, including the classification accuracy and the localization when the IOU threshold is 0.5 on the training set, the F-score and Frame-mAP on the validation set, and the Video-mAP on the test set. It can be clearly seen that the knowledge distillation training significantly improves the network perfermance. The non-local module further enhances the performance of the network in positioning tasks. After using knowledge distillation and non-local modules at the same time, F-mAP increased by 4.31%, and V-mAP increased by 1.9%. This proves that our method is effective and the enhancement of network performance is continuous.

Table 1. 3D backbone performance comparison with different motion enhancement methods. RGB only means to use only RGB training, K.D. refers to knowledge distillation training, K.D.+non-local refers to the use of non-local modules while using knowledge distillation.

Methods	Classif.	local.(0.5)	F-score	F-mAP(0.5)	V-mAP(0.5)
RGB only	96.02	92.70	91.11	77.98	44.30
K.D	96.10	93.30	91.70	80.28	45.00
K.D.+non-local	**96.10**	**94.0**	**92.40**	**82.29**	**46.20**

Short-Range-Motion-Enhancement. As we all know, 2D networks are good at extracting the apparent features of RGB images. Using optical flow and other motion information as input can also significantly enhance network performance. For action positioning tasks, we enhance the extraction of short-range time distance motion information by inputting the motion information close to the key

Table 2. 2D backbone performance comparison with different short range motion enhancement methods. RGB only means to use only RGB training, RGB + optical flow (n = 1) refers to input RGB and 1 optical flow frame together, RGB+SRM (n = 1) refers to input RGB and 1 SRM frame together, RGB+SRM (n = 3) refers to input RGB and 3 SRM frame together.

Methods	Classif.	local.(0.5)	F-score	F-mAP(0.5)	V-mAP(0.5)
RGB only	62.4	79.4	51.57	30.11	13.50
RGB+optical flow (n = 1)	68.2	82.1	57.59	36.90	14.96
RGB+SRM (n = 1)	**75.2**	**87.7**	**68.15**	**50.36**	**29.35**
RGB+SRM (n = 3)	**79.9**	**88.9**	**73.09**	**52.91**	**30.61**

frame into the network. We use Yolov2 as the 2D backbone network to conduct experiments on the UCF101-24 dataset, and we compare the performance of the network under different input conditions. We first input only the RGB image, and found that the results are poor. Then we input a frame of optical flow together with the RGB image into the 2D network, the F-mAP of the network has increased by 6.79%, and the V-mAP has increased by 1.46%. Then we input a frame of SRM, which greatly improves network performance, compared with optical flow, its F-mAP has increased by 13.46% and V-mAP has increased by 12.9%. Taking into account the noise between the information of the two frames of images, we finally use four frames of images to generate 3 SRM output. With RGB key frames as input, the experiment results demonstrate this further enhances the performance of the network, F-mAP increased by 22.80%, and V-mAP increased by 17.11% (Table 2).

4.4 Comparison to the State of the Art

We compare with other state-of-the-art S-T action localization algorithms. It should be noted that we did not compare with the VideoCaptureNet [36], because its video-map calculation method is different, it doesn't generate action tubes via linking strategies to calculate Video-mAP. To be fair, we did not compare with YOWO plus LFB. YOWO plus LFB use 8 LFB [27] features which extracted for non-overlapping 8-frame clips using the pretrained 3D ResNeXt-101 backbone, total number of 64 frames are utilized at inference time. Our nerual network architecture is based on YOWO, since we aim to explore how to better use motion information, we did not use the special strategy of LFB at inference time.

As shown in Table 3, on the UCF101-24 dataset, our algorithm has achieved advanced results in various metrics. We have achieved the current best F-mAP 83.5%. Compared with the original YOWO, our MENet has improved significantly in all indicators. MENet without SRM, F-mAP reached 83.5%, the current

Table 3. Perfermance comparison with state-of-the-art algorithms on the UCF101-24 dataset.

Method	F-mAP(0.5)	V-mAP		
		0.1	0.2	0.5
Peng w/o MR [37]	64.8	49.5	41.2	–
Peng w/ MR [37]	65.7	50.4	42.3	–
ROAD [38]	–	–	73.5	46.3
T-CNN [39]	41.4	51.3	47.1	–
ACT [40]	69.5	–	77.2	51.4
MPS [41]	–	82.4	72.9	41.1
STEP [5]	75.0	83.1	76.6	–
YOWO [4]	80.4	82.5	75.8	48.8
MENet w/o SRM (ours)	**83.5**	**82.1**	**75.9**	**49.5**
MENet w/ SRM (ours)	**83.2**	**82.4**	**76.7**	**50.8**

best, 3.1% ahead of second YOWO; under IOU 0.2 threshold V-mAP reached 75.9%, leading YOWO 0.1%; V-mAP reaches 49.5% under the IOU 0.5 threshold, leading YOWO by 0.7%. MENet with SRM further improved V-mAP at multiple thresholds, especially V-mAP at high threshold, V-mAP reaches 50.8% under the IOU 0.5 threshold, leading YOWO by 2%. There is a slight drop in frame-mAP, which may be due to the fact that the first few frames of the video are reused due to too few numbers, and SRM enhances noise. MENet considers motion information and strengthens the extraction of long-range dependent information in the video, various indicators have been significantly improved.

As shown in Table 4, on the J-HMDB-21 dataset, our algorithm has achieved advanced results in various metrics too. We have achieved the current best F-mAP 82.3% and best V-mAP(0.5) 61.7%. MENet without SRM, F-mAP reached 82.3%, the current best, 7.9% ahead of second YOWO; under IOU 0.2 threshold V-mAP reached 92.7%, the current best, leading YOWO 4.9%; under IOU 0.5 threshold V-mAP reached 90.9%, the current best, leading YOWO 5.2%; V-mAP reaches 57.9% under the IOU 0.75 threshold, within an inch of YOWO. MENet with SRM further improved V-mAP at high threshold, V-mAP reaches 61.7% under the IOU 0.75 threshold, leading YOWO by 3.6%. The J-HMDB-21 dataset is much smaller than UCF101-24 dataset, it has a lot of shorter video clips. It is easier to overfit, so the F-mAP and V-mAP under low threshold drop more. But it is clear that our method has achieved the best results currently on this data set, this proves the effectiveness of our work.

Table 4. Perfermance comparison with state-of-the-art algorithms on the J-HMDB-21 dataset.

Method	F-mAP(0.5)	V-mAP		
		0.2	0.5	0.75
Peng w/o MR [37]	56.9	71.1	70.6	48.2
Peng w/ MR [37]	58.5	74.3	73.1	–
ROAD [38]	–	73.8	72.0	44.5
T-CNN [39]	61.3	78.4	76.9	–
ACT [40]	65.7	74.2	73.7	52.1
P3D-CTN [42]	71.1	84.0	80.5	–
TPnet [43]	–	74.8	74.1	61.3
YOWO [4]	74.4	87.8	85.7	58.1
MENet w/o SRM (ours)	**82.3**	**92.7**	**90.9**	**57.9**
MENet w/ SRM (ours)	**78.3**	**90.5**	**88.1**	**61.7**

5   Conclusion

In this paper, we focus on learning motion representation efficiently without using optical flow. We use the knowledge distillation training method to enable the network to learn motion information from RGB input, and use non-local modules to better improve the network's ability to integrate motion information. To emphasize the motion information closer to the key frame, we use the SRM module to extract the motion information of the neighboring frames of the key frame. Good results prove the effectiveness of our method. In the future, we will explore more effective and more efficient ways to extract motion information to boosting video analysis and understanding.

Acknowledgments. The work is supported by the National Key Research and Development Program of China (No. 2018YFB1600600)

References

1. Yang, Z., Gao, J., Nevatia, R.: Spatio-temporal action detection with cascade proposal and location anticipation. arXiv preprint arXiv:1708.00042 (2017)
2. He, J., Deng, Z., Ibrahim, M.S., Mori, G.: Generic tubelet proposals for action localization. In: 2018 IEEE Winter Conference on Applications of Computer Vision (WACV), pp. 343–351. IEEE (2018)
3. Ye, Y., Yang, X., Tian, Y.: Discovering spatio-temporal action tubes. J. Visual Commun. Image Represent. **58**, 515–524 (2019)
4. Köpüklü, O., Wei, X., Rigoll, G.: You only watch once: a unified CNN architecture for real-time spatiotemporal action localization. arXiv preprint arXiv:1911.06644 (2019)

5. Yang, X., Yang, X., Liu, M.Y., Xiao, F., Davis, L.S., Kautz, J.: Step: spatio-temporal progressive learning for video action detection. In: Proceedings of the IEEE Conference on Computer Vision and Pattern Recognition, 264–272 (2019)
6. Zhang, D., He, L., Tu, Z., Zhang, S., Han, F., Yang, B.: Learning motion representation for real-time spatio-temporal action localization. Pattern Recognit. **103**, 107312 (2020)
7. Soomro, K., Zamir, A.R., Shah, M.: A dataset of 101 human action classes from videos in the wild. Center Res. Comput. Vis. **2** (2012)
8. Jhuang, H., Gall, J., Zuffi, S., Schmid, C., Black, M.J.: Towards understanding action recognition. In: International Conference on Computer Vision (ICCV), pp. 3192–3199 (2013)
9. Gu, C., et al.: Ava: a video dataset of spatio-temporally localized atomic visual actions. In: Proceedings of the IEEE Conference on Computer Vision and Pattern Recognition, pp. 6047–6056 (2018)
10. Redmon, J., Divvala, S., Girshick, R., Farhadi, A.: You only look once: unified, real-time object detection. In: Proceedings of the IEEE Conference on Computer Vision and Pattern Recognition, pp. 779–788 (2016)
11. Redmon, J., Farhadi, A.: Yolo9000: better, faster, stronger. In: Proceedings of the IEEE Conference on Computer Vision and Pattern Recognition, pp. 7263–7271 (2017)
12. Redmon, J., Farhadi, A.: Yolov3: an incremental improvement. arXiv preprint arXiv:1804.02767 (2018)
13. Liu, W., et al.: SSD: single shot multibox detector. In: Leibe, B., Matas, J., Sebe, N., Welling, M. (eds.) ECCV 2016. LNCS, vol. 9905, pp. 21–37. Springer, Cham (2016). https://doi.org/10.1007/978-3-319-46448-0_2
14. Girshick, R.: Fast R-CNN. In: Proceedings of the IEEE International Conference on Computer Vision, pp. 1440–1448 (2015)
15. He, K., Gkioxari, G., Dollár, P., Girshick, R.: Mask R-CNN. In: Proceedings of the IEEE International Conference on Computer Vision, 2961–2969 (2017)
16. Cai, Z., Vasconcelos, N.: Cascade R-CNN: delving into high quality object detection. In: Proceedings of the IEEE Conference on Computer Vision and Pattern Recognition, pp. 6154–6162 (2018)
17. Ren, S., He, K., Girshick, R., Sun, J.: Faster R-CNN: towards real-time object detection with region proposal networks. In: Advances in Neural Information Processing Systems, pp. 91–99 (2015)
18. Singh, G., Saha, S., Sapienza, M., Torr, P.H., Cuzzolin, F.: Online real-time multiple spatiotemporal action localisation and prediction. In: Proceedings of the IEEE International Conference on Computer Vision, pp. 3637–3646 (2017)
19. Weinzaepfel, P., Harchaoui, Z., Schmid, C.: Learning to track for spatio-temporal action localization. In: Proceedings of the IEEE International Conference on Computer Vision, pp. 3164–3172 (2015)
20. Klaser, A., Marszałek, M., Schmid, C.: A spatio-temporal descriptor based on 3D-gradients (2008)
21. Simonyan, K., Zisserman, A.: Two-stream convolutional networks for action recognition in videos. In: Advances in Neural Information Processing Systems, pp. 568–576 (2014)
22. Carreira, J., Zisserman, A.: Quo vadis, action recognition? A new model and the kinetics dataset. In: proceedings of the IEEE Conference on Computer Vision and Pattern Recognition, pp. 6299–6308 (2017)

23. Tran, D., Bourdev, L., Fergus, R., Torresani, L., Paluri, M.: Learning spatiotemporal features with 3D convolutional networks. In: Proceedings of the IEEE International Conference on Computer Vision, pp. 4489–4497 (2015)
24. Lin, J., Gan, C., Han, S.: TSM: temporal shift module for efficient video understanding. In: Proceedings of the IEEE International Conference on Computer Vision, pp. 7083–7093 (2019)
25. Crasto, N., Weinzaepfel, P., Alahari, K., Schmid, C.: Mars: motion-augmented RGB stream for action recognition. In: Proceedings of the IEEE Conference on Computer Vision and Pattern Recognition, pp. 7882–7891 (2019)
26. Sun, D., Yang, X., Liu, M.Y., Kautz, J.: PWC-net: CNNs for optical flow using pyramid, warping, and cost volume. In: Proceedings of the IEEE Conference on Computer Vision and Pattern Recognition, pp. 8934–8943 (2018)
27. Wu, C.Y., Feichtenhofer, C., Fan, H., He, K., Krahenbuhl, P., Girshick, R.: Long-term feature banks for detailed video understanding. In: Proceedings of the IEEE Conference on Computer Vision and Pattern Recognition, pp. 284–293 (2019)
28. Hinton, G., Vinyals, O., Dean, J.: Distilling the knowledge in a neural network. In: STAT, vol. 9, p. 1050 (2015)
29. Wang, X., Girshick, R., Gupta, A., He, K.: Non-local neural networks. In: Proceedings of the IEEE Conference on Computer Vision and Pattern Recognition (CVPR) (2018)
30. Teed, Z., Deng, J.: Raft: recurrent all-pairs field transforms for optical flow. arXiv preprint arXiv:2003.12039 (2020)
31. Dosovitskiy, A., et al.: Flownet: learning optical flow with convolutional networks. In: Proceedings of the IEEE International Conference on Computer Vision, pp. 2758–2766 (2015)
32. Hui, T.W., Tang, X., Change Loy, C.: Liteflownet: a lightweight convolutional neural network for optical flow estimation. In: Proceedings of the IEEE Conference on Computer Vision and Pattern Recognition, pp. 8981–8989 (2018)
33. Wang, L., et al.: Temporal segment networks: towards good practices for deep action recognition. In: Leibe, B., Matas, J., Sebe, N., Welling, M. (eds.) ECCV 2016. LNCS, vol. 9912, pp. 20–36. Springer, Cham (2016). https://doi.org/10.1007/978-3-319-46484-8_2
34. Zhang, C., Zou, Y., Chen, G., Gan, L.: Pan: towards fast action recognition via learning persistence of appearance. arXiv preprint arXiv:2008.03462 (2020)
35. Kuehne, H., Jhuang, H., Garrote, E., Poggio, T., Serre, T.: HMDB: a large video database for human motion recognition. In: Proceedings of the International Conference on Computer Vision (ICCV) (2011)
36. Duarte, K., Rawat, Y., Shah, M.: Videocapsulenet: a simplified network for action detection. In: Advances in Neural Information Processing Systems, pp. 7610–7619 (2018)
37. Peng, X., Schmid, C.: Multi-region two-stream R-CNN for action detection. In: Leibe, B., Matas, J., Sebe, N., Welling, M. (eds.) ECCV 2016. LNCS, vol. 9908, pp. 744–759. Springer, Cham (2016). https://doi.org/10.1007/978-3-319-46493-0_45
38. Saha, S., Singh, G., Sapienza, M., Torr, P.H., Cuzzolin, F.: Deep learning for detecting multiple space-time action tubes in videos. Pattern Recognit. (2015)
39. Hou, R., Chen, C., Shah, M.: Tube convolutional neural network (T-CNN) for action detection in videos. In: Proceedings of the IEEE International Conference on Computer Vision, pp. 5822–5831 (2017)
40. Kalogeiton, V., Weinzaepfel, P., Ferrari, V., Schmid, C.: Action tubelet detector for spatio-temporal action localization. In: Proceedings of the IEEE International Conference on Computer Vision, 4405–4413 (2017)

41. Alwando, E.H.P., Chen, Y.T., Fang, W.H.: CNN-based multiple path search for action tube detection in videos. IEEE Trans. Circ. Syst. Video Technol. **30**(1), 104–116 (2018)
42. Wei, J., Wang, H., Yi, Y., Li, Q., Huang, D.: P3D-CTN: pseudo-3D convolutional tube network for spatio-temporal action detection in videos. In: 2019 IEEE International Conference on Image Processing (ICIP), pp. 300–304. IEEE (2019)
43. Singh, G., Saha, S., Cuzzolin, F.: Predicting action tubes. In: Proceedings of the European Conference on Computer Vision (ECCV) (2018)

Author Index

Printed in the United States
By Bookmasters